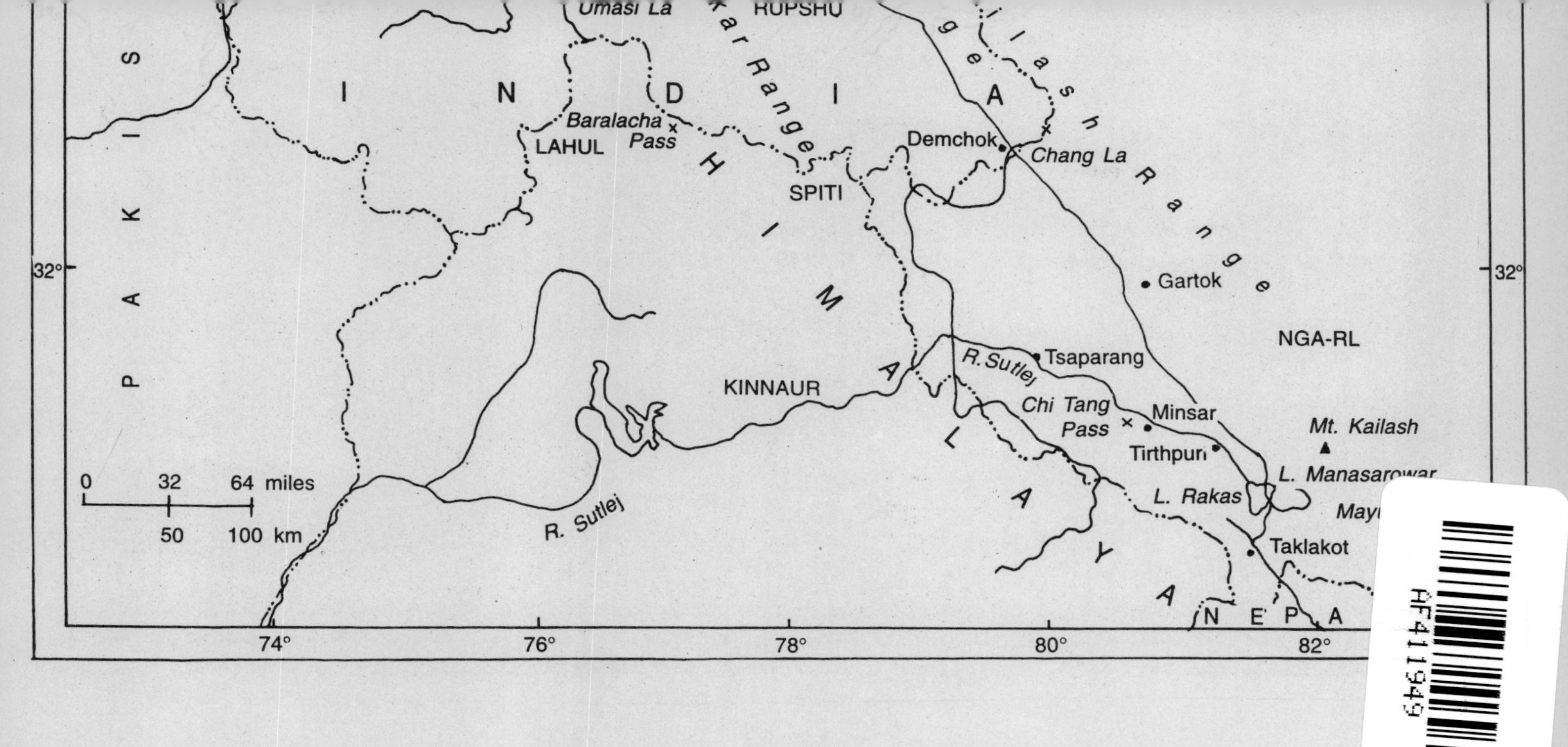
PAKISTAN
INDIA
Umasi La
RUPSHU
Kar Range
Kailash Range
Baralacha Pass
LAHUL
Demchok
Chang La
SPITI
HIMALAYA
Gartok
NGA-RL
KINNAUR
R. Sutlej
Tsaparang
Chi Tang Pass
Minsar
Tirthpuri
Mt. Kailash
L. Manasarowar
L. Rakas
Mayu
Taklakot
NEPAL
R. Sutlej
0   32   64 miles
50   100 km
32°
74°   76°   78°   80°   82°

THE MOUTHS OF PEOPLE,
THE VOICE OF GOD

THE MOUTHS OF PEOPLE, THE VOICE OF GOD

Buddhists and Muslims in a Frontier Community of Ladakh

Smriti Srinivas

DELHI
OXFORD UNIVERSITY PRESS
CALCUTTA   CHENNAI   MUMBAI
1998

Oxford University Press, Great Clarendon Street, Oxford OX2 6DP

Oxford New York
Athens Auckland Bangkok Calcutta
Cape Town Chennai Dar es Salaam Delhi
Florence Hong Kong Istanbul Karachi
Kuala Lumpur Madrid Melbourne Mexico City
Mumbai Nairobi Paris Singapore
Taipei Tokyo Toronto

and associates in

Berlin Ibadan

ISBN 0 19 564229 5

Typeset by images, Chennai 600 0018
Printed at Saurabh Print-o-Pack, Noida
and published by Manzar Khan, Oxford University Press
YMCA Library Building, Jai Singh Road, New Delhi 110 001

Acknowledgements

This book is largely based on field research done for my doctoral dissertation at the Department of Sociology, Delhi School of Economics, where I was financially supported by a fellowship from the University Grants Commission. I would like to thank my Ph.D. supervisor Andre Béteille for his support, comments and time. I would also like to thank J.P.S. Uberoi for encouraging me to pursue the idea of the 'frontier' in the first place.

Many people have supported me intellectually and emotionally as this book has evolved over the years. I would like to thank Sangeeta Chattoo, Kalpana Vishwanath, and Savyasaachi. Punam Zutshi and Anuradha Shah have shared with me so much of the excitement, pain and laughter of this study and I have no words to express my feelings of kinship with them. Dr. V.N. Pandit and Krishna Pandit have been like parents to me. The Zutshis, Nairs and Halarnkars kept an open house for me and I am grateful to them for their succour. I never knew Shiv Visvanathan in Delhi and I am grateful for this lag in our friendship! I also want to thank my friends and colleagues at the International Association for Ladakh Studies and the Central Institute of Indian Languages for their comments on different versions of this work.

I will never be able to repay the generosity and affection of the Kalon family in Leh: they gave me a home where I knew I was always welcome in the status of a grandchild. All of them and, in particular, Abbale, Wangchuk, Dr. Lahdol, Mutup, and Rigzin Angmo, shared their knowledge, experience and love of Ladakh with me. There is almost no part of this study which can be separated from my memories of walks, journeys, delicious meals and conversations with them. I hope they will approve of this final product.

My family in Tegar put up with my endless questions, my fumbling attempts to learn Ladakhi, and my efforts to help them in the field and in the kitchen. Wangchuk and Yangchen treated me like a younger sister and there are shared memories of good and troubled times with them and their families. Gelong and Chamshing have a place in my affections and understanding of Nubra which I cannot even begin to express. Abbe Putty and Tsewang Lullu sat for hours with me explaining the intricacies of various genealogies in the village. So many families extended their hospitality to me during various visits to Nubra–Jorapa, Hilbepa, Zimskangpa, and Kharponpa. I miss my friends in Tegar–Lullu, Tsewang Lhamo, Yangchen, and Spalzes. Master Razaak's family in Hundar extended to me their welcome and my experience of Ramzan there with Abba Razaak, Shafi, Amina, and others will always be memorable. I remember Mr. and Mrs. Verghese Samuel with so much affection. I also want to thank General Tomar and Major Srivastava for their thoughtfulness and support during my stay in Nubra.

Sohrab calmly continues to deal with my panic stricken calls about the computer. Nina and Babbi have provided so much good food and fun during the past few years.

I would like to dedicate this book to five people: to my father, who wrote me regular letters which sustained me in Ladakh, quietly sharing with me many of the anxieties and decisions about the production of this study, and for his belief in me. To my mother, who will recognize the joy of carrying this baby to full-term and for her patience in dealing with me while working on this book. To Smita, of whom I am so proud, and who was terribly ill on our first visit to Ladakh! To Geetha–for inspiration, the poetry and a shared history. To Jeh–for all the melodies, and with hope.

A note on the translation of local terms

Local terms are italicized in the text of this book. Their meaning, as explained to me contextually by villagers, is also given. I am reasonably fluent in understanding Nubra Ladakhi and whenever I failed to understand certain terms, I sought their explanation from bilingual villagers in Hindi (or what they call Urdu) which I am fluent in. No diacritical marks are used in this book and the plural form is usually indicated by 's' at the end of the word. I make no claims to linguistic precision and many subtleties of pronunciation have been probably lost in this method of transcription but, as I try and explain below, what is lost in such technicalities is made up by the fact that this procedure captures the variety and polysemanticity of social existence. For example, the Muslims translate the word *Bardo* as 'hell', although the Buddhists mean by this term 'the intermediate region between this world and the next'; similarly, the word *lha* is translated by Buddhists as 'god' and Muslims as 'angel'. Rather than indicating an imprecision of meaning, such translation points to the family resemblance between terms used by members of various social groups. Only in certain cases have words been transcribed according to the Wylie system: this merely preserves the mode of transcription used by the particular author cited as a reference.

At the end of the book, a glossary of Ladakhi terms has been made for the reader's reference. Local words which are names of persons, places and gods are not italicized in the text. Again, certain terms which are generally understood, such as 'Sunni' or 'Gelugpa', are not italicized. I have italicized certain Muslim words such as *Ramzan* because most scholars familiar with Ladakh tend to be familiar with Buddhist terms but not necessarily Muslim ones although my ethnography covers both religious groups.

The reason that terms are not transcribed according to the rules of Tibetan grammar, as tends to be the practice among those researchers working in Tibetan-speaking societies, is that the language in Nubra bears significant differences in vocabulary from Tibetan and many local words find no place in Tibetan-English dictionaries. To my knowledge, although there exists a standard Ladakhi dictionary and grammar, it is the language of Leh and increasingly, that used by the administration and media. The colloquial language of Nubra differs in many ways from this language and while both Tibetan and standard Ladakhi are considered prestigious and 'high' languages (one being the language of scripture and the other of the capital), they are not the language of the common people of Nubra.

There is the further danger that by transcribing the local language according to the rules of Tibetan or standard Ladakhi grammar, Muslim speakers of colloquial Ladakhi, whose vocabulary contains words that are neither always Persian, Arabic nor Tibetan, will be considered 'outsiders' or their language a distorted form of some 'high' language like Arabic. Rather than to participate in the hegemonic project of creating a single 'pure' language, my position is that the language of Nubra, like its society, is a locus of cross-cutting ties and, therefore, both Muslim and Buddhist terms used by the local people are transcribed chiefly according to the way they are pronounced. Classical religion of either group may provide a completely different meaning to some of the terms used, but my justification is that this study does not locate itself within a classical discourse.

The names of households in the two villages of my study are real ones. Only in the case studies have the names of persons and households been altered to preserve their anonymity.

Contents

Chapter 1

Introduction

THE CONTEXT OF THIS STUDY

In 1936, Marco Pallis visited Ladakh with Richard Nicholson, the Islamicist. Pallis had, on a previous trip in 1933, visited Gangotri and followed the Ganges and the Sutlej rivers to their source. His trip to Sikkim preceded his journey to Ladakh. The former included the objective of scaling one or more peaks situated near the margin of Zemu glacier before the arrival of the monsoon in June. The party of climbers were unable to scale the peak and retreated to Lachhen monastery. There, one day, the abbot asked Pallis why they tried to climb the snowy mountains. And he replied that they sought solitude there. 'You will never find it thus', the abbot stated. 'You have no idea how to seek it. It cannot be won by such methods. It will not be obtained nor acquired nor gained nor procured nor encompassed'.[1] Pallis then decided to go to Ladakh and learn the art of painting scrolls from Konchhog Gyaltsan of Phiyang and to study with the bursar of Spituk monastery in the Indus valley. He says, 'We wanted to absorb the spirit of the tradition by direct experience subjecting ourselves to its laws to the greatest possible extent; for there comes a time when it is difficult to rest satisfied with the part of observer; one must participate...'[2] The Lachhen abbot's response to Pallis transformed him from an adventurer, who regarded the Himalayas as a vast sporting ground, to a pilgrim who allowed himself to undergo an ontological transformation, the heart of which was, the communication of sacra of the tradition. Pallis remains till date, one of the most sympathetic students, though marginal, of Ladakhi culture.

It was in the nineteenth century, after the British established themselves in India, that systematic efforts were made to visit and document facts about Ladakh. Most writers on the region, like myself, are confronted by a plethora of travelogues and other documents which date from this period. When I first went to Ladakh in the autumn of 1989, on what I described in my conversations with others as a 'reconnaissance' trip, I little realized how embedded Ladakh studies were in this history and how unusual Pallis' account was.[3] Sociological and anthropological works on the area necessarily have to deal with a narrative context, whose background is a political and commercial contest for Ladakh. As I discovered in the long hours spent at the District Library in Leh, this contest has long determined a perspective on Ladakh which sees it either as a cultural periphery of Tibet, or as a geo-political frontier between empires and nation-states. The accounts of this period belong to what has been generally described as the 'Great Game', i.e. the contest between Russia, China and Great Britain for possessions in Central Asia and the complex alliances and manoeuvres between empires and local kingdoms within this 'Game'. An important aspect of this contest was the determination of boundaries – to discover where the authority of Britain began and ended, what designs Russia or China had in the Himalayan region, the extent of their powers and what fortifiction mountain barriers could be said to provide.[4]

Ladakh ceased to be an independent kingdom when the rulers of the kingdom of Jammu invaded and destroyed it in 1834. This act was a thread in the complicated skein of machinations in this region. Under Dogra rule, carried out in agreement with the British, customary patterns of life more or less continued at the local level though some high taxes and forced labour were imposed. It was arranged that a British representative, the Joint Commissioner, would supplement the authority of the Wazir of Kashmir in Leh. This dual authority continued till the British withdrawal in 1947 when Ladakh became part of the Indian state.[5]

Most early accounts of Ladakh attempted to create a map of the region which could serve imperialist interests by filling in blank spaces on maps, locating watersheds, aligning mountain ranges, discovering peaks and drawing fixed limits for its topos and peoples.[6] As Robert Shaw expressed it, 'We do not desire to know a country in order to map it, but we map it in order to know it'.[7] The shadowy contest which began in earnest in the 1830's when Tsarist armies were driving eastward towards the Pacific and southwards towards India, and the British were pressing northwards towards the Himalayas, was embodied most cogently in Lord Curzon's frontier policy.[8] Paralleling this outward delimitation was an internal one which, through land settlements, tolls, taxes, and cartographical surveys, was rendering the area of Ladakh into a bounded topos by the combined efforts of the geographer, the explorer, the administrator and the trader.[9] Within Ladakh, the Land Settlement begun under the Dogras was finally completed under the supervision of the Settlement Commissioner, Mr. Talbot. The *Bandobast*, as it was called, was prepared for every village in the area, fixing ownership, noting and levying taxes, and completing a survey of land holdings of entire families, villages and monasteries.[10] Nearly all the older accounts of Ladakh belong to this attempt to map the frontier, the intentions of various merchants, explorers, and administrators coinciding to a remarkable degree, and providing a reference point for later analyses.

Only the accounts of the Roman Catholic and Moravian mission-aries read differently. This is because the missionaries had an interface with the lives of the local people in ways not connected with rule, though linked with evangelization. The missionaries' relationship with peasant life was often more intimate than that of the various other sojourners to this area. The Moravians began a school, a dispensary, and an orphanage in Leh. They taught the women knitting, an occupation which continues to be important in the long winters in Ladakh; and they intro-duced a rectangular stove in the kitchens. The first pastor at Kyelang, August Wilhelm Heyde, was said to have brought two or three kilos of seeds of potatoes and other vegetables from Germany which were introduced into local fields.[11] A convert, Yoseb Gergan, wrote a history of Ladakh which supplements A.H. Francke's historical researches in the area. Gergan also translated the Bible into Tibetan and the growing need for a specialist in language led H. Jaeschke to come to Ladakh; he completed a Tibeto-German dictionary, an English version of which appeared in 1881.[12] The short-lived Roman Catholic mission (1888-98), which founded a mission station called St.Peter's, was also engaged in educational and medical work.[13]

The missionaries, however, did not really have a great presence in Ladakh. It is at another level, i.e. in the form of an interface with

Orientalist studies, that they had a more lasting influence. Orientalism is based on an ontological and epistemological distinction between the Orient and the Occident as the starting point for elaborate conceptual enterprises.[14] The Orientalist paradigm has functioned in expansionist politics of the West and in cultural domination over the non-West. The literature on Ladakh is largely influenced by the above distinction and entwined in a complex manner with domination of other kinds. The Moravians, as well as the Catholic missionaries, considered their academic work complementary to their mission. For example, linguistic skills were essential to the work of Bible translation.[15] Also, the Government of India, through the offices of the Director-General of Archaeology, sponsored the first cultural mission of a highly scholarly character in 1909. This was carried out by Dr. A.H. Francke of the Moravian Mission Board.[16] Many contemporary works on Ladakh share the emphasis with this earlier literature that the area forms a homogeneous culture, primarily Buddhist and Tibetan in inspiration, preserving a continuity in its form from the past to the present period. Other cultural influences–Muslim, nomadic or Central Asian–are largely ignored.[17]

The withdrawal of British power from India in 1947 resulted in immediate hostilities between new India and new Pakistan. Pakistani forces invaded Baltistan and Ladakh early the following year. From 1948, the Ladakh region has become a vulnerable and strategic tract for India. In 1950, China invaded Tibet and occupied it; in 1959, the Dalai Lama fled Tibet for India; and in 1962, China invaded India and occupied the eastern and north-eastern parts of Ladakh, a portion of which was called Aksai Chin. Ladakh now has a large Tibetan refugee population and a huge presence of the Indian army, following a tense border situation both with China and Pakistan. The records for the period after 1947 are rather poor partly for these reasons. Due to the changed political conditions in Kashmir, a result partly of hostilities between Pakistan and India (with China as a third player in the game), census records are extremely uneven. The censuses of 1961 and 1971 were conducted and include district census reports for Ladakh district. The 1981 census contains only the bare details for this area and because of the political trouble in Kashmir valley, the 1991 census was not carried out.[18]

The consequences of these events have been two-fold. With the closure of the consulate in Kashgar, the restrictions on travel to Xinjiang and the imposition of a cease-fire line in Kashmir which continues to be tense, the links of this area with others have been transformed. Trading operations, on which the prosperity of Ladakh largely depended, have nearly ceased and Indian army goods and Punjabi and Kashmiri merchants largely control the market.[19]

The second consequence is less easy to understand: there has been a transformation of the cultural connections (pilgrimage, ritual prestations, language, etc.) of this area with others, side by side with the perception of separate identities on the part of various groups in Ladakh. With the fixation of external political borders, internal cultural boundaries emerge as a conjoint product. This is not an outcome of a single historical conjuncture; 'Buddhist' identity in Ladakh, for example, is a representation which is embedded in practices of administration and classification, both colonial and nationalist.[20] Not only geo-political processes, but processes of the state, and the symbolic and material remaking of identities by communities are crucial in understanding these cultural shifts.

THE ORGANIZATION AND AIMS OF THIS WORK

This study is the first sociological monograph about the Nubra valley. I carried out fieldwork for this study in Nubra, the northern-most valley of Ladakh, between August 1990 and July 1991, after a preliminary trip in 1989. I returned to Ladakh for three weeks in August 1993. Till my second period of fieldwork between 1990-1, I was confronted with an intellectual and popular perspective on Ladakh which structured frontier areas according to two sets of oppositions. The first opposition is between centre and periphery, making the frontier population marginal.[21] The second opposition is between homogeneity and heterogeneity: the area within the frontier or on one side of the boundary line is considered a homogeneous community with a single identity, while the one outside it is considered heterogeneous from it.[22] One of the aims of this work is to go beyond this perspective.

During the period from 1990-1, my fieldwork experience provided me with a way of countering this framework. The very processes which prevented me from travelling across the Karakoram into Central Asia or to Baltistan, because of the contest over national borders in this area, made me choose two villages on one side of the cease-fire line. This resulted in an attempt to 'dialogise' my study in terms of internal contrasts and parallels between social groups in the region. My fieldwork was done in two villages, one on the travel route to (formerly) Soviet Central Asia and the other on the travel route to Chinese Central Asia. Tegar lies on the banks of the Nubra-Siachen river, while Hundar is on the banks of the Shyok river. Both villages are large, with about two hundred households each. The first is nearly completely Buddhist (except for four Muslim families); the second has a mixed population of Buddhists and Muslims (both Sunni and of the Nurbakshia sect). Both villages are along routes that were important in the past in matters of trade, pilgrimage, and other kinds of exchange and, in the present period, are along the main routes to the sites of conflict with Pakistan in the east and in the west. I resided with a Sunni Muslim family in Hundar and with a Buddhist family in Tegar. I was thus able to observe at close quarters, the similarities and differences among the two most important religious communities in Ladakh. 'Participant-observation' meant that I not only attended and witnessed all important events in the two villages - dramas, visits to the monastery and the mosque, festivals, and so on – but that I also assisted the members of both families in tasks in the field and the house such as sowing, making of beds, gathering vegetables for sale to the army or for use in the house, or bringing water. The Nubra valley has one planting season in these parts, from March-April to about October or so, growing mainly barley, mustard, lucerne and vegetables. I also taught informally in the village middle school in Tegar for a while. My fieldwork experience in the Nubra valley allowed me to understand frontier areas as cultural zones with two features: a diachronic process which has created cross-cutting ties (whether these be linguistic, commercial, or religious); and the 'community' as constituted by different levels of integration depending on the nature of practice and exchange between and within social units. The community is defined in this work as a dynamic, historical entity whose organizational basis depends on the type of social praxis. It is not monolithic in nature, but is viewed as the site of a ceaseless struggle between centripetal and centrifugal forces; this is analogous to the definition of language followed by some authors.[23] An account of the social organization of the two villages in Nubra valley is given in Part One of this book.

In the winter of 1990, an event occurred which forced me to question my identity as a fieldworker in Ladakh: this was the possession of the priest of the village temple in Tegar, whence he became an oracle. It also clarified a number of issues which are central to the second aim of this work: to understand the pathways of language and communication in a culture as not only linguistic but also sensory and visceral. I hope to make a contribution in this study to the sociology of Ladakh and also to linguistic anthropology.

The issue of a fieldworker's identity has been examined in a great many studies.[24] Two anthropologists have looked at the issue of their and others' identities in areas which, like Ladakh, are frontiers having been subjected to similar geo-political pressures. J.P.S. Uberoi states that the Tajiks of Andarab district in Afghanistan have three main institutions – the Afghan state, Islam, and the family – producing an overall identity of unitary allegiance. In his fieldwork, Uberoi adopted two chief roles: that of a semi-permanent resident of the bazaar where he rented a room and where men from different villages visited him to exchange communications of various kinds; and that of a visitor to other parts of the district and to people's homes where he was received in the domains frequented by men. He was an outsider to each of the Tajik institutions: in relation to Islam, he was a non-believer, in relation to the Afghan state, he was a non-Afghan, and in relation to the family, he was a single male. His identity was defined as a series of negations of identity in the field.[25] Similarly, Frederik Barth describes how the Swat Pathans move between different ethnic groups by passing from one side of the cultural boundary to another. They adopt cultural markers of different groups, doffing and donning identities like masks.[26]

My identity in the field was constructed neither as a negation nor as a masquerade, but at various levels, as I moved from Leh to the Nubra valley. After spending many hours in the bazaar and libraries in Leh, a serendipitous meeting with Wangchuk Kalon and his family led me to decide on visiting the Nubra valley, so far unresearched by any sociologist. The Nubra valley is an 'inner-line' area, and permission to visit this militarily strategic region was not only difficult, but I was also confronted with the fact that maps published by the Indian government do not depict the valley in detail, except for the location of mountain ranges and rivers. So the valley was literally a 'blank' space in my mind's eye before I began the journey. When I reached the Khardung pass (18,500 feet) at the end of a day-long journey by truck in October 1989, equipped with an inner-line pass from the District Commissioner, Leh, bad weather and snowfall forced us to halt at the pass for the night. Temperatures were sub-zero, and I spent a cold night in a shed at 14,000 feet. The next morning I was embroiled in a controversy when the army discovered my presence there: a single Indian woman on the top of a mountain seemed suspicious (another 'spy' had been apprehended recently, soldiers told me). Although I had a permit from the district headquarters, I found that authority in an area like Nubra valley is ambiguous. The areas of civil and military jurisdiction are difficult to separate and for some hours it seemed that I would be forced to turn back. It was noon of the second day when I finally reached the village of Tegar. If I had learned in my library research that the frontier of Ladakh had involved a contest for territorial boundaries, I found that overlapping jurisdictions and claims characterize it today. If I had unconsciously described my journey as a 'reconnaissance', I had been unwillingly cast into the role of a spy. Like Kipling's Kim, I was to ask myself many times during my fieldwork, who I was and if I was there merely conducting some kind of 'cultural' espionage as a researcher.

In my second period of fieldwork, as I began to live in Tegar in the house of a farmer, the area and its people began to acquire a form through the activities I was engaged in with them – working in the field, participating in rituals, and so on. I had been requested by the priest of the village temple, familiarly called 'Gelong', to teach him English. Gelong was a monk at the Samstanling monastery close to Tegar village. He belonged to the neighbouring village of Chamshen and had been with the monastery for two-thirds of his thirty-odd years. He was rather unworldly, in comparison with some of the other monks I met, and would often come to chat with me on his way to the houses of villagers for performing different rituals. Most of those who join the monastery when young rarely travel far from it, their movements being strictly monitored, and their routines equally rigid. It appeared that he had only occasionally been out of the valley and, within Nubra itself, had not travelled very far down the Shyok's route. His countenance often bore a rather bashful expression or an enquiring one. When Leh politics, the Siachen war, Hindi films, or other topics were discussed by a group of us, he wore an expression of polite interest. He appeared to be friendlier with younger people in the village rather than those of his own age-group. In our household, three-year old Jigmet was his greatest rival, especially when it came to our English classes. It was generally agreed that he had little ambition, even within the monastery hierarchy itself, which was the object of mockery by other monks. He had been told by a village oracle that he had the ability to master 360 languages. That, coupled with the novelty of our conversations, fueled his desire to learn English. Did he believe the oracle, I asked. 'Everyone believes the oracle, and nobody listens to the monk!', he replied.

The two languages that I spoke at that time were English and Hindi, while the monk spoke Ladakhi and some Urdu. I had not learnt Ladakhi before going to Ladakh, but acquired it in a variety of local contexts as my fieldwork proceeded. Our lessons occurred in a mixture of Hindi and Urdu. Within a Hindi syntax, I used a largely Sanskritized vocabulary, substituting Ladakhi words as I went along. Gelong used Urdu. I was able to acquire the Tibetan script in which Ladakhi is written, which is somewhat similar to Devanagiri. I also mastered, to some extent, the syntax of Ladakhi which followed the same order of 'subject-object-verb', as did Hindi. I would transcribe an English sentence into the Ladakhi script for Gelong to pronounce since he found English phonetically mystifying. A similar process of transcription occurs in everyday life in Ladakh, when many Ladakhis transcribe a Ladakhi sentence into the Urdu or Persian script, which they learn at school. This is simpler than using written or literary Ladakhi which has elaborate rules of grammar.

Gelong, however, never fully learnt the English language as, in February of 1991, he became possessed by the deity of the village temple, Chamshing, and became an oracle. He made a transition that I had made, although in a slightly different domain: he substituted a new vocabulary in a syntax familiar to him – the speech of a deity in the syntax of spoken Ladakhi. However, he seemed to have renounced English in favour of another language of power, one which had its origins in the sacred sphere. I acquired a language of everyday life, whereas Gelong acquired a language of oracular possession.

A coordinate event occurred when I attempted to learn the Arabic script while residing with the family of the priest of the Sunni mosque in Hundar. While Ladakhi is the language of both religious groups of Muslims and Buddhists in this part of the Nubra valley, Arabic is regarded as the language of the Koran. The non-correspondence of Arabic, in phonetics and script, with any language I knew, made it difficult for me to acquire any mastery over it. However, since I was staying with a Sunni family during *Ramzan*, I participated in the fast of the holy month and the feast afterwards.

My status changed many times in the field. Initially, I was cast into the role of a spy, but my role changed in the second phase. For the first half of the year, I spent my days in near complete silence; I could not speak any Ladakhi initially and spent my days largely speechless in the language of the villagers, a pupil in their culture and ways. Most of the villagers in fact, called me *pomo* (girl child). The only time when I was not in a child-like role was when I was with Gelong. Our language lesson proceeded everyday till January of 1991 when a break occurred due to Gelong's possession. Our classes were never resumed.

Gelong and I were to participate in a ritual which occurs in the first month of the Buddhist calendar, roughly from 15 February to 15 March. The purpose of this ritual in the monastery is to cement ties of friendship between two strangers and bind them into 'ritual siblingship'. Two strangers thus joined are to assist each other from that moment, exchange gifts, and to be in a relationship of reciprocity. However, this did not take place because of Gelong's possession. Symbolically, however, I felt that we were bound into siblingship by the linguistic reversals on our parts and the synchronizing of the exchange of markers of language and identity. I found that by January, I could understand Ladakhi and could largely dispense with English and Hindi, while Gelong was 'speaking in tongues', the language of the spirit. I left Tegar for Hundar about this time to do fieldwork with Muslim families. Since I had arrived during Ramzan, I spent a great deal of my time as a neophyte, in fasting, silence and prayer, alongside members of the family I stayed with.

Thus, all kinds of role-reversals occurred during my fieldwork. Role-reversal has been described as a state when players become their 'others' — novices become priests, teachers become pupils, and vice-versa. My state also had the characteristics of initiation rites during which initiates go through a period of social death (to old roles and statuses), the signs of which are silence, invisibility and a child-like state. Much of what is given as axiomatic by society is interrogated and there is a reflection on core values of culture and religion; initiates are bound into comradeship, and there is a sense of correspondence between a religious paradigm and human experience.[27] My experiences during my fieldwork led me to translate the cultural processes of the valley in terms of such role changes and a multiplicity of domains and identities. Also, due to Gelong's transformation, I began to look at oracular possession, not just as a ritual process or as a symbolic reflection of complex political and material transformations in the frontier villages of Nubra valley, but as a semantic of the body – both social and individual.

It is true that the researcher is in part a collector of cultural artifacts; he/she follows the pathways opened up by the processes of a culture and by others, listens to numerous stories, and weaves them into images which satisfy the linear process of analysis. But this intellectual exercise is only a part of the total enterprise of understanding. An equally central portion belongs to the understanding of the visceral pathways of culture. What is it to grieve, lose one's soul, or laugh in a community? How people build houses, prepare the foods they eat, carry out the organization of work in summer and winter, or who they marry, occur as a result of social processes and commonly accepted cultural codes, to be sure. But as the researcher participates in various domains, he/she begins to understand jokes which are told, what it is to feel the cold and weariness after work, fears of being attacked by demons and ghosts at night, and any number of feelings which register themselves on the body.

This non-linear experience is often not captured in most descriptions of cultures. The cases described in Part Two of this book are an attempt to understand how social categories are a support not only of symbols but also structures of feeling. It also aims to understand the relationship between linguistic forms and the body, both the personal and the body-politic, thus forging links between the study of language and anthropology or sociology.

Notes

1. Pallis 1974 [1939]:168-9.
2. Ibid.,:200.
3. There are two well known histories of Ladakh written in Ladakhi (Gergan 1976 and Rabgyas 1984) and one in Urdu (Khan 1939). But these have been overshadowed largely by a Tibeto-centric perspective on the area. Social anthropological studies on Ladakh are recent. Till 1980, much of the literature was part of Tibetan studies influenced largely by Orientalist concerns. In the last

two decades, Ladakh has become accessible for study to sociologists and anthropologists. Till date, the most complete bibliography on Ladakh is Bray and Shakspo 1989. At Hernhut, the International Association for Ladakh Studies (IALS) was formed as a forum for scholars interested in Ladakh. It publishes an occasional newsletter, 'Ladakh Studies'. A number of colloquia under its aegis have been held: in 1981 in Konstanz (Germany), in 1985 at Pau (France) and in 1987 at Hernhut (Germany). These proceedings have been published (Dendalechte and Kaplanian 1985; Icke-Schwalbe and Meier 1990; Kantowski and Sander 1983). Four more colloquia have been held: in Bristol in 1989, in London in 1992, in Leh in 1993, and in Bonn in 1995. See Osmaston and Denwood 1996; Osmaston and Nawang Tsering [forth-coming].

4. Among the earliest travellers were William Moorcroft and George Trebeck, employees of the East India Company, who travelled through Ladakh in the early nineteenth century, ostensibly to buy Turkman horses for the cavalry, but covertly with the design of discovering and preventing Russian expansion in this area. The most comprehensive of the early surveys of Ladakh is Alexander Cunningham's *Ladak: Physical, Statistical and Historical with notices of surrounding countries* published first in 1854, a source many geographers continue to use. However, the *Gazetteer of Kashmir and Ladak,* first brought out in 1890, is the most reliable source on the cultural and topographical features of Ladakh in the nineteenth century. It was compiled by the Quarter-Master General's branch in Calcutta and is based on all the information provided by previous travellers, explorers and government officials.

5. Bray 1991:115-33.

6. See for instance, Drew 1976 [1875] and Thomson 1978 [1852].

7. Shaw 1984 [1871]:18. In 1868, Robert Shaw made a pioneering journey to Shahidulla, a frontier post in the Karakoram. His account expresses the strategic and commercial potentialities that this region had for the British. He was a tea planter who set out from Leh in 1868, the same year that the Russians added Samarkand to their possessions, to become the first Englishman to visit Chinese Turkestan. He was in a race to do so with another Englishman, George Hayward, whose sponsorship was official.

8. Curzon's basic thesis was that with the collision of two or more politico-territorial systems, a primary stage is reached in which the major contestants leave a vaguely defined frontier zone between them; a secondary stage occurs when the frontier zone acquires internal political form in the creation of buffer states; a tertiary stage is arrived at when the zone collapses due to peripheral political pressures and the alignment of buffer states to a boundary line capable of precise definition. (See Curzon 1907).

9. This is expressed by Fraser in his *Trans-Himalaya Unveiled.* The Karakoram mountains, according to him, form an inner-line of defence and along with desert, are a no-man's land which no one cared to penetrate. With the Russian penetration of Central Asia, the age-old commercial connection between various regions was threatened. The profits of the trade from goods like charas, a

narcotic, comprising about one third of the imports into Ladakh and another principal import, wool, from Tibet, were great. Fraser states: 'Present-day imports and exports' average about Rs.25,00,000 annually, nearly equally divided. In 1904-5, there were ten lakhs of merchandise either way...' (Fraser 1986 [1910]:124). This trade was subject to taxes of various kinds and attempts were made to increase trade through the building of roads, supply depots of food, horses, caravanserais, etc.

10. For the purpose of detailed information on villages, the best source of information in the pre-1947 period is the Land Settlement. This *Bandobast* was carried out for every village in the area and completed by 1908, fixing the ownership of the land among various owners, their social origins and status, the crops grown on the land under cultivation, the area which was barren, the various categories of land, and so on. Most of the changes in ownership were recorded in the *Jamabandi* which were produced every six years or so. The documents are to be found in the office of the Tehsildar of Leh. There are many gaps in the *Jamabandis* for some were destroyed in a fire in the post-independence period. They were not made after 1947.

11. These details are from an interview conducted in the winter of 1990 with E. Joldan, an early Christian convert of Leh.

12. See Jaeschke 1975 [1881].

13. Bray (forthcoming).

14. At a completely romantic level, the missionaries sometimes saw Ladakh as an inversion of the world at home. The Hebers speak of Ladakh as 'the veritable home of merry sprites and strange goblins' (Heber 1976 [1923]: 17), where things go the other way and are topsy-turvy.

15. See Bray 1990 and Bray (forthcoming).

16. A.H. Francke's articles on Ladakh, his *A History of Ladakh*, originally published in 1907 and reissued as an annotated edition in 1977, along with his two-volume work on the antiquities of the area, remain to date the most definitive works on the subject. Many of his assertions were supplemented by two other scholars, Luciano Petech and Guiseppe Tucci, in the 1930's.

17. Samuel 1982 has pointed out that what goes under the rubric of 'Tibetan' society was far more diverse and changing than has been assumed. He states that these societies, in and on the periphery of Central Tibet, had a greater variety in their social and political formations than is usually appreciated. It makes little sense to think of all these regions as lying within a centralized state ruled by a theocratic government at Lhasa.

18. The latest figures which are available for the population of this area for the period of my fieldwork are from the *Economic Review* published by the District Statistical Evaluation Agency, Leh, for the year 1990-1, and the annual reports of the Lead Bank of the State Bank of India, Leh. Since Leh and Kargil districts of Ladakh were given Scheduled Tribe status in 1991, figures have been collected of various cultural groups in this area but were unavailable to researchers at the time of writing this book.

19. See Rizvi 1995 and Warikoo 1995 for analyses of the role of Ladakh as an entrepot between 1846-1947, and Bray 1990a for the significance of Ladakh's trade relations with Lhasa.

20. See Bertelsen 1995, Srinivas 1991 and 1993, and Van Beek and Bertelsen 1995. Van Beek 1996, in particular, shows how different census documents and reports employed various categories—'race', 'caste', 'tribe' and 'religion'-for describing Ladakh and how these have been employed in the fashioning of Ladakhi identities. There are other kinds of reports and surveys, both by the British and Indian governments, which form part of the attempt to record the politico-geographical limits of this area and, in the post-1947 situation of conflicting jurisdictions in Ladakh between Pakistan, China and India, to establish prior claims of the various disputants. Some of these are dealt with in Fisher et.al. 1963; Gillard 1977; Mehra 1992 and Woodman 1969.

21. See for instance, the definition of the frontier provided by Lattimore 1968 [1956]:374.

22. It follows that for current theorists of the frontier (such as Lamb 1968), an unstable national boundary is one that does not coincide with the limits of national identity, however this is defined (in terms of language, ethnicity, or religion).

23. In this work, I follow M.M. Bakhtin's theory of language and the oeuvre associated with him, for instance, the works of V.N. Volosinov. Society is represented by Bakhtin as a polysemic, contradictory world, where different 'voices' (a world view, discourse, and practice) speak different tongues. His basic assumption is that society is inseparable from language because language is the primary medium of social interaction. See Chapter three, for the relationship between the definition of 'community' used in this book and the nature of signification in such a site. Part Two of this book also relies on the ideas of Bakhtin and Volosinov for an understanding of cultural processes in the Nubra valley.

24. A recent sensitive exploration of the issues involved in participant-observation and the fragility and interpersonal nature of fieldwork material is to be found in Okely and Callaway 1992. Atkinson 1990 deals with the textual modalities and rhetorical devices through which ethnographies 'produce' social reality.

25. See Uberoi 1964:78-89 et passim.

26. Barth 1969:9-38 et passim. In Rudyard Kipling's '*Kim*', we have the story of an Irish boy who travels along the Grand Trunk Road across India with a Buddhist monk. In chapter after chapter, he undergoes a series of metamorphoses which allows him to speak in many dialects and adopt many roles. His existential dilemma – 'Who is Kim?' – is solved by a strategy which Barth describes as 'passing'.

27.   Turner 1969:166-203 et passim. Contrast this explanation of the anthropologist's role with that of Nash 1963 who, deriving his analysis from the works of Georg Simmel and Alfred Schutz, casts the researcher into the role of marginality, rather than liminality, experiencing anomie and alienation. Cultural pluralism, according to him, occurs only in the anthropological community, while fieldwork is a struggle to be 'objective', rather than to maintain multiple identities. See also Srinivas 1995 which explores the idea of dialogism and role reversal in fieldwork.

Chapter 2

The Frontier Region of Ladakh

A BRIEF DESCRIPTION OF THE LADAKH REGION

Ladakh, the eastern region of Jammu and Kashmir state, covers an area of about 58,321 sq.km. (occupying approximately the grid from 32°15'N to 36°N latitude and 75°15'E to 80°15'E longitude). It is situated in the trans-Himalayan zone bounded by high mountains with passes located above 4,400 mts. It is a cold desert, presenting a system of alternating valleys and mountain ranges. Before the ceasefire line was drawn with China and Pakistan in 1949, the Ladakh region was composed of three tehsils – Leh, Kargil and Skardu – with an area of about 95,876 sq.km.[1] The area under effective administration today is a shrunken tract which is only about two-thirds of the area that existed before 1947. Ladakh was divided into two districts, Leh and Kargil, in 1979. A recent enumeration gives the percentage of Muslims in Ladakh division (including Kargil, Leh and Skardu tehsils) in 1941 as 86.71 percent and Buddhists as 12.89 percent. In 1971, these were 44.66 percent and 51.82 percent and in 1981, 46.05 percent and 50.88 percent, respectively. The drastic change in their proportions was a result of a variety of factors such as the occupation of certain territories by Pakistan and the out-migration of the Muslim population.[2] The exact distribution of various communities in each tehsil (now each district) in this decade is not available, though it is assumed that Muslims predominate in Kargil and Buddhists in Leh. The estimated population of Leh district, where the fieldwork for this study was conducted, was 89474 persons in 1991.[3]

The mountain ranges form the most important physiographic feature, running parallel to each other traversing the region from southeast to north-west. Most of the population is engaged in agriculture although the growing season is short, usually from about April to October.[4] Nearly all the villages are found in river valleys situated close to streams and springs. The Indus valley lies between the Ladakh and Zanskar ranges; the Shyok and Nubra valleys between the Ladakh and Karakoram; the Suru, Dras and Wakha valleys occupy the whole of the Kargil district towards the Great Himalayan range; the Zanskar valley is located between the Great Himalayan range and the Zanskar range; and the Hanle valley lies in the region of the Rupshu plains to the south-east of Ladakh.

While it is true that in one respect, the Ladakh region can be said to lie within the boundaries formed by the mountains of the Karakoram, Ladakh, Zanskar and Greater Himalayan ranges, a closer examination reveals that such a coincidence of natural and cultural boundaries is a fiction. In practice, the traffic of men and women, commercial products, religions, and languages across this region makes it difficult to demarcate strict cultural territories. For example, the nomads of Changthang moved in search of pastures across wide regions, respecting topographical features in their nomadic mode of life, but not necessarily political or cultural divisions between Ladakh and Tibet. Similarly, the history of Islam in Ladakh was linked closely with the history of Islam in Kashmir and Central Asia. It is said that a Turkish saint, Sharafuddin, converted a fugitive Ladakhi prince, Rinchen, the ruler of the Kashmir valley, in 1320. Many Muslim converts date from the time of Hazrat Syed Ali Hamdani, a Kashmiri scholar on his way to Kashgar in 1394, and Syed Mohammed Nur Baksh, a disciple of Hamdani in the early fifteenth century.[5] As many as seventy five travel routes traversing this area are mentioned for the period ending in 1900.[6] The old Yarkandi passage, for instance, crossed the Nubra valley through the Saser pass in summer. Many persons in the valley had made the journey towards Yarkand. Oral accounts state that the route from the Saser pass to Panamik was three days, and from Spang Chenmo, near the Khardung pass, to Leh, about a day. The Yarkandi traders brought wool, leather boots, silk and charas with them. They took back tea, cotton and precious stones. Usually, they came with a team of thirty or forty horses and camels before the grass-cutting season in the Nubra valley and would pay upto fifty rupees for pasture. Many of the Yarkandis were proceeding for the pilgrimage to Mecca. On the other route down the Shyok, the *Balti*, as the inhabitants of Baltistan were known, would come for work to the valley and also for some trade in grain.

Trade, art, pilgrimage and transhumance thus linked Ladakh with Tibet, Yarkand, Kashmir and Punjab, leading to diverse influences culturally. This is evident in the nature of the social groups in Ladakh today.

THE SOCIAL GROUPS IN LADAKH

In a critical introduction to Francke's history of Ladakh, S.S. Gergan and F.M. Hussain say that Francke is correct in stating that the present population of Ladakh is the result of a long process of blending of diverse peoples. Two of these are of Aryan 'stock', while one, which is numerically greater in number than the others, is of Mongolian origin. The Aryan peoples are the Dards of Gilgit and the Mons of North India, perhaps from Kashmir, but the Mongolians are of Tibetan origin.[7] The *Balti* have not been included by Francke in the Tibetan group in spite of the fact that they speak Tibetan, or that they had a Tibetan literary tradition before they adopted Islam. Their existence testifies that the relationship of language, ethnic origin, and religion is a complex one in Ladakh.[8] The older religion of the Dards was said to have been Mahayanic Buddhism and they converted to Shia Islam in the fourteenth and fifteenth centuries.

Islam was introduced into Baltistan about the same period and was probably, at first, a Sufi form of Shia Islam whose followers were called the Nurbakshia.

Shia communities, who dominate in Kargil district and are sometimes referred to as the *Balti* regardless of their geographical origin, are essentially agricultural and are similar to their Buddhist neighbours economically. Around Leh town, however, they tend to be quite poor, and are employed by Kashmiri Muslims for a variety of menial tasks, and as tanners, cobblers, and butchers. Other Shias, such as the richer Sayyid families, devoted themselves in the past to the profits of trans-Himalayan trade, the breakdown of which has forced them into seeking new occupational opportunities. Many of the links of Shia communities with

Buddhist ones were probably strengthened by the marriage of various Rnam-rgyal kings of Leh with women from Purig and Baltistan. Buddhist traditions survived long after Islam was adopted by them – for instance, the offering of lamps, and ceremonies to local deities.[9] By all accounts, Islamization of Ladakh was a complex process but it is certain that before the fourteenth century, Ladakh was Buddhist. The Buddhism of that period, however, did not bear resemblance to the institutionalized Buddhism of eastern Ladakh, especially from the seventeenth century onwards.[10] Further, although there is evidence that Sufi traditions from Persia and Kashmir (for instance, the Nurbakshia) and Central Asia (perhaps the Naqshbandiyya) influenced Islam in Ladakh, today there is greater orthodoxy than before in practices among Ladakhi Shia Muslims; this, however, has been paralleled by a certain revivalism among Buddhists in Ladakh as well.

Besides these groups, there are Buddhists who dominate in the east, north and south, i.e. in Nubra, Rupshu, Leh and Zanskar. Both the Reformed and Unreformed orders of Gelugpa and Drugpa are represented in Ladakh. Francke remarks that at the time of the Tibetan-Dard kingdoms (500–1000), there were two coexisting faiths – Bon and Buddhism. Buddhism entered Ladakh through two channels: the ancient Mons brought it from India and the Dards brought it from Gilgit. Buddhism was also strengthened during this period by the migration of many Buddhist monks from Kashmir, the most famous of these being the teacher Rinchen Bzangpo.[11] In the seventh century, with the arrival of the Buddhist teacher, Padma Sambhava, and the conversion of the Tibetan king, the primitive monastic community of Samye, south of Lhasa, developed into a key centre of the Nyingmapa. The Nyingmapa, more than any other order, appropriated many of the symbols and sciences of the Bon.[12] In the eighth century, Padma Sambhava visited Zanskar, Sakti and Phokar in Ladakh. It was during the reign of Lhachen Ngorub, in the early fourteenth century, that the practice of novices being sent to Tibet was introduced which not only dealt a death-blow to the Bon faith which had lingered on till then, but also was the end of the forms of Indian Buddhism; Lhasa became the cultural centre of Buddhism.[13]

The Kagyud sect was started by Marpa, whose teacher was Naropa. Marpa visited India three times to receive teachings and became famous also as a translator. In A.D.1010, Naropa came to Lamayuru and

Zanskar and in A.D.1100, Marpa, his disciple, built Marpaling in Zanskar. Even before the glorious period of that sect, during the reign of Seng-ge-rnam-rgyal in the early seventeenth century, this sect seems to have had a wide following in Ladakh. The Sakya sect began to spread in Ladakh from A.D. 1300. In the fourteenth century, the reformer Tsong Khapa came from the marches of Kansu to create the Gelugpa in Tibet, who are distinguished from the Drugpa by being less slack in their observance of certain rules. For example, abstaining from alcohol, marriage, meat-eating, paying more attention to daily ritual offices, and also in their orientation to Lhasa. Tsong Khapa built the monastery of Gaden in A.D.1413, while his disciples built those of Sera, Drepung and Tashilhunpo. In the first half of the fifteenth century, two ascetics arrived in Ladakh from Tibet sent by Tsong Khapa. The king began to patronize the Gelug sect and the Spituk monastery was built then.[14] Some monasteries in Nubra, for example at Diskit, were also built during the fifteenth century. Monasteries continue to exist as important religious and cultural centres in Ladakh. In Leh district, nearly every large village has a monastery close to it. The monasteries own a considerable amount of land, each with a number of villages affiliated to it.

Apart from these groups, whose links with other regions and religious orders has been complicated by a turbulent political history, there is a smaller group comprising of those who are known locally as *Arghuns*, who are a group born of marriage between Muslims (usually from Central Asia or Kashmir) and Ladakhi Buddhists. While the term refers generally to descendants of ethnically mixed marriages, it has come to refer to the descendants of Kashmiri Muslim fathers and Ladakhi Buddhist mothers, most of them Sunni Muslims adhering to the Hanafi school of law. Although there are a number of rich Shia families who trace their descent to great trading houses of the pre-1947 period and claim they came from Central Asia, it is the Sunnis who have more diverse origins. Many came as officials and traders in shawl wool in the seventeenth century and traded until 1950 with the Central Asians. Some of them married local Buddhist women, and their links with their families in Central Asia, Kashmir or Tibet, made them valued commercial mediators. Many of the traders were palace traders and received special privileges in return for services to the royal family. The Rnam-rgyal king, fearing an invasion from Aurangazeb, agreed to construct a Sunni mosque in Leh (this was finally completed about A.D.1666–7). It was, however, after the Ladakhi king was forced to seek the assistance of the Mughals to drive away the combined forces of the Tibeto-Mongol army in 1679 that many Kashmiri Muslim traders began to settle in Ladakh. Some Sunnis also came later as refugees from Chinese Turkestan.

A number of Sunnis came with the Dogra administration, as in Zanskar, or migrated to Ladakh as crafts people, such as makers of coins. There is also a pocket of Hanafi Sunnis at Dras.[15]

There is a very small Christian population who were converted chiefly from Buddhism when the first Moravian missions were established in Leh around the middle of the nineteenth century. The total number of Moravians, according to the Moravian pastor in Leh, was about 165 in 1993.[16]

LADAKH AND ADMINISTRATION BY THE INDIAN STATE[17]

In 1846, Kashmir was handed over to Maharaja Gulab Singh by the British through the Treaty of Amritsar and Ladakh became a part of Jammu and Kashmir. The king of Ladakh, at the time of General Zorawar Singh's invasion of the region in 1834, Tondup Namgyal, was made a titular head and on his death, a minor, Jigmet Namgyal, was appointed king in 1840. Till 1846, however, no administrative apparatus could be set up due to continuing insurrection in Baltistan, Purig, Zanskar, Skardu and Ladakh. Military garrisons were set up and afterwards, administra-tive heads, designated 'Thanedars', continued to exercise civil and military powers. By the time of the last two administrators, Radha Krishen Kaul (1882-6) and Chandri Khushi Mohammed (1902-5), it had become customary to call these heads, 'Wazirs'. The last two were responsible for initiating, revising and completing the Land Settlement of Ladakh and Zanskar. The Land Settlement was, perhaps, the most influential measure undertaken by the Dogras. The Maharajas, who were Hindus, banned cow slaughter in Ladakh and in the early 1870's, an effort was made to start a school in Leh and propagate Hindu scriptures. Hinduism, however, had little impact on Ladakh in contrast to Kinnaur and Lahaul. Monasteries continued to function as usual with the government granting them privileges and officials attending monastery festivals. Even the *Lopchak* (triennial trade missions) to Tibet continued. The king retained his apex position within the social hierarchy and, during the New Year festival, was allowed to set up court in the royal palace. New associations emerged: the Ladakh Buddhist Association was founded in 1934 (registered in 1937) on the instigation of Kashmiri Pandit neo-Buddhists. It was active in local politics at that time as well, chiefly through social reform campaigns. The relations between Muslims and Buddhists, however, were not overtly hostile.

With the partition of the Indian sub-continent and the accession of Kashmir to India, Ladakh became part of the Indian union in October, 1947. A popular government was installed under Sheik Mohammed Abdullah at Srinagar when war broke out with Pakistan. By 1948, parts of Skardu and Gilgit were under Pakistani occupation and the rest of the region under civil rule from Srinagar. The Ladakhis felt, as expressed in delegations to the centre, that on the transfer of power from the descendants of Maharaja Gulab Singh to the National Conference of Kashmir, the constitutional links between Ladakh and the state were broken; Ladakh could not be bound by any decision of plebiscite by Kashmir.

At this point, it must be recognized that the effects of the incorporation of the Ladakh region into a modern state framework had a profound impact, unprecedented in past history. The change in the status of Ladakhis to citizens and the democratization of the political process led to certain elites – the Buddhist clergy and the landed class, chiefly – organizing themselves to promote certain political demands. Although economic factors were important, the form and content of political contest in the period after 1947 is understandable chiefly in the context of the widening and deepening of state intervention in Ladakh as well as the destruction of its previous economic role as a Central Asian entrepot: this not only displaced a number of persons connected with the old trade – Kashmiri Muslims, Central Asians, and so on — it also forced others – *Arghuns* and *Baltis* – to seek new economic niches.[18] It is also important to note that the various forms of organization that developed were not premised always on the same idea of community, 'Buddhist' or otherwise. There is evidence of alliances and cleavages of various sorts in addition to class differences between Shia and Sunni Ladakhis, Buddhists and Muslims, and state and central governments.

Under the Sheik's rule, Ladakh was represented by Kushok Bakula, a head monk of Spituk monastery. He was the President of the Leh unit of the National Conference and a member of the Legislative Assembly till the government of Sheik Abdullah fell in 1953. Under Sheik Abdullah's regime, Ladakh continued to be neglected and the services of the Panchayat and cooperative systems or utilities like electric power, hospitals, or canals, were not forthcoming. Further, the demand that Zanskar should be transferred to Leh tehsil from Kargil (on the grounds that its culture was more akin to Leh than Kargil) continued to be ignored (as it is even today). Neglect of this region and misrepresentation by the Kashmiri government about figures of various religious communities in Ladakh could well have been the beginning of demands for regional autonomy.

It was as a result of demands for representation in state services, provision of utilities, and the recognition of Ladakh's strategic political value, that led to the grant (for each tehsil) in 1952, of a district committee with a Deputy Commissioner, a Superintendent of Police, and an MLA (Member of the Legislative Assembly).

With the Bakshi Gulam Mohammed government assuming office in Srinagar, some changes occurred. Bakula was inducted into the state's Council of Ministers as a Deputy Minister in charge of Ladakh Affairs in 1953. Later, a Ladakh Affairs Department was created with funds provided by the state budget, the schemes of which were to be discharged by the Deputy Commissioner. After the 1962 Chinese aggression, the region assumed a greater strategic importance than before. The army presence in Ladakh increased and has never diminished since. The Bakshi Gulam Mohammed rule (1953-63) ended with G.M. Sadiq taking over as the next Prime Minister (later designated as Chief Minister). Sadiq was responsible for a further decentralization in Ladakh's administration. Bakula was inducted into the Council of Ministers as a Minister of State for Ladakh Affairs, Health and Local Self-Government. A Development Committee was set up as well.

In the 1967 general elections, the Leh Assembly ticket was given to Kushok Bakula's nominee, Sonam Wangyal, and the Kargil ticket to Agha Mohammed Khan. They faced contest from Kushok Thikse in Leh and Kacho Mohammed Ali Khan in Kargil, both of whom were supported by Srinagar. The Sadiq-Bakula antagonism had clearly come to the fore. Till this period, the National Conference was the only political party in the state and the Democratic National Conference under Sadiq merged with it. The Congress made an appearance in Leh with the merger of the two Conferences in Leh and Srinagar. With the latter party being wound up in Leh, it was replaced by the Congress.

Differences emerged and two factions were formed in this party – Congress 'A' and 'B' – each asserting itself as the de-facto party. The legislators, Ali Khan and Sonam Norbu (Member of the Legislative Council (MLC) and earlier Deputy Commissioner), belonged to one faction and were felt to be supporters of Sadiq, while Wangyal and Bakula were allies. When Norbu was appointed Ambassador to Mongolia, the position of MLC was filled by his associate, P. Namgyal.

The two factions were, at this point, largely divided in their support of religious communities – one (Congress 'B') led by the Thikse monastery's reincarnate monk, regarded the region as comprising of Muslim and Buddhist Ladakhis, while the other (Congress 'A') led by Kushok Bakula of Spituk monastery, increasingly advocated that Ladakh, or Leh tehsil at least, was a Buddhist culture area.

In Ladakh, the definition of Ladakhi identity was, thus, a contested site between monasteries and secular powers, and traditionalists and modernists. This was complicated by a background of personal rivalries.

A movement gathered momentum under the Buddhist Action Committee after 1969 over a local incident. The agitation launched by the committee included the demand for the declaration of Ladakhis as a Scheduled Tribe, settlement of Tibetan refugees in Ladakh, and the recognition of Ladakhi in schools. Except for the induction of Wangyal (who was elected to the State Assembly in 1967) into the Council of Ministers, no real concessions were made. In 1971, with the demise of G.M.Sadiq, Syed Mir Qasim was sworn in as Chief Minister of Jammu and Kashmir. Developmental efforts continued to be sluggish and in 1973, a movement headed by Lama Lobzang for Union Territory and Scheduled Tribe status for Ladakh was launched. It was opposed by leaders like Sonam Wangyal and P. Namgyal on the grounds that it represented a threat to national integration. There were also statements made by Kushok Bakula that Ladakhis were opposed to the demand for a restoration of the pre-1953 position in Jammu and Kashmir state and that the experience of Ladakh under successive state governments called for an abrogation of Article 370, a demand which came to naught.

In 1975, a government backed by the Congress in Delhi of Sheik Abdullah and the National Conference was installed in Srinagar and some attempts at a rapprochement were made. Kushok Bakula, however, declined to rejoin the National Conference, driving a further wedge in political relations in Ladakh between Srinagar and Leh, between the National Conference and the Congress, as well as the two Congress factions. This was followed in July 1979 by a bifurcation of the district of Ladakh into two districts (a predominantly Buddhist district of Leh and a predominantly Muslim district of Kargil, with the Buddhist area of Zanskar attached to it), adding distinctive communal tones to other kinds of divisions. In the 1977 Assembly elections, Leh tehsil had already elected a Buddhist Congress (I) candidate and Kargil, a Muslim National Conference candidate. It is important to note at this point that while electoral patterns in Leh and Kargil for the seats of MLA went to the respective majority community, the Member of Parliament seat in the Lok Sabha (until 1989) went to the Leh Buddhist candidate. Nor did the National Conference and the Congress merely reflect religious divisions in Ladakh: the Congress itself for more than a decade was deeply divided between A and B factions, a division that often cross-cut religious lines.

Personal rivalries continued as well. Norbu, who had contested the State Assembly elections from Ladakh as a Congress candidate, defected to the National Conference.

Kushok Bakula was appointed a member of the Central Minorities Commission in 1979. The Commission was opposed by Sheik Abdullah who held that under Article 370, the state was provided immunity from the Commission. In the 1980 Parliamentary election, as a result of seat adjustment between the Congress (I) and the National Conference, the single Ladakh seat was given to the National Conference which fielded Kacho Habibullah; the two Congress leaders from Leh and Kargil, P. Namgyal and Kacho Mohammed Ali Khan, contested the election as independents. With the Muslim vote divided, Namgyal won the elections. This event was complicated by the fact that in 1980, an incident which occurred in Zanskar (over a diesel generator brought to the area for the Dalai Lama's visit and later removed to Kargil by the district authorities) assumed proportions of an agitation launched by the All-Party Ladakh Action Committee headed by Kushok Bakula for regional autonomy and Scheduled Tribe status. Even P. Namgyal joined in allegations of discrimination against Buddhists by the state government. The Action Committee, which was active from about this period to 1989 when it was informally dissolved, included Buddhists and, for the most period, Muslims from Leh and Kargil. The Committee's appearance largely signified the end of A/B factional politics in Ladakh.

In the event of a indefinite agitation being launched in January 1981 by the Action Committee, the State Government appointed a ministerial sub-committee and the Sikri Commission to investigate the issue of regional imbalances. On the assurance that the recommendations of the committee would be implemented and the request for Scheduled Tribe status considered, the agitation was suspended. It was resumed in January 1982, leading to some deaths in police firing, the imposition of Section 144, and a curfew.[19] In September 1982, Farooq Abdullah became Chief Minister on the demise of his father, Sheik Abdullah, and the Action Committee continued to hope that the previous government's commitments would be honoured. On the basis of Farooq Abdullah's assurances that the State Government would make a recommendation to the Centre and the demand for regional autonomy would be placed before the Prime Minister, the ten month old agitation was suspended. The demand for financial autonomy was not conceded and the demand for tribal status continued to lie with the Centre.

In 1983, the Congress and the National Conference failed to work out satisfactory seat adjustments in the Assembly elections ending the rapprochement between the state and the centre. Farooq Abdullah placed before the electorate the distinct identity of the state, wooing voters on communal lines, while the Jammu region rallied around the Congress. In Ladakh, the Congress (I) Buddhist candidate, Sonam Gyalchen, was elected in Leh district while the National Conference's Muslim candidate, Munshi Habibullah, was elected from Kargil. Farooq Abdullah, who was returned to power in the State Assembly elections, announced in June 1983 that tribal status for Ladakh would not be granted unless it was granted to the people of Kargil, Zanskar and Jammu as well. When the Abdullah government was replaced by that of G.M.Shah in 1984 with Congress (I) support, it was expected that the Shah Government would accede to the demands for Scheduled Tribe status to Ladakh. The Government made a recommendation to the Centre under Article 342 to this effect.

The 1984 parliamentary elections returned the Congress (I) to power. But due to weather conditions, the election for the parliamentary seat in Ladakh was not conducted till April 1985. P. Namgyal of the Congress

(I) won this seat defeating Qamar Ali of the National Conference (Farooq), despite charges that the voters list in this area had been seriously tampered with. With the defeat of the National Conference in 1984, the Congress also withdrew its support to the Shah Government in 1986 and imposed Governor's rule in the state. In the 1987 elections, there was an electoral alliance between the Congress (I) and National Conference (F); the Leh constituency election was won by T.Samphel of the Congress (I) and the Kargil one by Qamar Ali of the Conference. The two parties shared power till January 1990, when Farooq Abdullah resigned against the appointment of Mr. Jagmohan as Governor of Kashmir state.

In July 1989, an agitation was launched by the Ladakh Buddhist Association (LBA) headed by Rigzin Jora and Thubstan Tshewang in Leh arising from an incident where the former was assaulted by four Muslim youths. The culprits were apprehended by the police but released later. A procession was taken out by Muslims on rumours that stones had been pelted at the Leh mosque and by Buddhists when the Hemis monastery property was damaged. Firing occurred when Buddhists set fire to government buildings and Section 144 and a curfew were promulgated. Tension rapidly escalated with Buddhists asserting that Kashmiri Muslims were responsible for instigating the Sunnis of Ladakh. An indefinite protest was launched by the LBA pressing forth demands for a Commission of inquiry into the incidents. Repeated demands were also made for Scheduled Tribe status, the necessity of Ladakhi becoming the medium of instruction and improved educational facilities, increase in representation for Buddhists in state services, action against conversion of Buddhist women to Islam, and the neglect of Buddhist culture. There was a boycott of Muslim shops and commercial establishments; the Muslims in turn retaliated with a counter-boycott. There were other repercussions – the lack of participation of the two groups in common cultural activities, the adoption of the Kashmiri garb by many Muslim women, and Buddhist-Muslim marriages being prevented. Villagers' houses and property of both communities were also damaged and in many villages with a single or few Buddhist or Muslim families, migration and sale of property occurred. Chowkhang Vihara in Leh bazaar was a centre of the Buddhist agitationists.

Signs of the fact that there had been trouble in Leh were visible through posters on its walls which were also to be found elsewhere in the town: 'Ladakh is not a colony of Kashmir'; 'Union Territory status for Ladakh is the only solution'. The fact that law and order were being maintained by the Jammu and Kashmir police – chiefly Sunni Muslims – did not help to diffuse the situation.

Eventually, tripartite talks were called (in the wake of the LBA threatening to boycott the 1989 parliamentary elections) and the Central Government issued a Notification on 7 October, 1989 conferring tribal status on eight 'ethnic tribes'.[20] The LBA withdrew its election boycott and tripartite talks were held in Leh on 29 October, 1989 between the LBA, the Union Home Minister and state officials. As a result, the LBA withdrew its four month-old agitation for Union Territory status. The meeting decided in principle that an Autonomous Hill Council would be provided for the region.

The National Conference, in the wake of the agitation and the LBA boycott of Muslims, succeeded in dividing the region on communal lines before the 1989 Parliamentary elections. The independent candidate, Mohammed Hassan Commander, was supported by the Conference in spite of its electoral understanding with the Congress and despite allegations that the elections were rigged. He succeeded in defeating P. Namgyal, the Congress (I) candidate.

Incidents continued to occur throughout 1990 in the situation of a delay in implementation of the decisions of the tripartite meeting. Scheduled Tribe status for Ladakh was implemented slowly, the formal order only occurring on 3 January, 1991. In view of the failure to attain Union Territory status, the LBA agreed to settle for an Autonomous District Council for Leh which was granted on 10 October, 1993. The 'Ladakh Autonomous Hill District Development Council Act of 1955' was signed by the President on 8 May, 1995. The boycott has been withdrawn since 1991 and some rapprochement between the leaders of the two religious groups has occurred in order to work towards the implementation of such a Council. The Council will exercise powers in all areas connected with the development of Ladakh excepting law and order and the judiciary (which will remain with the state government). It is composed of thirty members, twenty six elected and four nominated members, and in 1996, elections to it were completed.[21]

Notes

1. As mentioned in chapter one (note 18), available statistics for the Ladakh area are extremely meagre. No census was carried out for this area in 1951; the 1961 and 1971 census was, however, carried out. The census of 1991 was not carried out in the area, and the 1981 census contains only bare details for the region. For this reason, and the fact that the area is a disputed territory politically, many of the figures mentioned in this chapter and later ones must be treated as approximations.
2. See Zutshi 1994.
3. *Economic Review* 1991:4. According to the 1961 census, the population of Ladakh was 88000 persons, while in 1971 it was 105259 persons. In 1981 it rose to 132966, but by this time, Ladakh had been divided into two districts. One estimate of the 1991 population using 1981 growth rates is about 175000 for the whole of Ladakh (Van Beek 1996: 185).
4. In the 1981 census, Leh district had a population of 68,380 persons. Nearly 87 percent of the population (59,662) was rural and 13 percent, urban. Out of the working population (43.55 percent of the total population), 58.48 percent were cultivators, 7.36 percent, agricultural labourers, 2.35 percent, engaged in manufacturing and processing, and 31.81 percent in other occupations such as tourism, in government employment as teachers, nurses, soldiers, and so on. The region is overwhelmingly agricultural although the landholdings are small and only 0.10 lakh hectares are sown against the net area of 0.445 lakh hectares. Land under cultivation cannot be increased unless irrigation facilities are improved, and new canals constructed. Nearly all the existing canals are customary ones. The same is true for livestock which can increase from its present number only through increase in area under fodder. The potential of this area for industries is poor; only small industrial units (602 in 1991) and some handicraft centres exist, though in terms of tourism, Ladakh has, with the tensions in the Kashmir valley and Tibet's occupation by China, become a focus for an industry marketing this area as the last 'Shangri-la' or 'the Hermit kingdom'. In 1990-1, 6,738 tourists (mainly foreign) visited the district (*Economic Review* 1991).
5. See Dollfus 1995, Grist 1995, Rizvi 1987, and Sheik 1996 for a treatment of Muslims in central and western Ladakh.
6. These routes are dealt with in The *Gazetteer of Kashmir and Ladak* 1974 [1890].
7. See Francke 1977 [1907]:4-5.
8. The *Imperial Gazetteer* (1908:390-4) brings out the hybrid nature of languages in Ladakh. Ladakhi, which is a Tibeto-Burman language, under the general rubric of Indo-Chinese languages (notice the hyphenated label of the language groups), contains also several sub-groups. There are a number of related varieties from Sikkim, Ladakh, and the Bhotias of Tibet, which bear family resemblance to Ladakhi, as Jaeschke's dictionary attests (Jaeschke 1975 [1881]).
9. See Dollfus 1995, Grist 1990 and 1995, Shakspo 1996 and Sheikh 1996 for details of Shia communities in Ladakh.
10. See Grist 1995:60
11. See Francke 1977 [1907]:81.

12. See Pallis 1974 [1939]:370.

13. See Francke 1977 [1907]:94.

14. See Gyaltsan 1993 for a history of Buddhist orders in Ladakh.

15. See note 9.

16. See Bray 1990 for a history of the Moravian church's Bible translations and an analysis of the linguistic issues underlying this effort.

17. The material for this section is based on somewhat scanty secondary literature since most works on Ladakh cover its nineteenth and twentieth century political history or aspects of its religious and cultural life in the twentieth century. I rely on Bertelsen 1995, Bray 1991, Kaul 1992, Srinivas 1991 and 1993, Van Beek and Bertelsen 1995, and numerous newspaper reports, interviews with locals and authorities and first hand experience of events after 1989, for constructing a narrative of this recent history. See especially Van Beek 1996 for an excellent analysis of different phases of agitations in Ladakh and changing notions of 'Ladakhi-ness'.

18. It has been calculated that trans-Himalayan commerce fell from ninety three lakhs of rupees in 1920 to 78,000 in about twenty years (Dollfus 1995:47).

19. Section 144 of the criminal procedure code is an order promulgated by a magistrate to regulate and control the assembly of people; it is a prohibitory order which bans an assembly of five or more persons, and processions in order to maintain law and order.

20. The basis for the classification of 'eight tribes' was probably a mini-census carried out in 1986-7 and a report by the Registrar General of India (which remains classified information) about the same time. These 'tribes' are about 2.5 per cent of the population of the state of Jammu and Kashmir, and 88.7 per cent of the total population of the Ladakh region (about 1,83,963 in 1989). The eight 'tribes' are Balti, Beda, Bot, Brokpa, Changpa, Gara, Mon and Purigpa, some of whom include both Muslims and Buddhists. The 'tribe' category bears a complex relationship to other categories and identities–religion, region, rank, 'race' etc. – in Ladakh (Van Beek 1996; 252–3). Certain groups, such as the Arghuns have not yet been recognized as a 'tribe'; the reasons for exclusion are racial in nature (Srinivas 1993).

21. As Van Beek 1996 points out, the hill council faces all kinds of problems; old and new factions confront each other in the state; perceptions of urban and rural Ladakhis differ; and all kinds of identities–regional, gender- and class-based–seem to be gaining ground through the inherent contradictions in the structure of the council. Further, lack of financial autonomy is a great stumbling block for the council as it remains subject to approval from the state government for its plan and budget.

PART ONE

Chapter 3

The Household, Integration and Exchange

'A long time ago, Siachen glacier was an open plain. It was therefore subjected to marauders from Central Asia and beyond, espe-cially the Mongols. Finally, a wandering hermit from the Gonbo area collected coal, walled the plain, and covered it with ice. Since that time, the northern part of the Karakoram has been inaccessible. In Diskit monastery, there is preserved the head of a Mongol raider who managed to reach Nubra, but was struck down by the goddess, Paldan Lhamo.'

– a Nubra Story

THE ETHNOGRAPHIC SITE

The valley of the Nubra and Shyok rivers, north of the Khardung pass across the Ladakh range of mountains, is traditionally referred to as 'Nubra'. The Nubra river is a tributary of the Shyok river which joins the Indus before Skardu and flows through Baltistan (now in Pakistan-Occupied Kashmir). Historically, this region was an important source of passage through the Saser and Karakoram passes to Shahidulla, Kashgar and Yarkand in Central Asia; and, following the course of the the Shyok river, towards Hunza, Gilgit and Chitral. Today, the area is bound by the cease-fire line with Pakistan in the west and the Siachen glacier and Aksai Chin in the east, both sites of military conflict.

There is very little information on Nubra before the fourteenth century but, from the time of Grags-pa-'bum-lde (1400-40), there are various historical references. The king's ambitious brother, Grags-pa-'bum, in the hope of seizing power, is said to have paid a visit to Nubra. A local ruler, Nyi-ma-grags-pa, reigned there at that time and it is said that he assisted a Gelugpa exponent, Shes-rab-bzang-po, who came from the Leh valley, in building the monastery of Diskit and installing a statue of Tsong Khapa, the founder of the Gelug order.

In 1500, Bkra-shis-rnam-rgyal, the first Namgyal king, ascended the throne in Ladakh and faced the troops of the famous invader from Central Asia, Mirza Haider, both in Nubra and around Leh. There was much bloodshed before the Turk army was defeated. This event was significant in Nubra's history because after this, the area came under the king's rule totally although local nobles, such as those of Hundar and Diskit, continued to have some powers. The palaces of the two villages were taken over by the king and became residences of the royal family. The king's son, Tshe-dbang-rnam-rgyal, came to the throne in 1530, and brought Skardu and Shigar under his rule. He planned to invade Xinjiang but was persuaded to give up the idea by the people of Nubra who feared that trade with Yarkand would dry up. It is recorded that from the reign of the next king, 'Jams-dbang-rnam-rgyal (1560-90), the people of Nubra began to pay a regular tribute to the king. At this time, Muslims, mainly Shias, began to settle in Nubra. In the reign of Seng-ge-rnam-rgyal, the next ruler, the *gompa* (monastery) of Hemis acquired land in Nubra, becoming a landlord to a number of households in the villages of Hundar, Charasa and Yarma.

The Rnam-rgyal kings seemed to have paid attention to religious matters besides being periodically embroiled in wars with Baltistan. Thus Nyi-ma-rnam-rgyal not only rebuilt the palace of Charasa, but also revered the relics of Pan-chen Lha-btsun. The king, Tshe-dbang- rnam-rgyal, who came to the throne in the middle of the eighteenth century, offered Diskit *gompa* to Thikse *gompa* hear Leh and this arrangement has persisted to this day. He also went to war against the Balti invaders and was assisted by Nang-gso-bkra-shis, a member of the leading family of Charasa. For the latter's help, he presented him with land and other items. The king, Tshe-brtan-rnam-rgyal, who came to the throne in 1780, was said to have been a polyglot and knew Yarkandi as well. It is possible that he lived in Nubra for some time.[1]

From the time of Tshe-dpal-don-grub-rnam-rgyal in the 1830's, when the traveller Moorcroft visited Nubra, we find many accounts of Nubra and Ladakh, some of which have already been referred to in the first chapter. By the time the Dogra invasions were over, Ladakhi independence was coming to an end. The Dogras destroyed many monasteries and religious relics, besides destroying the political authority of the king. In Nubra, a village named after the Dogra king, Pratap, came into existence populated by retainers and other servants of the Dogras, nearly all of whom were Shia Muslims. It was left to the heads of the various monasteries and the monks to try and re-establish certain traditions. Thus, Tshul-khrims-nyi-ma founded the monastery of Samstanling near Tegar in 1834. It is the second largest *gompa* in Nubra with about thirty-five monks led by the incarnations of Tshul-khrims-nyi-ma. It lays emphasis on the observance of the Vinaya and has a far stricter discipline than many other *gompas*.

This event notwithstanding, the forces of change were already set in motion by the events of the Great Game and the continuous threat that was perceived by the rulers of India from Russia on the northern borders of Nubra.[2] Trade did not, however, come to an end and the routes to Central Asia passing through Tegar towards the Karakoram pass and between Nubra, Baltistan and Tibet, continued to be active. The locals supplied pasture for caravans and horses and also some *begar* (carriage requirements) for travellers between the passes. It is said that some kind of tax was collected by the government in kind and deposited at trading and halting posts, for example, at Panamik. British officials occasionally toured this area in the summers.

The traffic on the travel routes abruptly halted when in 1948, Nubra became a battlefield, along with other parts of Ladakh, between Pakistan and India. When the enemy occupied Skardu and came as far as Skuru, about 20 kms. from Diskit, the Nubra Guard was organized locally to resist the invaders. Some nobles and Buddhists fled while other Buddhists converted to Islam fearing that Nubra would be run over by Pakistan. Villagers rallied with old matchlocks, grain, horses and their men drove back the Pakistanis as far as Bogdang, about 80 kms., from Diskit. In 1971 again, Nubra faced another attack, but this time there was an organized military which recaptured some of the earlier occupied territories such as Thang, Turtuk, and Taksi. At the present moment, the borders of Nubra have been sealed militarily as Indian and Pakistani armies confront each other in the east and west. There is a huge army presence in the valley in a partly symbiotic relationship with the local people. The army buys vegetables from the villagers, uses its labour for building roads and for other construction activity, and also includes a sizeable number of the local men in the Ladakh Scouts regiment.

After the inclusion of Ladakh in the Indian state, certain administrative boundaries have been created. Firstly, in 1979, the region was divided into the two districts, of Leh and Kargil, with Zanskar, Dras and Suru as part of Kargil district, and Rupshu and Nubra as part of Leh district. The political unit is composed of blocks. The block where I did my fieldwork was Nubra with its headquarters in Diskit. Towards the south and west lie the other blocks of Leh district i.e., Leh, Khalste, Nyoma and Durbuk. Nubra has an estimated 10,667 persons (all rural) according to the 1981 census with six Gram Sabhas. This area is mainly oriented towards agriculture. Out of a total reported area of 11,936 hectares, the net cultivated area, which is also the net irrigated area, was 1882 hectares in 1989-90. The main crops grown are wheat, gram, fodder and mustard, and also some orchards of apricot and apple trees.

Towards the line of actual control near Pakistan-Occupied Kashmir, the climate and mode of cultivation resemble that of Kargil, and cherry, walnuts, and grapes grow here. There is a single agricultural cooperative marketing society for Nubra which is affiliated to the central one at Leh and handles the marketing of vegetables, fodder, and fruits from villages to the army. There are thirty four small-scale industries and some village and household industries like pashmina weaving, spinning, carpet and wood units, oil mills and smitheries.[3]

The two villages in which my fieldwork was done lie at an average height of about 10,000 feet along the elbow formed by the main ridge of the Ladakh mountains and the Karakoram which meet at the Khardung pass. Hundar is located along the Shyok river. At the base of the Karakoram range and the Nubra river is Tegar. Diskit lies at the junction of the two rivers. The two villages derived their significance in the past from being on important travel routes. They are now defined by being on the route to the sites of conflict between India and Pakistan to demarcate fixed administrative jurisdictions – the Siachen glacier in the east and the Baltoro range in the west. Diskit has a bazaar of sorts, the offices of the

Assistant Commissioner of the district, a television station, the local police headquarters, and a high school, i.e. it is a locale of *mulazzim* (officials) of various kinds. Hundar has a middle school, as does Tegar, but neither has a bazaar, only dispersed shops situated on the highway. Most of the population is composed of those who work on land but each village has some occupational differences which will be discussed in the next chapter.

A record, published first in 1890, says of the village 'Taghar' that it is a village in the Nubra district situated on the left bank of the Nubra river containing twenty houses. It is a halting place on the summer route from Leh to the Karakoram and lies eighteen miles below Panamik and seven above the junction of the Nubra with the Shyok. Barley and lucerne, apricot, willow, poplar and elm are cultivated here. The river runs in divided streams over a wide bed of shingle and sand on which there are island patches of buckthorn and bushwood. It is frozen over in winter.[4]

Hundar, the account states, lies on the left bank of the Shyok, and about seven miles below its junction with the Nubra river. It is a halting place on the route from the Nubra valley to Skardu. It is one of the most populous villages in Nubra with fine orchards of apricot trees.

The village has about sixty houses, forty of which pay taxes. The inhabitants are said to possess seven horses, sixty-four horned cattle and five hundred and fifty goats and sheep. A road from here leads up the Hundar stream dividing into two branches; one goes to Leh via the Thanglasgo pass and the other to the Snimo and the Likir valleys. The camping ground is an orchard and supplies are procurable for travellers.[5]

Presently, Tegar has three hamlets and the one I resided in contains Buddhists and four Muslim families. The third hamlet contains a separate *manekhang* (village temple), and also families who form, in the eyes of villagers, another group. It also has its own *Zimskang*. This is a family distinguished by some act of bravery, social largesse or duty to the king, and has, thus, been given that title in the past. All these factors lead one to conclude that this hamlet was included within the bounds of Tegar as a purely administrative measure. It even has its own set of members for the village council in recent times (perhaps because it is spatially separated from Tegar by a few kilometres). In this book, when I refer to Tegar, I mean only the first two hamlets with a population of about ninety-three households. Hundar has five hamlets, each with

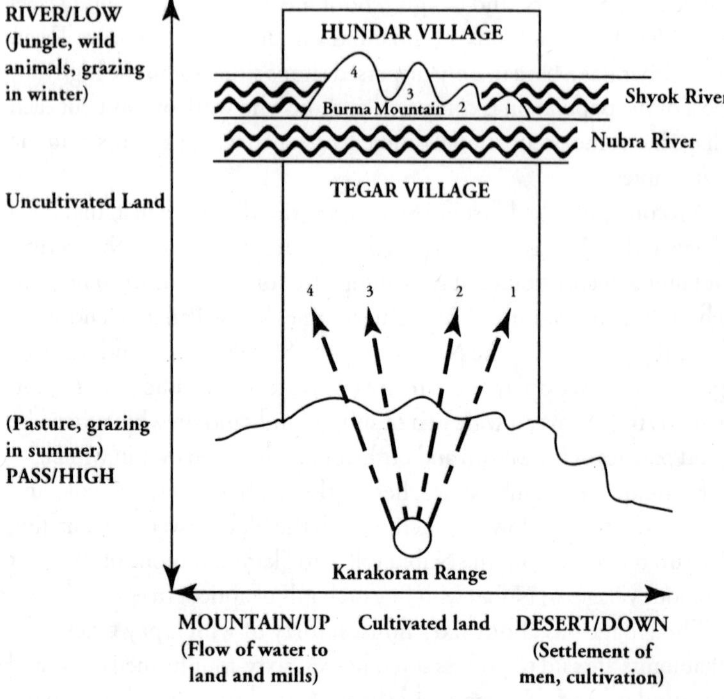

Figure 1: The Agricultural Clock

Buddhists and Muslims living together. The number of Muslim households is about fifty-five, the total number of households in the village being about 200.

THE AGRICULTURAL CALENDAR

In both the villages and indeed, for most of the villages in the surrounding area land, has a conceptual significance. In this section, I shall look at the conception of ecological time and agricultural space in general terms for both religious groups and both villages.

The concept of land derives from two pairs of terms: there is first a pair formed by mountain and desert (*ri* and *thangskam*) and the second pair formed by passages through tracts, pass and river (*la* and *tsangspo*).

There is a further distinction of land into cultivated and uncultivated land, but this distinction includes and suggests more than is detailed by the Land Settlement, the *Bandobast*. By placing the pair, mountain and desert, and direction (up and down), under 'cultivated land', and the pair, river and pass, and direction (high and low), under 'uncultivated land', we create a polarity as well as a gradient. There are thus two axes. In the first axis, the dominant relation seems to be of man to land, and in the second, man to animals. The two axes together give a map drawn by a farmer for me in Tegar reproduced in Figure 1. This is not merely a spatial map but also one which accommodates temporality within it, both of work and ritual. (1) and (4) are two ritual points in two different villages next to Tegar – one is a *lhato* (a shrine where a deity resides) and the other is a *mane* wall – a long wall of stone and mud on which stone plaques inscribed with sacred words are placed by passers-by, travellers, and others. These are the farthest points between which the rising and setting sun oscillates daily in the year. (1) is the furthest point on the landscape which the rays of a rising sun can strike in winter, while (4) is the corresponding point in summer. (2) is a house in the village and when the rising sun's rays begin to strike it, they mark the time for sowing barley in spring and harvesting it in autumn when the sun is on its return journey. (3) is a round *mane*; in early summer or late spring, the rays of the sun strike it to mark the time for sowing mustard and a pulse called *kertse*. The Burma mountain across the river has a jagged outline which also acts like a clockface for the points (1)-(4). In winter, for example, the rising sun's rays will not exceed (1) just as in summer it will not exceed (4). Farmers in Hundar will read the 'clock' on the mountain, which lies across their river, in the reverse order. The mountain, in fact, intervenes between the two villages I resided in; on either side of it there is a river.

The dynamics of time and space in this topos can be seen according to the nature of agricultural and pastoral work. This is, in its general features, common to both villages although the ritual use of the land differs partly between Muslims and Buddhists. The Tibetan Buddhist ritual calendar is the point of reference for agricultural work; it is a compromise between the solar and the lunar cycles.

The year is divided into lunar months, i.e. the time between the sun and the moon coinciding (the new moon). During this time, there is a lag in which the moon falls behind the sun about 12 degrees everyday so that the lunar cycle is 29.53 solar days. A calendar date sometimes advances by a day or is omitted or is repeated. Full moon occurs on the fifteenth day of the month and new moon on the thirtieth. The lunar year has a net loss of five or six days (with about 354.36 days) against the notional 360 days of twelve cycles of thirty days. In comparison with the Gregorian calendar, there is a loss of ten or twelve days which is corrected every third or fourth year by adding an extra month.[6] The Muslim calendar is lunar and moves 'backwards' a few days every year in comparison to the Gregorian one, to return to the same starting point after thirty-six years. In addition to Tibetan Buddhist lunar cycles, agriculture is also governed by the astrological almanac (which is based both on the signs of the zodiac and the constellations or moon-houses). An astrologer, the *onpo*, is deputed to select a ritually propitious moment to start ploughing independent of soil and weather conditions. The actual work may take place weeks later. For this purpose, farmers select a date based on the rising and the setting of the sun as determined by their practical knowledge and traditional lore in the way described earlier – using 'marks' on the landscape or built up environment as a natural sun dial. I present below the dynamics of the use of the space and time in agriculture and the pastoral economy for Buddhists and Muslims in the two villages of the valley. This is represented in table form in Figure 2. There are various types of cooperative groups or work units for carrying out agricultural work: the form of cooperation and exchange characterized by a collective work implement is described in this study as a 'complex group of cooperation'; 'simple cooperation' involves individually owned implements and identical or analogous labour; 'extended simple cooperation' is practised in agriculture in major tasks; and 'restricted simple cooperation' is practised in daily maintenance work in agriculture.[7]

Dawa Tangpo (first month of the Buddhist calendar; roughly 15 February–15 March): manure is taken out to the fields from a heap outside the house. Sometimes before *Tangpo*, the individual household owners and their families take out waste and manure from animal stalls and the dry toilets of the house and put it out in the sun, covered with soil. This manure is taken from the house to the field on bulls and donkeys pooled together either area-wise or serially for each house in the village. Among the Muslims of Hundar, because of the boycott, all

Figure 2 : The Agricultural Calendar

Month (Dates are approximations)	Agricultural Activity and Work Group.
1. *Dawa Tangpo* (15th February-15th March)	Individual households fence fields with thorns and bushes, take manure out of dry toilets and animal stalls.
2. *Dawa Neespa* (15th March-15th April)	Extended group of cooperation takes manure to fields. Complex group cleans the main water channels of village. Individual houses clean small water channels, stall-feed cows and take goats/sheep to jungle. Extended group does the ploughing of furrows and sowing of barley.
3. *Dawa Sumpa* (15th April-15th May)	Extended group continues with manuring, ploughing, and sowing. Individual houses make paths between fields, stall-feed animals or take them to the jungle; nursery for vegetables is made.
4. *Dawa Jipa* (15th May-15th June)	Individual houses and extended group make beds for flow of water to barley fields after barley sprouts. Individual houses stall-feed animals or take them to the jungle; vegetables are transplanted to gardens.
5. *Dawa Sngapa* (15th June-15th July)	One member of a family or of complex group or extended group takes sheep/goats to pasture in the mountains. Extended group does the sowing of mustard. Extended group of women weeds fields.
6. *Dawa Tukpa* (15th July-15th August)	Extended group does grass-cutting in field fringes and lucerne meadows. Individual houses pluck and dry apricots and apples.
7. *Dawa Dunpa* (15th August-15th September)	Extended group harvests mustard and barley. Individual houses thresh the above and leave cows/donkeys/horses to graze in the fields.
8. *Dawa Gyatpa* (15th September-15th October)	Individual houses leave goats/sheep (which return from the mountains) to graze in the fields; thresh barley; mill barley/mustard; women of the household pickle cabbage, carrot, onions, etc. Extended group does the (winter) ploughing of fields.

Month (Dates are approximations)	Agricultural Activity and Work Group.
9. *Dawa Gupa* (15h October-15th November)	Individual houses mill baorley/mustard; make woollen clothes; go to Leh/army canteen for supplies; remove and store root-vegetables underground; winnow seeds; collect dung/wood for fuel; stall-feed *dzos*/cows and take other animals to village meadows.
10. *Dawa Chupa* (15th November-15th December) 11. *Dawa Chukshikpa* (15th December-15th January) 12. *Dawa Chuknispa* (15th January-15th February)	Individual houses go to jungle for wood/dung; goats/sheep are taken to the river to graze in meadows while *dzos*/cows are stall-fed; spinning and carding of wool by women as well as knitting continues.

Muslims pooled their labour and animals together for this purpose. The other activity which occurs during this period is the fencing of fields with a pitch-fork with thorn bushes brought from the jungle. (Only Nubra has a jungle). In Leh, all the fences are made of stone which may or may not be permanent. Men and women participate in both movements from jungle to field and house to field, either as a household or a group of restricted simple cooperation, during fencing, and in a group of extended simple cooperation for the task of manuring. The cows and *dzos* (a cross between a yak and a cow) are stall-fed and goats and sheep are taken to the jungle daily, the river being fordable in winter. At all times, it is women who cook unless there is no female member in the family. At this time there is no water in the channels so a member of the family fetches water from the river for household purposes.

Dawa Neespa (second month of the Buddhist calendar; roughly 15 March-15 April): removal of manure can continue into this month. At the end of this month, roughly when the snow melts and water appears in the channels, the canals are opened and for ten-fifteen days, all the main canals, smaller channels and the pond are cleared of silt by a complex group of cooperation. One member from each household (*tutbing*) is represented in the work team daily in the village. For the main canal, even in Hundar, both religious groups participate in the village activity. Little channels near the house or the field are cleaned by the household as a separate unit. The cows continue to be stall-fed and goats and sheep are taken to the jungle. At this time, as ploughing of fields also begins, there may not be anyone to take them to the fields and they are left in meadows. When the water begins to course through the channels, parallel activities of watering the earth and ploughing of furrows takes place. The households individually, or a group of two or three households as a extended simple work unit, do the ploughing. In Nubra, villages at a slightly lower height use a pair of *dzos* for the spring and autumn ploughing. Mills are used for grinding the flour after winter.

Dawa Sumpa (third month of the Buddhist calendar, roughly 15 April-15 May): ploughing and sowing take up the major portion of this month and part of the next. Before this, manuring takes place. Manure is placed in heaps on the field. It is spread out with spades and when water flows there, wide beds are made for it to spread over the field. Around this time, paths are made between individual fields. Both these operations are usually done by a single household. After a few days, ploughing is done by a man running the plough. He may have another man leading the pair of *dzos*. Behind him is a woman broadcasting seeds into the furrows. Two or three men and women rake the soil over the seeds or drag a nettle over the ground as a rake. The animals are stall-fed or sent to the jungle or meadow. At this time, a nursery for vegetables is also made.

Dawa Jipa (fourth month of the Buddhist calendar; roughly 15 May-15 June): after barley sprouts, which may be in about seven-ten days time, beds are made for the flow of water. Water is let in for the first time after manuring because by then the ground is dry and it is done serially for each house in Tegar. In Hundar, water does not need to be distributed like this either by day of the week or at night, because it is plentiful. The beds are made by the household or a extended simple group of cooperation of a few households. About this time, the *dzos* and cows are fed branches and fresh leaves of trees, and goats and sheep may be sent into the jungle or put in meadows near the village. Saplings of vegetables like cabbage and cauliflower, are also transplanted to the garden from the nursery.

Dawa Sngapa (fifth month of the Buddhist calendar; roughly 15 June-15 July): at about the beginning of this month, *dzos*, goats and sheep go towards the pastures. Families in Tegar make up a party and one member and sometimes children go towards the passes. The goats and sheep are entrusted with a shepherd of one of the families or with certain people of a neighbouring village in the lowland or upland who are traditionally *dogpas* (nomads/shepherds). In Tegar, these were sometimes entrusted with a shepherd of the village or with men of villages near the Khardung pass. In the case of Hundar, it was a lowland village, all of whose men took their cattle to the pastures. Cows are stall-fed or put in meadows. About this time, the sowing of mustard also takes place. No manuring is done for mustard fields. In this month, the weeding of the fields of barley begins. There might be weeding of the vegetable garden if vegetables are grown on a large scale. Weeding is done by women of the household or the extended simple group of kin and neighbours.

Dawa Tukpa (sixth month of the Buddhist calendar; roughly 15 July-15 August): grass cutting begins in this month both on the fringes of fields and in alfalfa meadows. The group includes men and women of the extended simple group. Grass is brought to the roof and dried there as stall-feed for winter and early spring. Grass is left on the land on the fringes of the river or in pastures on the fringe of the jungle (common to the entire village). Apricots and apples are plucked towards the end of the month and the beginning of the next, and dried on roofs. Some of the vegetables like tomatoes are also dried in this month.

Dawa Dunpa (seventh month of the Buddhist calendar; roughly 15 August-15 September): harvesting begins towards the middle and the end of this month. Households within the extended group, like those at the time of grass cutting, assist each other. All the fields are first harvested of mustard. This is brought to the *yultak* (threshing ground) immediately lest the seeds fall on the ground. The threshing is done by households individually by spreading a parachute sheet on the ground or simply placing it on the mud-baked surface of the *yultak*, pounding it with long poles by hand, and then winnowing it to separate chaff from seed. This is then made into oil by the sole oil grinding machine in Tegar. For the next two months or so, the machine is at work all the time there is water in the stream because it works by diesel oil and has a boiler which needs flowing water. After the harvesting of mustard, black peas and barley are also harvested. This is done by the simple extended group. The cut grain stalks are however left on the fields till every household has finished its cutting. It is then brought simultaneously, and in a synchronized movement, to the *yultak* by each household for threshing.

The gates to the fields are opened and the cows, donkeys and horses are left to graze there.

Dawa Gyatpa (eighth month of the Buddhist calendar; roughly 15 September-15 October): in this month, goats and sheep also return from the pass up-mountain. They are left to graze on the stubble in the field while threshing of barley begins. At times, threshing takes upto a month. During threshing all cows and donkeys of a house are yoked together and driven round in an anti-clockwise motion by a man on the *yultak*. The animals stamp the grain with their feet while it is pitchforked into the centre. After the stalks have been separated (this is later used as stall-feed along with grass during winter and early spring), winnowing of husk from grain takes place with a board. In the process, barley and black peas are separated. This is a household activity involving both men and women. This is a windy month and all across the valley, whistling of tunes by villagers can be heard. At the end of the threshing month, each household takes the grain on donkeys to the mill. The *dzos* also return towards the end of the month (they normally find their way home from the pastures like the camels in Hundar which find their way back from the jungle). They are used for ploughing the field. By this time, all the stubble has also disappeared and a couple of men of the household or extended group do the ploughing. This is done in the direction opposite to the spring ploughing, i.e. from low to high. During this month, some vegetables like cabbage, carrot and onions are also pickled by the women.

Dawa Gupa (ninth month of Buddhist calendar; roughly 15 October-15 November): this is a busy month as milling continues in the various mills near the village till the water stops flowing. Then people are forced to go higher up towards the *spang* (pasture) where channels continue to flow for milling. Woollen clothes are woven and stitched for winter by the local weaver of wool that is sheared in spring before the sheep depart for the pasture. Woollen shoes are made by one or two people in the village. Men also go to Leh before the pass becomes difficult to cross, or to various army canteens to buy supplies such as butter, flour, sugar and rice. This is also the time when root vegetables like carrot, potatoes, onions, radish and turnip are removed from the field and stored underground in a field close to the house; onions are usually dried on the roof first and then put into the store. Seeds of onions and other vegetables are also removed, winnowed by hand (usually woman's work), and stored. The *dzos* are stall-fed while the other animals are taken to the meadows on the fringe of the river, common lands of the village, or left to graze in household meadows and fed with the stalks of threshed grain. Dung from the fields and the jungle may also be brought by poorer households to use as fuel; it is also sent to Leh where there is a shortage of fuel. Wood cutting from the jungle begins.

Dawa Chupa (tenth month of the Buddhist calendar; roughly 15 November-15 December): all through winter, men and women of each household can be seen going to the jungle with their *dzos* to bring wood which they have cut there. This is a scrub jungle and the wood provided is used as fuel for stoves in winter. The *dzos* also graze there during the day. The water in the river is fordable and little bridges are made of stone and nettle at convenient points. Goats and sheep are taken by a member of the family across to the river to graze there in the *nangskor* (meadows) or near the village. Spinning and carding of previously shorn wool continues throughout winter. This is done by women on tiny spindles which they can be seen carrying around in baskets with fluffs of wool. The winding of small balls of wool into large balls with tighter threads is also done by men. Knitting is done by women.

Dawa Chukshikpa (eleventh month of the Buddhist calendar; roughly 15 December-15 January): during this month, the gathering of wood continues. Goats and sheep are taken to the jungle pastures while cows are stall-fed. This procedure is the same in the next month. Spinning and knitting continue. This is the month of *Sonam Losar* (the People's or Farmer's New Year) for Ladakh: this is the first day of the eleventh month, ideally the winter solstice (22 December), but varies between 5 December and the 3 January.

Dawa Chuknispa (twelfth month of the Buddhist calendar; roughly 15 January-15 February): the activities are similar to that of the previous month.

There are thus various movements across the river to the pass, from settlement to jungle, and from house to field. In summer and spring, the dominant movement is up to down, water to land, from mountain to desert, and settlement to fields. The river acts as a barrier and the movement of animals is in the other direction, i.e. from low to high, jungle and meadow to mountain or pasture. In winter or late autumn, the process is reversed and the mountain passes become barriers. There are, of course, individual differences between households, but in a formal sense, these movements apply to all households.

LEVELS OF INTEGRATION

The composite style of life created by the agricultural calendar in Nubra is cross-cut by differing socio-cultural orientations. For instance, it was pointed out in the previous chapter that the history of Islam and Buddhism in Ladakh is a complex affair and there are present, in various valleys, religious groups with differing allegiances. Thus, the Buddhists in Tegar, for example, largely belong to the Gelug order and are locally associated with the main *gompa* of the area, Samstanling. There are some families in a hamlet of the village who belong to the Diskit *gompa*. Both these *gompas* own some land in the village. What this means in practical terms is that the monthly ritual called the *lapsang* (cleansing the gods) performed by each household, and certain other rites, will be performed by a monk of the order to which the household belongs. Each village also has a *manekhang* and the *gompa* to which it belongs appoints a monk there as a priest. Tegar has two *manekhangs*, each with a priest of a different *gompa*. But all major festivals of a monastery are attended by villagers of any religious affiliation; in the past, even by Muslims who took part in the fair and the festivities of a monastery event. The villages in the valley have *masjids* (mosques) only where there are Muslim families in fairly large numbers. Tegar has no *masjid*, but Hundar has three: one belonging to Sunnis, one to Nurbakshias and another to a family which has adherents who are both Sunnis and Nurbakshias, although the current household head claims to be Sunni. The *masjids* and the *gompas* have ties with Leh as well as with other centres. The Gelug order owes its allegiance to the Dalai Lama of Lhasa traditionally, while the Drugpa have had close ties with the Dharmaraja of Bhutan. At present, each *gompa* has its own sphere of influence in the villages around it while Hemis, the 'royal' *gompa* of Ladakh, continues to be fairly important.

The prevalence of both Shias and Sunnis as well as Nurbakshias, who the local people say is a cultural group lying between the Shia and Sunni sects, makes the orientation of Muslims a complex affair. The Nurbakshias are held to be less orthodox than the Shias found in villages further down the Shyok river, and retain many beliefs connected with Syed Mohammed Nur Baksh. The term 'Shia' in this area is used to refer to the *Balti* and to

Muslims from Kargil. Although many of these terms are used contextually, it is my understanding that Sunni Muslims in this area are descendants of Kashmiri Muslim fathers and Ladakhi Buddhist mothers (called locally *Arghun*); Nurbakshias are usually descendants of migrants from Baltistan, or Purig, some parts of which form Kargil district today, many of whom married Buddhist women. All these divisions complicate the unity of the Muslims in Nubra. For instance, during *Ramzan*, the month of the holy fast, the Sunnis in Hundar began their fast on a day that their Nurbakshia neighbours began it, only to find that the *imam* (priest of the mosque) in Leh had not given a call for the fast. The Nurbakshias continue to follow the dictates of the *imam* of Skardu (now in Pakistan-Occupied Kashmir) to whom they are customarily affiliated. On the day of *Id* as well, this kind of ambiguity was evident for the fast was broken by the Nurbakshias a day earlier than the Sunnis. The fact that large numbers of people were congregating in the *masjid* for the *Id–ul–Fitr* (the feast breaking the fast) prayers, however, led the *imam* of the Sunni *masjid* to celebrate *Id* twice – once according to the calendar of Skardu and the Nurbakshias and again according to the calendar of Leh (and Delhi) and the Sunnis.

When the choice of the village, Tegar, was made, I had proceeded with the somewhat naive assumption generated by previous works on Ladakh that the 'community' lay within the boundaries of the village. I began to live with a Buddhist family in Tegar, a village that contained a single family of Sunni *Arghun* Muslims and three Nurbakshia families (called sometimes Shias by the villagers). As the fieldwork proceeded, I learnt of the past year's tensions between Muslims and Buddhists in Ladakh, as a result of factors described in the last chapter, the out-migration of a few families of Muslims, as well as a social boycott between the two groups. I decided that, in order that I might understand how diverse groups (religious or otherwise) inhabited the same space of the village and the nature of the interaction between them, I would live with a Muslim family for a while as well.

In Tegar, however, it was difficult to reside with a Muslim family for two reasons. Firstly, as the boycott was in force, my moving between the Muslims and Buddhists in the village created difficulties for me as an uneasy participant-observer in a time of strained relations. Their mutual suspicions created a certain restraint. I was privy to events which had occurred in the village and to confidential information which made my position extremely delicate. Secondly, as there were only two Muslim families (as another family in the village had left since the boycott started and two sons of a third family had converted to Buddhism just then), I felt that I would not really be able to observe the practices of Muslim households in any detail. So I arranged to move for a while to another village across the river, to Hundar, which had a large number of Muslim families as well as Buddhist ones in order to observe life from the 'other side'. I chose to live with a Sunni Muslim family since they were a stigmatized category directly affected by the boycott. Already, the idea that a community was a coherent whole was beginning to be questionable. A shared residential space did not mean a shared perception of commonality. A common practice of some sort, for example, work within a shared agricultural calendar, could exist with another sort of practice that divided the same group, for example, ritual orientation. How then is 'community' to be defined?

The idea that the 'community' can be formed at various levels has been advanced by different authors.[8] In this study, it is used to describe how, in Nubra, different sorts of practices lead to various levels of social integration making the community an entity which is the site of centripetal and centrifugal forces. At any given moment, its organizational basis is cross-cut by ties that may decentre it at another moment. The household is the atom of social life in Nubra. It is differentially related to other households in ascending levels of integration. Levels of integration occur through various modalities of exchange and practice both within and between households – either exchange of work, men and women in marriage, ritual services, or political support.

We may distinguish between three levels of integration in local life depending on the type of exchange or practice within and between households. The 'primary level of integration' is the household composed of men and women related by consanguinity and affinity, labouring in the field and at the hearth, opposed to all other households in the village. Within the household, the exchange of work between members and gender and age-based division of labour, create a domain of social life firmly anchored within the territory of the domestic group. In this individuated aspect, households are related to other categories of persons and institutions -- the *chospun* (ritual siblings) of members of the household, the monk from the *manekhang* or the *gompa*, and the *imam* of the local *masjid*.

The 'secondary level of integration' relates a household to other households in the village through diverse practices. These include the exchange of work through various kinds of work groups for harvesting, manuring, etc.; ritual exchanges through the *phaspun* (a group of families in the village bound by the idiom of fictive kinship) among Buddhists and the *iftarspun* (usually an agnatic group) among the Muslims; and the practice of constituting authority in the village. The secondary level of integration also includes the occupational division of the community in Ladakh into various ranked categories. Within the secondary level of integration, i.e. the domain of the village, there may also exist, the division of the households in the village into two overarching religious groups, as was the case during the social boycott. The social boycott of Sunni Muslims (chiefly) by Buddhists in Ladakh ensued as a result of an agitation which began in 1989 arising from an incident in Leh where Buddhist leaders were allegedly assaulted by four Muslim youths. This boycott continued to be in force, in various forms, until 1991. (See chapter two).

The 'tertiary level of integration' relates a household to other households by marriage creating the category of the 'kindred.' This level of integration occupies a domain greater than the village, given the dominant practice of village exogamy. A household is also related to other households in political organizations of the Ladakh Buddhist Association and the Ladakh Muslim Association (LBA and LMA). This kind of integration relates Muslims and Buddhists, and Leh town and the villages politically, resulting in various sorts of cleavages and coalitions.

The idea that various levels of integration can constitute a community is connoted by two words used locally for indicating the sense of place and members of a group. *Yul* is a multivocal term and can indicate a hamlet, a village, a region, this world, or the world of the gods or spirits. A speaker using such a term normally uses it contextually depending on who he is speaking to. Two villagers of a valley may use it with reference to themselves and the other as referring to a village or a hamlet as the case may be. A Kashmiri would be defined as belonging to *Kache-yul* in reference to a Ladakhi when the issue of his 'place' is discussed. The second term that indicates that various levels of integration can exist is *pa* (people) used in such diverse contexts as *Kalon-pa* (people of the Kalon family), *Nubra-pa* (people of Nubra), or *Kache-pa* (Kashmiri Muslims) indicating that people can be members of many kinds of groups. The levels of integration, i.e. primary (domestic), secondary (within the village), and tertiary (outside the village, within the valley or outside the valley), could alter depending on various cultural factors and the extent of the spatial unit being considered.

Within the space of this ecological niche in Nubra, inside and outside, coalition and cleavage are not absolute but contextually situated because integration occurs as a result of different social practices and cross-cutting ties. In British social anthropology, from the post-Second World War period upto the late 1960's, society was conceived of not as a consistent, organic structure premised only on fusion, consensus and societal homogeneity, but also on fission, conflict and cleavage. Different modes of relating structurally equivalent units – two households, two hamlets or villages, two cultural groups, or men and women – were seen as creating social fields. Two groups were seen not as facing each other as monolithic entities but as implicated in various networks of relations so that each position in the network became intercalary. It was pointed out that in a society with cross-cutting ties, men allied in terms of one customary rule of association were grouped under a different rule with others who have a different allegiance under the first rule. Social cohesion was rooted in the conflict between people's different allegiances. A person's role or position could exist at many different levels and was not unitary because each social position or unit was the site of conflicting interests. Further, in a society with cross-cutting ties, mystical symbols played an important role in performing the function of unity.[9]

The issue, therefore, of how differences (whether linguistic, religious, or otherwise) come to be articulated in Nubra is related to this principle: because of cross-cutting ties of many types in Nubra due to a variety of historical and cultural reasons, alliance is created by one rule between social groups and roles, and separation by another. Distance and proximity are continually created or negated between units and roles, and dynamism is inherent in the way boundaries are worked out between them. Variety is inscribed in social existence and cultural processes reflect this multiplicity. The construction of meaning and symbolic processes refract in a complex way, the intersection of differently oriented social interests. Like symbols themselves, one's self-role is constituted in interpersonal territory.[10]

This constitution of self-role may take various forms. For instance, in the relationship of villages in the Nubra valley to monasteries, it occurs by shifting the locus of festivals from one monastery to another; and by the participation of religious groups in complementary ways.[11] In February, the main festival of the Diskit monastery, at the junction of the the Nubra and Shyok rivers, takes place. It goes on for three days at the end of *Dawa Chuknispa*. The veils of the deities in the monastery are removed and villagers from the entire valley come for a glimpse of them. This marks the transition of winter to spring in Nubra, but it is also part of a structure of monastery festivals. From the festival at Samstanling on the Nubra river's left side in winter, the site of the festival moves to Diskit on the Shyok river's right in winter-spring and then to Yarma on Nubra's right. After Yarma in late spring, it moves to Rongdo on the Shyok's left. In summer, when the passes are fordable, there occurs the Hemis festival in Leh which attracts large groups of villagers. Thus valley and town, inside and outside, and the different far-flung villages are, by this circling of the festival site at different calendric points, brought into relation. The *masjid* seems by contrast static; but some of its festivities are complementary to those occurring among the Buddhists. For example, a festival of flowers occurs in spring when the wild roses have begun to blossom sometime after sowing in May. In Tegar, this is the occasion of a fair and the making of garlands for decorating the *manekhang* and *chortens* (places for housing holy relics). In Hundar, it is the occasion for Muslims to decorate the *masjid* and also for laying garlands on the tombs of their dead.

Ladakh has been largely seen as a homogeneous culture area, primarily Tibetan Buddhist in character, with personal identity being a series of mutually enveloping layers radiating from a Buddhist core, as it were. It is possible, however, to look at the area as a site of cross-cutting ties with various levels of integration. This is because it has slowly come to be recognized that 'Tibetan society' was not centralized in political economy or culture as previously conceptualized. The figure of the monk or shaman possessing magical powers and the possibility of his inter-vention in social affairs, the existence of numerous Buddhist orders, and the presence of networks of trade routes made Tibetan society, a web of interconnections.[12] Further, in the case of Ladakh itself, it has come to be recognized that there are various kinds of horizontal and vertical ties in its communities, as is the case with other frontier communities.[13]

Notes

1. The preceding few paragraphs draw chiefly on Shakspo 1990.
2. The Great Game, strikingly portrayed by Kipling in *Kim*, began in the middle of the nineteenth century when Britain and Russia faced each other across the mountains and deserts between their empires, as they struggled for hegemony in Asia.
3. All the figures (which refer to population, acreage and industries in the Nubra block) in this paragraph are from the State Bank of India 1991. The statistics which refer to the two villages where I did my fieldwork are from a census which I conducted from 1990-1 and from genealogical information which I collected during the same period. There are no other recent statistics for the two sites.
4. *Gazetteer of Kashmir and Ladak* 1974 [1890]:806.
5. Ibid., 1974 [1890]:366-7.
6. See Rabgyas and Osmaston 1994:111-19 et passim.
7. I use these terms as defined by Terray (1972 [1969]:115) in his analysis of Claude Meillasoux's works.
8. For instance, Evans-Pritchard 1940 and those of the Manchester school of social anthropology (see note 9). The concept of 'levels of socio-cultural integration', however, is most closely associated with the name of Steward 1955. Steward suggested that one could view the culture of a society at various levels. At the lowest level, a culture could be based upon certain natural and technical conditions; at the same time, it could develop forms of participation in institutions which included it in wider society. Although he used this idea to explain how different groups at different stages of evolution could co-exist (against the idea of unilinear stages of other evolutionists and the idea that a culture area could contain only a single culture within its boundaries), in this study, the idea that a community can be integrated at various levels does not have this evolutionary bias.
9. Gluckman 1965:90-104 et passim; In the works of others of the school, these concepts of cross-cutting ties were developed to describe all kinds of frontier situations: Frankenburg's work (1957) showed how differences are bridged between various groups because no two villagers are at the center of the same group. The groups overlap and intermesh and therefore, no one is an outsider to all groups and everyone is a stranger to at least one. The ties that cross-cut can be those of neighbourhood, marriage, kinship and face-to-face interaction (Frankenburg 1957), or the exchange of the gift (Uberoi 1962). The border situation can create ties between villages on one side of the border and villages on the other side as well as link them to the processes of nation-state formation giving these villages an intercalary status (Cohen 1965).

10. 'Heteroglossia' is a word used by Bakhtin 1981 to stress the primacy and constant interaction between meanings and languages in society. Further, he sees dialogism whether for individuals, texts or social forms, as 'the characteristic epistemological mode of a world dominated by heteroglossia' (Bakhtin 1981:426). The semantic content of words and language itself is seen by Volosinov 1973 [1930] as the site of struggle and social change rather than as a set of immutable forms.

11. A similar point is made about the Tallensi on the Gold Coast of Africa by Fortes (1940:238-71), where there appears to be no structural unit larger than the clan to create social cohesion and nothing to mark precise linguistic, political or social boundaries between large groups. See also Srinivas 1995a exploring the theme of social conjunction and disjunction between Muslims and Buddhists in Nubra.

12. See Miller 1961; Samuel 1982.

13. See Aziz 1978; Dollfus 1989.

Chapter 4

The Primary Level of Integration

The household

The fundamental category of social organization in Nubra's villages is the household. There are many terms for this idea: the individual homestead is the *khampa;* the family is called *nangmi,* literally, 'people of the inside', i.e. those who share a common residence; rhe Nubra-pa differentiate between whether the people of a particular family who bear a common name live in the big house or small house – the *khangchen* or *khutu.* The *khangchen* and *khutu* are typically made of baked mud bricks and stone with beams of wood as rafters and thick walls. They may have several floors with the animals on the ground floor or in the stalls next to the house. Each house has a compound outside it which is walled off from the outside by a low wall or a thorn fence. The organization of houses in a village varies. Houses may be built along a path serially with their respective compounds and their fields below or around the nucleated settlements (as was the case in both Tegar and Hundar) or as a dispersed settlement of houses each with fields of its own around it, fairly self-contained, as was the case in the village neighbouring Tegar. Both patterns are common to villages in other parts of Ladakh.[1] The *khangchen* or *khutu* are separated by a wall in some cases or not in others.

Four features of social organization can be identified here: a) Various stages in the developmental cycle of a household by the breaking away of virtually any member of the family. The rules of primogeniture are not as strictly observed here as reported for certain other areas, for example, Zanskar.[2]

b) On the marriage of a son or daughter, the household possessions are divided up between parents and unmarried children as one unit, and the newly married couple as another unit. The latter are now the *khangchen* and ritual representatives for the family; the sacra stays with them. The *khangchen*, organizes the *phaspun* dinners at *Losar* (see chapter five for a description of the *phaspun*), and after harvest at an occasion called *Shrupla*. It is also counted as the symbolic head whom the gods visit at *Losar* and the head of the extended group of families, at *Id*. I shall call all the *khangchens* and *khutus*, who are considered descendants from some ancestor in the village, a kin group. A household will be used to denote a separate production and consumption unit.

c) The eldest sibling (a brother, but also in many cases, a sister) of the present reproductive generation usually resides in the *khangchen* with or without other siblings. In only one case (in Tegar) was it a polyandrous family and in none was there a polygynous one. The *khutu* usually contains parents, brothers and sisters, and sometimes unmarried children or additional relatives. The estate thus passes from one generation of siblings to another, all junior brothers and sisters having de facto rights to the land even if they are not the main inheritors of it. Division of land takes place from one generation to another.

d) The presence of the *khangchen* and *khutu* also points to the minimum unit of joint housekeeping, ownership of land and property, commensality and privacy. The minimal unit of production which coincides with the consumption unit is the household organized around the domestic fire or hearth, possessing tools such as the spade, pickaxe, sickle, or pitchfork, for work in the fields.

The above features of social organization are similar to those reported for other areas in the Indus valley and Zanskar, although the number of polyandrous and polygynous households differ based on a number of economic and social factors as well as the extent to which they have been affected by forces of change. A larger number of such units as well as the passage of the estate undivided from generation to generation has been reported for Zanskar. It has been argued that traditional rules of primogeniture continue to operate in a classical way in Zanskar, which is less affected by change than the villages in the Indus valley.[3]

There are certain terms related to the idea of the household and the kin group which need to be considered here: *nyen, ruspa, spun* and *gyut*.

As stated earlier, *nangmi* refers to those who share a common residential unit. Those who marry out of the household to other households come to be considered *nyen* (kin) to those of the natal one. This term is a general one used to mean those whom one is related to both through the mother and the father, bilaterality being more important here than anything else. While links with relatives of both side are expected to be strong, it is social intercourse that prevents them from disappearing. Relatives are expected to be present or to assist in household feasts at birth, marriage and death. They will be invited to such occasions, and when a person travels to another village, he or she may stay and expect hospitality from the *nyen*. *Nyen* may also, of course, belong to the same village. But the term, for an individual, will differ from generation to generation. The idea of *nyen* is more or less equivalent to the sociological concept of the kindred in Nubra (to be described in chapter six). To some extent, the idea of *ruspa*, 'people of one bone', overlaps with that of *nyen*: kin subsumed by the idea of *nyen* are generally those with whom there is a shared substance, 'bone'. But unlike some Tibetan-speaking societies studied by others (see chapter six) where the idea of *ruspa* refers to a substance inherited from the father (blood or *tag* being the parallel substance from the mother), in this area and the Indus valley, *ruspa* denotes kinship at the most basic level. The 'sharing of bone' makes people unmarriageable, since it is necessary that one does not marry anyone to whom one is related (through the father or the mother) within seven degrees of a common ancestor. It is at a more abstract level that the *ruspa* are those with whom one shares a common descent, although it does not therefore become a descent group. Some of those in the *khangchen* and the *khutu* would also, thus, be *ruspa*. The *ruspa* in practical terms marks the limits of exogamy for an individual. Muslim households practising cross-cousin marriage would be seen by Buddhists as marrying their *ruspa*.

The most minimal use of *ruspa* refers to siblings who are of a 'shared bone' because they are born of the same parents. These *spun* (siblings) cannot intermarry, nor can their children. Siblingship is an important theme for other kinds of relationships of individuals and households, some of which will be discussed later. During the course of the developmental cycle of a household, a sibling group divides and brothers or sisters may leave the household to form their own. This does not, however, weaken the link 'through the bone', and visits and gifts continue on most ritual occasions. Almost all writers on Ladakh agree that after the marriage of a sister, the link between a brother and sister is transferred somewhat to the link between her child and its mother's brother, *ajang*. This *ajang* has an important role to play in the birth and marriage of his sister's son or daughter, and they visit him on occasions such as the New Year, *Losar*. On the death of an *ajang*, the children also have a significant role. To refer to someone as *ajang* is to infuse a certain informality in the relationship with one who is not a kinsman. The term *gyut* has a range of meanings in Tibetan-speaking societies (see chapter six). In this area, it refers to people who belong to a particular household bearing its name and to a group of *khangchen* and *khutus* as well. The idea of *gyut* thus refers to descent in a limited sense; but while looking for prospective spouses, one may enquire more generally into a person's *gyut* or ancestry. This refers to a person's family background, extraction, and 'lineage'. In selecting marriage partners, the notion of *gyut* is important but not in terms of unilineal descent. It is believed that personal traits, temperament, and substance are transmitted through heredity and *gyut* is important in that context. For certain households, especially those who are tied to specializations such as astrology, healing, smithery, music, or those of high status, such as the nobility, *gyut* comes to have a more specific reference. Only some households and members of that *gyut* can perform certain tasks or occupations. In the case of the nobility, not all households can aspire to a high status *gyut*.[4]

The *thap* (stove) is the central focus of the household, just as the kitchen is the largest room in the house in both villages. Cooking is nearly always done by women in both villages. The woman of the house sits at the *thap* tending the fire, making tea or food. The one thing that she abstains from is (usually) chopping meat. The position around the fire signifies all kinds of relations: guests are seated (if they are not seated in the guest room) on the side opposite the woman of the house. On other days, children or others may sit there. Rugs are placed on the floor, the best rugs being reserved for the guest room; in the case of wealthy families, they may be fine rugs from Yarkand, Tibet or Kashmir. The place where a guest sits is also where a *lama* (monk) or the *imam* may be seated. In summer, when it is warm, most families move to a summer kitchen and sleeping room. This is usually permanent and can be refurbished with fresh leaves and stalks as it is a structure made of wood, leaves and hay; most families move there in early summer and move back in late autumn. In winter, most of them sleep together around the fire of the stove which dies out after cooking at night or around the *bukhari* (a heater). Wood is collected from the scrub jungle during the winter months after harvesting, threshing, and storage of food are over in the field. Every morning, men and women of a household in both the villages set off with their donkeys and *dzos*, and in the case of Hundar, also with camels, to the jungle.

Water for cooking purposes in the households of Tegar and Hundar is brought from streams flowing close to a house. From March-April till November or so, water appears in the main channels of the region at this altitude. Cultivation is simultaneous with the timing of the water. When it freezes over, families can be seen going to the river for water with their army procured jerry cans in Tegar, though in Hundar, the main channel never freezes. There is almost no category of waste in the household; vegetable peel and left over food are either put into the dry toilet or fed to the cows and other animals. All human and animal waste is recycled as manure for the fields by mixing it with ash and mud; it is taken out at the beginning of the agricultural cycle. Some vegetables are planted by nearly every family in both villages for domestic use. Most families provide vegetables on a regular basis to the agricultural cooperative, even if it is a small amount, which then sells it to the army. Some make minor personal sales, which seemed to be more common in Hundar than Tegar. Most have just about enough to cover domestic consumption and once they run out of vegetables, they borrow from others in exchange for labour or because of kin ties. Those who have surplus vegetables are also the ones who consume more meat. Most others, according to my figures, consume about one or two goats per year, mostly in winter, at *Losar,* or during *Id.* Mustard and barley are two other crops which are grown and only a few families in Tegar and Hundar are self-sufficient in both. Small quantities of mustard and barley grain are milled throughout the year in the 'water months', but chiefly before and after winter. Mills are located at fast-moving streams or on the slopes of channels – some of these are privately owned and others are owned by monasteries.

There are five processes of cooking in the valley which are common to both communities. These are: **brewing**: four kinds of liquids are brewed – butter tea, *khunak* (a salty tea decoction), *chang* (barley beer) and arrack (a spirit); **baking**: *markur, khambir, papolo* and *tagi* are the main types of breads; **steaming**: *mok-mok* and *ti mok-mok* (both dumplings) are the main steamed items; **frying**: *poori* and *kura* are fried items; **boiling**: *chutayi* and *skew* are two kinds of dumplings; *zan, kholak* and *marzan* are three porridges; *ngamtuk, paktuk* and *gyatuk* are three kinds of noodles and soups.

These foodstuffs can be differentiated according to the occasion, festive or work related, on which they are served, the category of people to whom it is served, and the season of the year. In all eating and drinking, there is a practice of *tzangs,* i.e. when people are invited to partake of food, there is a show of disclaiming the need to eat. People have to be, when they are guests, repeatedly urged to eat – extravagant offers of food and drink have to be made and equally extravagantly, refused. The higher the person in the social hierarchy vis-à-vis the person offering or eating, the greater the *tzangs* involved and the greater the amount wasted on the plate. Between those among whom social reciprocity and proximity prevails, there is little display of *tzangs*. There are five types of food in Tegar – the daily fare (contrasted to festive food), food for the gods, food for the spirits, food for guests and strangers, and for those in the work group and the kindred (defined in chapter six) who are sometimes placed in the first category or in the fourth depending on the degree of proximity or distance between the household and these groups. Among the Muslims in Hundar, the category of foods for the gods and the spirits are absent while the other three categories are present. There is also another category, i.e. food shared pre-eminently during *Id* and at other festivals, which affirms the body of the Islamic community. *Dua* (prayer) is said before and after each meal. A picture of the *Kaaba* (the holy building in Mecca housing the sacred black stone) adorns the wall in the kitchen or the guest room facing west. A *Koran* is usually placed in the kitchen though not all peasants can read it because of lack of instruction especially in areas distant from Leh. It is used by the *imam* when he visits the house.

In Buddhist households, there is a *choskhang* (altar) placed either in the kitchen in poor households, or in a separate room in rich ones. In this *choskhang* are placed pictures and idols of various *lhas* (gods/deities), ritual cups filled with water, a lamp, and incense sticks. In the morning, these cups are filled with fresh water and the lamp is lit. The altar also houses the god to whom the family owes ritual allegiance, the *phaspun lha* to whom the in-marrying member, male or female, is also affiliated. During major festivals, the *khataks* (ceremonial scarfs) around the idols are changed, foodstuffs offered, and obeisances paid. But the hearth is also considered sacred. One of the first acts in the morning, after the fire is lit in the Buddhist households in Tegar, is to put a little fresh tea or food in a small cup for the *lhas*; this is usually done by women. This *thap-lha* (god of the hearth) is not usually named but is acknowledged on many ritual occasions. For instance, when members of a natal household visit a newly married member, gifts of food from one hearth are taken and placed before the *thap-lha* of the other household. Again newly married sons and daughters are expected to give salutations to the *lha* of their natal household at *Losar*. There is also a small earthenware container into which flour mixed with butter or milk is burnt with coal.

It is kept outside on a wall or in a niche in front of the house. This is for spirits such as the *idak* who have large stomachs, small mouths and voracious appetites living in *Bardo* (an intermediate realm between this world and the next); or for other sorts of spirits which humans cannot see.

The domains of hearth and field and consumption and production of a household involve other groups for work and ritual purposes. These belong to the secondary level of integration to be described in the next chapter. The household is dependent on the labour of men and women both jointly and individually. Within the household the division of work is as follows: men butcher meat, wind wool into balls, and plough; and women cook, spin wool, weed kitchen gardens, and knit.

Men and women of the household, i.e. the unit of restricted simple exchange perform the following tasks: take manure to the yard from the toilets and animal sheds, fence the field, fetch water and wood, take animals to pasture in the forest or mountains or feed them in the yard, make paths around individual fields, spread manure on fields, water the fields,pluck and dry fruits like apricots and apples and seeds of onions, thresh grain, winnow grain, mill barley and mustard, bring supplies from the ration shop or army canteen, and store root vegetables under the soil.

Children learn these tasks as soon as they are old enough and follow the division of labour outlined above. In addition, many take care of their siblings regardless of their gender, though increasingly, most children are withdrawn from many of these tasks, at least for part of the day, since they attend school. I observed no discrimination between male and female children about being sent to school. In the charts 3A and 3B given in this chapter, figures for this gender differentiation in work are given: as can be seen, both male and female members of a household participate in work in the field, although as the figures show, gender biases are visible in non-agricultural work with a greater male presence in that domain.

THE NUMBER AND TYPES OF HOUSEHOLDS IN HUNDAR AND TEGAR

According to the *Bandobast* (the Land Settlement) for Hundar, in 1908, there were fifty-three houses whose owners were classified as owners of land, *malik*. Tenants appear only tangentially in the *Bandobast* since they were not tax payers and it was difficult for me to acquire details about the number of tenants. Out of these *malik*, forty-four were Buddhists, eight Muslims (one Shia Muslim, two *Arghuns*, i.e. Sunni Muslims, five *bedas*, i.e. musicians who could be either Sunni or Shia but are here considered

Nurbakshia) and one *Isahi* (Christian). Hemis and Chemrey *gompas* in the Leh valley and Diskit and Samstanling *gompas* in the Nubra valley were also owners of land. In addition there were seven other families who were tenants or servants. There were the following Muslim families in the village, now grown into a large number of *khutus* from their original families.[5]

1. Razak was the owner of the land in 1908. His father came from Srinagar and was a *Bandobast* official. He married a Buddhist woman from Terste village in Nubra. In 1990-1, there were five households regarded as members of this kin group.

2. Ali was the second owner. The family belonged originally to Stok in the Leh valley and an ancestor married a Buddhist woman of Hundar. In 1990-1, there was only one household of this name, resident in Leh, whose members came occasionally to oversee their land. Both Razak and Ali were Sunnis.

3. Gangphel and Ali were joint owners of a piece of land: Ali belonged to (2) and Gangphel was probably a member of a Buddhist family.

4. The ancestor of this *beda* (musician) family from Purig married a Buddhist woman, village not known, and settled in Hundar. In 1990-1, there were twelve households in this kin group.

5. Rahim Biwi was the wife of a *beda* man.

6. Azim Biwi was the daughter of the same man and was a separate owner of land. She had no children and the eldest brother had also died childless so the land went to the youngest brother. In 1990-1, there were two houses belonging to this kin group.

7. Ali's family were *beda*, origin not known. In 1990-1, they had split into two households.

8. Kulli was also a *beda*. He sold land to Buddhists and migrated across the river.

   All the above families are considered to be Nurbakshia. Besides these families, there were seven other families and their descendants who were not mentioned in the Settlement as *maliks* either because they were tenants and after the land reforms in India became owners, or because they had other occupations when they settled in Hundar. These were:

9. The Stao-*pa* who were merchants from Leh. Their ancestor married a Buddhist woman from Sakti village in the Indus valley, and at some later date, bought land from the *Zimskang* in Hundar. There was only one household of this name, Sunnis by faith, in 1990-1.

10. Ramzandar came as a merchant from Srinagar. He married a Nurbakshia woman from Partapur village in Nubra, though he himself was a Sunni and many of his descendants are members of both sects. In 1990-1, there were fourteen households in the kin group out of which four or five are Sunni.

11. The Khirochan-*pa* got land after the land reforms from the monastery. Their ancestor came from Kargil and worked as a shepherd for Buddhist families. He married a Buddhist woman. In 1990-1, there were two households who were his descendants. Possibly originally, this family was considered Nurbakshia, but many descendants are married into Sunni families.

12. The Stao-*pa* were an old couple who used to work for the *Zimskang*. The man was married to a Nurbakshia woman from Partapur. In 1990-1, there were three households who were their descendants, considered to be Nurbakshia.

13. Miti Hasan came as domestic help from Kargil and married a Buddhist woman (village unknown). In 1990-1, there were three descendant households.

14. Gulam Nabi came from Purig as a shepherd for the *Zimskang*. He married a Buddhist woman (village unknown) and in 1990–1, there was only one household of this family.

15. Chini was a *beda* from Purig, married a Buddhist woman and in 1990-1, there were ten households who counted as his descendants.

All the previous three families of Miti Hasan, Gulam Nabi and Chini are considered Nurbakshia. In the above cases, if certain details are omitted such as villages of origin or marriage, it is because these details were unavailable.

At the time of my fieldwork there were eleven kin groups of Muslims excluding families of (2), (3) and (8) and counting (5) and (6) as one unit. The total number of Muslim households at the time of my census was fifty-five, counted as separate *tutbing* (smokes) in the villagers' enumeration, i.e. as separate production and consumption units. They did not comprise a separate territorial area but tended to live in between their Buddhist neighbours, sometimes in clusters and sometimes as solitary houses. There were 121 males and 118 females and the average household size was 4.35 souls. There were basically two types of households – nuclear and composite – though really part of different demographic stages of development of a household, the occurrence of impermanent accretions giving an appearance of greater diversity in structure and size.[6] The nuclear household might be simple, consisting of husband, wife and children, or accreted, consisting of those budding and declining accretions such as a son-in-law residing with the father-in-law, or a widower/widow living with a son/daughter. The composite household consisted of a growing nuclear family at its broadest stage of development prior to division – either through parents and married children or through siblings. Both *khangchens* and *khutus* can be composite or nuclear in their structure as shall be discussed.

Accordingly, among the Muslims of Hundar there were forty simple nuclear households; ten accreted nuclear households; and five composite households. The break-up within these broad types is given in appendix A at the end of this chapter.

According to the *Bandobast* for Tegar, in 1908 there were thirty-eight households in all three hamlets classified as owners of land, *malik*. Out of these, thirty-seven were Buddhist and one was *Arghun*. Diskit and Samstanling *gompas* were also holders of land. In 1908, in the area that we call Tegar for the purposes of this book, the number of *malik* were twenty-three (also the number of kin groups); the total number of households were thirty-five out of which three were Muslim (one was *Arghun* and two were considered Nurbakshia). Details of these households can be found below.

1. The Kalon family, also called the *Kharpon* (the master of the castle in the past), were the largest owners of land. In 1990-1, there were two households in the village, one of whom were residents of Leh although they owned land in the village.
2. The *Zimskang* family; in 1990-1, there were two households of this name, also large farmers.
3. The Lunzur family; in 1990-1, there were three households of this name.
4. Three households who were part of a kin group called Nyirpa-*pa*; in 1990-1, there were four households in the kin group.
5. Two Mayur-*pa* households of a kin group by that name; in 1990-1, there were six households in the kin group.
6. The Gyan-*pa*; in 1990-1, there were five households.
7. The Chulikirkir-*pa*; in 1990-1, there were six households.
8. The Rabgias-*pa*; in 1990-1, there were two households.
9. The Makpastampel-*pa*; in 1990-1, there were ten households including the household of the sister of the original family which is now called by a different name but is considered part of the same kin group.
10. The Phorokh-*pa* in which three brothers (of whom two were

Figure 3A : Census of Muslim Households in Hundar Village

Sl. No.	Ref.No. of Kin Group	No. of Households	Members		Occupation	Adults		Children	
			M	F		M	F	M	F
1.	1	5	20	15	Farmer	1	7	12	7
					Teacher	2	1		
					Doctor	1			
					Shopkeeper	1			
					Driver	1			
					Govt. employee	2			
2.	4	12	28	30	Farmer	8	13	14	17
					Musician	1			
					Soldier	5			
3.	5 & 6	2	3	4	Farmer	2	2	1	2
4.	7	2	5	7	Farmer	1	4	2	3
					Soldier	1			
					Labourer	1			
5.	9	1	5	5	Farmer	2	3	2	2
					Merchant	1			
6.	10	14	29	25	Farmer	2	16	14	9
					Shepherd	1			
					Moulvi/Imam	2			
					Merchant	1			
					Soldier	5			
					Nurse		1		
					Teacher	1			
					Govt. employee	2			
7.	11	2	1	3	Farmer	1	3		
8.	12	3	9	5	Farmer	2	3	4	
					Teacher	1			
					Guard	1			
					Soldier	1			
					Servant		2		
9.	13	3	6	7	Farmer	4	5	1	1
					Soldier	1			
					Servant	1			
10.	14	1	2	2	Farmer	1	1		1
					Shepherd	1			
11.	15	10	13	15	Farmer	11	9	2	6
	Total	55	121	118		69	70	52	48

Average household size: 4.35

Figure 3B : Census of all Households (89 Buddhist, 4 Muslim) in Tegar Village

Sl. No.	Ref.No. of Kin Group	No. of Households	Members		Occupation	Adults		Children	
			M	F		M	F	M	F
1.	1	1	3	1	Farmer	1		2	
					Teacher		1		
2.	2	2	7	8	Farmer	2	3	2	4
					Soldier	1			
					Teacher		1		
					Govt. employee	2			
3.	3	3	12	7	Farmer	3	4	4	3
					Teacher	3			
					Driver	1			
					Contractor	1			
4.	4	4	10	11	Farmer	6	5	2	6
					Soldier	2			
5.	5	6	11	16	Farmer	7	11	2	5
					Lama	1			
					Govt. employee	1			
6.	6	5	7	8	Farmer	3	6	1	2
					Lama	2			
					Soldier	1			
7.	7	6	7	15	Farmer	4	7	2	7
					Labourer	1			
					Teacher		1		
8.	8	2	4	3	Farmer		1	1	2
					Lama	1			
					Shopkeeper	1			
					Govt. employee	1			
9.	9	10	21	16	Farmer	6	9	8	4
					Govt. employee	3			
					Soldier				
					Driver				
					Travel agent	2			
					Teacher	1	3		
10.	10	4	10	7	Farmer	5	6	5	1
11.	11	5	13	8	Farmer	3	5	5	2
					Lama	1			
					Soldier	1			
					Teacher	2	1		
					Govt. employee	1			

Sl. No.	Ref.No. of Kin Group	No. of Households	Members		Occupation	Adults		Children	
			M	F		M	F	M	F
12.	12	3	11	10	Farmer	3	3	5	5
					Lama	1			
					Nurse		1		
					Teacher		1		
					Soldier	1			
					Miller	1			
13.	13	3	10	5	Farmer		3	6	2
					Govt. employee	2			
					Soldier	1			
					Nurse		1		
14.	14	5	11	13	Farmer	3	6	4	5
					Soldier	4			
					Labourer		2		
15.	15	1	5	4	Farmer	2	2	1	1
					Teacher		1		
					Nurse	1			
					Clerk	1			
16.	16	6	21	16	Farmer	8	9	6	7
					Lama	2			
					Shopkeeper	1			
					Soldier	2			
					Office peon	2			
17.	17	3	7	3	Farmer	4	2	2	
					Soldier	1			
					Teacher		1		
18.	18	13	33	25	Farmer	11	17	11	8
					Lama	3			
					Shopkeeper	3			
					Soldier	2			
					Teacher	2			
					Mason	1			
19.	19	2	4	1	Farmer	2	1	2	
20.	20	3	7	8	Farmer	5	4	2	3
					Labourer		1		
21.	21	2	6	6	Farmer	1	4	3	2
					Soldier	2			
22.	22	1	2	1	Farmer	2	1		
23.	23	3	6	5	Farmer	2	3	4	2
	Total	93	228	197		148	126	80	71

Average household size : 4.57 Average without Muslim households : 4.58

minors) owned land in common; in 1990-1, there were four households.

11. There were four families of the name Takchan-*pa* of which I was only able to trace two. No one recalls the other two. There is another large family who may belong to this family but that is just speculation. In 1990-1, there were five households of this kin group.

12. The Phargun-*pa*; they may have been called by another name in the past – the family members are not sure if they were called Jora-*pa* and the family by that name was not traceable. In 1990-1, there were three households of this name.

13. The Hilbe-*pa*; there was another family called Pili-*pa* related to the above but there are no traces of that family now. In 1990-91, there were three households of this kin group.

14. The Changtuk-*pa* who were carpenters and peasants; in 1990-1, there were five households in the kin group.

15. One *Arghun* family descended from the same ancestor as the first Muslim household in Hundar; in 1990-1, there was only one household of this name.

16. The Gyamkar-*pa* and Nyachu-*pa* which have now merged and are called Gyamkar-*pa*; in 1990-1, there were six households of this kin group.

17. The Nisit-*pa*; in 1990-1, there were three houses in the kin group.

18. In addition there were about six households who may have been tenants in the past and now own some land; in 1990-1, there were thirteen households of the Bangajan kin group.

19. The Tsaspang-*pa*, Nurbakshia by faith; in 1990-1, there were two households of this kin group.

20. The Tashi Tsering-*pa*; in 1990-1, there were three households of this kin group.

21. The Amma Zangmo-*pa*; in 1990-1, there were two households of this kin group.

22. The Rasul-*pa*, Nurbakshia by faith; in 1990-1, there was only one household by this name.

23.   The Zingyok-*pa*; in 1990-1, there were three households in this kin group.

The total number of males in the households in Tegar was 228 and the total number of females, 197. There were ninety-three households counting serial number one as one household because the other is non-resident; the average household size was 4.57. If the Muslim households are excluded, then the total number of males in Tegar, now all composed of Buddhist families, is 217 and the total number of females, 191. The number of households would be eighty-nine and the average household size, 4.58. For further details kindly refer appendix A.

The information in the preceding sections and appendix A deal with a number of concepts and descriptions which refer to the nature of the household in Tegar and Hundar. The *khangchen* and the *khutu* are local terms which refer to the various stages in the developmental cycle of a household formed by the splitting off of sons, daughters, siblings, and so on; usually the eldest sibling of a generation (son or daughter) resides in the *khangchen* after marriage, and the rest of the siblings and parents, in *khutus*. *Khangchens* and *khutus* are of two types – simple (nuclear or accreted) and composite. In the tables given in Figures 3A and 3B, certain aspects of the relationship between *khangchens* and *khutus* and the types of households, as well as of their developmental cycle can be summarized. These features are partly a result of the life-histories of families through the processes of marriage, birth, death, and residence; and partly a result of historical factors – for instance, land reforms in the area, the opportunities for cash employment, and so on. Five features can be delineated more specifically. These are:

1.   The reference number of the kin group (according to the description above) is given in Figures 3A and 3B. The number of households and the number of men and women in each group is also given. The first household in each kin group is the *khangchen* of the group. There is great diversity in the types of *khangchens* and *khutus* in Hundar and Tegar.

(a)   In Hundar, among the Muslim households, there were:

Simple nuclear *khangchens*	8
Accreted nuclear *khangchens*	2
Composite *khangchens*	3
Simple nuclear *khutus*	32
Accreted nuclear *khutus*	8
Composite *khutus*	2

(b) In Tegar:*

Simple nuclear *khangchens*	18	(1)
Accreted nuclear *khangchens*	3	
Composite *khangchens*	2	(1)
Simple nuclear *khutus*	39	(1)
Accreted nuclear *khutus*	23	(1)
Composite *khutus*	8	

* The figures in the brackets indicate the number of Muslim households among the total figures given.

2. The gender difference in agricultural and non-agricultural occupations is also shown; the implications of this for the community is discussed in the next few chapters. Basically, there is a predominance of females in non-cash and agricultural occupations, while males are more prevalent in cash and non-agricultural occupations.

3. Most children in the village attend school upto at least standard eight and school-going is influenced quite often by the proximity of the school and household status rather than any merit on the part of the child.

4. Households which are engaged in a greater number of high-income non-agricultural occupations, such as merchants, doctors, school teachers and contractors are those who also had a greater amount of land and were of higher status in the pre-1947 period. Those who are totally confined to agriculture or have labourers or peons among their members are households who were small farmers and had a lower status in the past. There are no hereditary occupations except for those of the carpenter, blacksmith and musician (and sometimes the astrologer). Even in households which traditionally follow any of these occupations, it is usually a single member who does so while the rest do other jobs.

5. The increase in the number of households in Tegar and Hundar between 1908-90 or 91, i.e. a period of about eighty-two years has differed in the two villages:

Firstly, while the increase in the number of households in Hundar has been from eleven to fifty-five, i.e. about five times, the percentage increase has been about 400 percent. The increase seems to have been the largest among two types of households – the merchant group (kin group no. 10), and those who are descendants of *bedas* or musicians married to Buddhist women (kin group no. 4 and 15). The large increase in the number of households in the former category appears to have been through the division of landed and other assets; in the latter category, the households are poorer ones, and the increase in the number of households appears to have been through the acquisition of some land after the land reforms, and through a minimal diversification into non-agricultural occupations. The latter two households are Nurbakshias, while the former category has households who are both Sunni and Nurbakshias.

Secondly, the increase in the number of households in Tegar from 1908-1990/91 is from thirty-five to ninety-three households, i.e. about 2.7 times. The percentage increase has been about 166 percent. If we exclude the Muslim households whose number has increased from three to four households (i.e. 33 percent), the percentage increase among Buddhist households is 178 percent. The increase has been the largest among five kin groups (no. 6, 7, 9, 14, and 16). All of these are Buddhists, and are middle level peasantry. The increase in the number of households has been both through the sub-division of land as well as the diversification into non-agricultural occupations. There is thus an important class and religious difference in the nature of the increase in eighty years. Some of the reasons for this are discussed in chapter six. One reason for the slower rate of increase among Buddhist households appears to have been due to the fact that at least one male member of the household till recently became a monk. The poorer Nurbakshias, whose number has increased dramatically in the last eighty years, appear to have taken to non-agricultural occupations in ways similar to Buddhist middle-level peasant households; but they appear to have had as many uxorilocal marriages as virilocal both in this and the previous generation contributing to a larger number of households in the village in comparison to Buddhist households. Among the other Sunni Muslims in Hundar, the number of virilocal and uxorilocal marriages seem to be more or less similar to Buddhists.

THE LAMA AND THE IMAM

The complexities of the relationship of the *gompa* to the village, or a study of the monastic system is not analysed in this book. This has been the subject of reflection of other works on Ladakh.[7] In my ethnography, I make no attempt to unravel the intricacies of this mosque/monastery-village relationship apart from referring to those aspects which impinge directly on the content of the case studies, especially the spirit possession of the *manekhang* priest. I make only two observations. Firstly, the villagers are in no way economically dependent on the monastery, except for some loans as they were in the past, nor are they dependent on mosques. *Gompas* do not 'own' villages in this part of the valley although they do have some land which they lease out to tenants in return for certain services. Mosques in the Hundar area do not own land. Secondly, the Samstanling monastery continues to draw monks and novices from the surrounding villages since it is a fairly prestigious monastery but monks are rarely elder sons of a family. The practice of women becoming nuns seems very limited in comparison to regions such as Zanskar where there are a great many nunneries probably for demographic and other reasons. I found no nun in the Buddhist sample in Tegar but the number of monks out of the total number of 217 Buddhist males was eight, i.e. about 3.5 percent. Priests of mosques are lay persons and are not formally trained in theology.

There are two individuals related to the household exchanging with it various ritual services. First, the *gelong* (an initiated full monk) of the village *manekhang* who is appointed by the *gompa* under whose control the *manekhang* falls or a monk who is from the *gompa* to which the household owes allegiance. Second, the *imam* or priest of the nearest *masjid*.

The monk of the *manekhang* is the officiant appointed by the monastery to perform ritual services at the *manekhang* and conduct daily ablutions of the idols there. He may belong to the Gelug or the Drug order, both of which are present in Nubra. He, more than any other monk, has a constant interface with the local people on an everyday basis. Normally three kinds of services are performed by him for a household:

(a) the monthly *lapsang*, the purification or cleansing of the gods of the household. Once a month, for every house in his jurisdiction, which may cover more than one village, he performs the monthly prayers at the *choskhang* or sets up an impromptu altar in the kitchen. In Tegar, the *gelong* performed *lapsangs* for two hamlets as well as one or two neighbouring villages, the third hamlet being associated with Diskit *gompa*. During the *lapsang, chotpa* (dough offerings) are made with butter, tea and barley flour, incense and lamps lit, and prayers chanted to the beating of a gong and cymbals.

(b) He also performs the annual *skangsol* ceremony with other monks of the monastery for the *khangchen* of each kin group Once a year, this ceremony is performed by the *khangchen* as the ritual representative of the kin group normally around or before harvest time, although they are supposed to perform it four times a year. This is a ceremony of offering to the gods, a payment of ritual debts, and a warding off of evil.

(c) The third kind of ceremony that is performed by the *gelong* is the life-crisis ritual – that of birth and death being the central ones. In return for these services, the household gives at harvest time, one *bo* (a large wooden mug used as a measure) of barley to the *gelong* when he comes around.

The *imam* of the *masjid* also has similar duties to perform. He may be Shia, Nurbakshia or Sunni. As stated earlier, there are three *masjids* in Hundar, one Nurbakshia, one Sunni and the other is a family *masjid*, the family having adherents of both sects although the head claims to be Sunni. The *imam* of the Sunni *masjid*, whom I observed, does not perform any monthly prayers for a household but there are two other parallel services he does perform: (a) during sowing and after harvest, the grain is brought by Muslim households to the *masjid* and the *imam* reads a prayer over it. (b) He is the main officiant at life-crisis rituals – birth, circumcision, marriage and death. In return, households give gifts in kind or in small and stable amounts of cash to him when he visits their house. In Hundar, during winter, there was also a *moulvi* (one trained in theology at Deoband) from a village near the cease-fire line in residence to teach the children of some of the families the *Koran*. This was a purely private arrangement since it was felt that these *moulvis*, many of whom were trained at Deoband, were learned.

There are of course collective rituals where the entire village or community participates; households are not individuated in their relationship then.

There are other kinds of specialists whose association with the household is sporadic and based on need. The *onpo* (astrologer) is consulted on a variety of afflictions facing a person, a family, or a village and also asked at times to carry out exorcisms, fix auspicious dates, or diagnose diseases. The *larje* (doctor) is consulted on a variety of ailments and prescribes herbal and mineral remedies. The *gara, beda, shinkan*, i.e. the blacksmith, the musician and the carpenter, respectively, are others. Exchange for their services by the households is mainly in kind – with grain, vegetables, or labour.

THE CHOSPUN

A rite creating ritual siblingship occurs in the first month of the Tibetan Buddhist calendar in Tegar, a month when many important Buddhist festivals occur. *Chospun* are ritual siblings created by a rite in the monastery. Two strangers – villagers or outsiders, who are not bound by kinship – undergo this sacred binding into siblingship by an exchange of gifts. On an appointed day, they put a personal item – a sash, a ring, a watch, etc. –

into a large container along with those of others in the monastery. A *lama*, after chanting prayers, picks up any two items as in a lottery and joins them. The owners of these two objects, male or female, then become siblings. They are enjoined to assist each other in times of crisis, children's marriages, or extend hospitality and patronage. Persons may have more than one *chospun*, though generally it is one. Like siblings, *chospun* and their children do not intermarry, but unlike the *spun*, the ties of the *chospun* are non-biological.

Other such cases have been documented for the Himalayan region: the Nepali 'mit', the Tibetan 'ganye', the Lepcha 'ingzong', and the Tibetan mutual aid society called 'kidu'.[8] These ties are couched in terms of fictive kinship and involve, at times, prohibitions regarding marriage. They may function as a mechanism for cohesion in a multi-ethnic or multi-religious community (the 'mit'), establish trade links across borders (the 'ingzong') or create and solicit attendance and contributions towards rituals (the 'kidu'). Their composition may cut across ethnic, religious, occupational, regional and status differentials. They do not, it seems, coalesce into inclusive political groups. In the area in which I did my fieldwork, this institution seems to have fallen into disuse and I could not determine whether it was only a Buddhist institution.

Appendix A
Break-up of Muslim household types in Hundar

1. SIMPLE
   - a. SIMPLE NUCLEAR:
     - – husband-wife unit (old or young) — 9
     - – husband, wife and children — 31
   - b. ACCRETED NUCLEAR:
     - – Widow and daughter — 1
     - – Widow alone — 1
     - – Widower alone — 1
     - – Widowers with married/unmarried children — 2
     - – Widower with adopted daughter — 1
     - – Widowed half sister with brother's family — 1
     - – Two unmarried brothers — 1
     - – Widow with married son — 2
2. COMPOSITE
   - – Husband, wife and at least one married son — 4
   - – Husband, wife and at least one married daughter — 1
   - TOTAL — 55

Break-up of household types in Tegar

The following are the types of households including the Muslim families in Tegar – one composite family with a married son and other members, two nuclear families with husband, wife and children and one with a widow and her two sons. The details are as follows:

1. SIMPLE
   a. SIMPLE NUCLEAR:
      – Husband and wife group   4
      – Husband, wife and children   53
   b. ACCRETED NUCLEAR:
      – Widow with married daughter   1
      – Widow alone   6
      – Widower alone   2
      – Widow with married son   2
      – Woman divorcee with daughters   1
      – Male divorcee with daughter   1
      – Widow with niece and her married son   1
      – Mother and son   2
      – Father and son   3
      – Unmarried man   1
      – Two brothers with elder's family   1
      – Widower with married daughter   3
      – Widow with daughters   1
      – Widow with two sons   1
2. COMPOSITE
      – Husband, wife and children including
        at least one married son   7
      – Husband,wife,children including
        at least one married daughter   3
      TOTAL   93

Thus, the number of simple nuclear households were fifty-seven, the number of accreted nuclear households were twenty-six, and the number of composite households were ten.

Notes

1. c.f. Fraser 1977.
2. See the various studies of different villages in Zanskar in Crook and Osmaston 1994.
3. See Crook and Osmaston 1994 for villages in Zanskar and Goldstein and Tsarong 1987 for villages in the Indus valley.

4. Phylactou 1989 also broadly makes the same kind of assumptions in her thesis about household structure in the Indus valley.

5. (I was not able to trace the Shia household). I make a distinction here between a household and its members, *nangmi* in local terms (the family in sociological terms), and a group of *khangchens* and *khutus* descended from an ancestor in the village which I have called a kin group. The villagers do not themselves have a term for this unity, except perhaps to call them 'the people of' a particular *khangchen*, thereby indicating descent from it. Occasionally, they may call it a *gyut* to mean parentage rather than a lineage. I call it a kin group and not a descent group because they are formed bilaterally without strong patrilineal and matrilineal tendencies.

6. My analysis of household structure follows that of Uberoi (1964:29-33) with some minor changes in terminology.

7. c.f. Crook and Osmaston 1994. Part Four of the book is devoted to monastic institutions and belief-systems in Zanskar; See also Nawang Tsering 1979; Pallis 1974 [1939]; and Singh 1977.

8. See Miller 1956; Okada 1957.

Chapter 5

The Secondary Level of Integration

Grouping households together on the basis of their religious orientation, as was done in the previous chapter, suggests that the unity and singularity of the household is cross-cut by other ties that integrate it within the territory of the village, i.e. at the secondary level. This kind of grouping assumes some importance particularly in the background of the boycott of Muslims, especially Sunnis, by Buddhists, and the LBA agitation which gathered momentum after 1989. The separation into overarching religious groups is, however, not necessarily permanent and after February 1991, the social boycott in the villages was lifted so that in terms of practice, if not in emotive content, this kind of separation disappeared.

The kind of integration at the secondary level which associates a household with other households in the territory of the village exists in four modalities: the first is the system of ranks in the village, basically occupational in nature; the second is the work group for all major activities in agriculture; the third is the ritual group, the *phaspun* among the Buddhists and the *iftarspun* among the Muslims for the performance of life-crisis rituals; the fourth is the minimum locus of political power – the village. In this chapter, I will consider these four modalities at the secondary level of integration.

THE OCCUPATIONAL CATEGORIES IN THE VILLAGE

Households are differentiated into various social categories in the two villages. The *Bandobast* is one basis for the classification of social strata.

There is a mapping of two kinds of spaces in this Land Settlement: firstly, the mapping of a social space which defines the various grades and sections of village society; secondly, the mapping of land into different categories, humanized for the purpose of subsistence and settlement. The placing of both these maps onto one another, then, results in a frame which defines both ownership in land (and transfers in ownership) and sources and items of revenue.

The *Bandobast* for Tegar in 1908 classified households according to the following categories:

(a) one household, called the *Kharpon*, belonged to the *Kalon* category (Chief minister);

(b) one household, called the *Zimskang*, was classified as *Lonpo* (minister);

(c) Thirty-two households were *zamindars* (land owners) and one out of these was *Arghun*;

(d) one household was *onpo* (astrologer);

(e) two households were considered *shinkan* (carpenters);

(f) one household was *Mussalman* (Muslim); and

(g) two *gompas* held land – Diskit and Samstanling.

The *Bandobast* for Hundar classified the households into the following categories:

(a) one household belonged to the *Lonpo* category;

(b) Forty households were *zamindars* including one *Balti* household, two *Arghun* households and one *Isahi*;

(c) one household was *larje* (doctor);

(d) two households were considered *gara* (blacksmiths);

(e) five households were *mon* (musicians and carpenters);

(f) Diskit, Chemrey, Samstanling and Hemis *gompas* were also landowners.

There is a further classification of land as that under settlement (houses and canals), *Abad-i-de*, and that which was government land (roads, market areas, gardens and Muslim cemeteries), *Khalsa Sircar*.

What is significant about this classification is that it is partly defined by religion, as for instance in the classification of certain households as *Isahi*, partly by social role or function, as *zamindar, larje, gara, onpo*, etc.; and partly by social status, the *Kalons* and the *Lonpos* being the highest in the social hierarchy and *mons* being the lowest. It is also defined partly by the ownership-tenancy polarity with the *gompas* and the *Sircar* (government) also being landlords and tenants being a sub-category. It is defined occasionally by family name, for example, *Kalon*. By contrast, some writers describe Ladakhi society as being composed of ethnic groups. According to them, among the Buddhists, these groups include the *Botos* or Ladakhis (agricul-turists), *gara* (blacksmiths with some land) and *mon* (musicians who have no land and only sell their labour); among the Muslims are the *Balti* (Shias) and the *Arghuns* (of Kashmiri/ Turkestani and Ladakhi parents) who are agriculturists and the *beda* (wandering minstrels).[1] Besides these, there are the *Changpas* (pastoralists) and the Dards (agriculturists, a section of whom are Buddhists). These authors fail to see that social classification occurs in Ladakh not according to one dominant criteria but according to various factors not all of which coalesce, as can be seen from the varied categories that the *Bandobast* uses to define the population. The actual position is that there are a number of criteria for classification – ethnic origin, territory, occupation, religion, and rank – which cross-cut each other.

The households in Tegar and Hundar present some disparities in wealth, occupation, prestige and influence. In the past, there were ranked social groups sustained by rents and customary obligations. Society was classified into different strata in any local context (including, therefore, ethnic groups). These strata are generally referred to as *rigs*. In Jaeschke's dictionary, this term is translated as family, lineage, extraction, birth or descent; also as nation or tribe; in a special sense, it is used to mean caste, class in society, or rank. He further states that there are five ranks in Tibet – the royalty, the caste of priests, the nobility or aristocracy, the citizens, and the common people. When applied to India, he argues, these appellations are applied to castes of Brahmanism although they do not correspond in every respect.[2] While the use of the term caste may or may not be applicable in ancient Tibetan-speaking societies, in contemporary Ladakh, most writers agree that the definition of *rig* is strata or rank, and divide Ladakhi society into four such strata: the royalty (*rgyal rigs*), the aristocracy (*skutag*), the middle-ranking peasantry (*mimangs*), and the low-caste artisans and musicians (*rigsnan*). The distinction between the royalty and the nobility may not be significant anymore in Ladakh, and one may say that there is only one *skutag* category now.[3] This rank certainly continues to enjoy a great deal of respect even today, and in the village, their status is most clearly defined on ritual and other festive events in the village where they are given a precedence in seating arrangements and other honours. Their family genealogies are also the most vividly remembered, but in practical terms, they do not necessarily wield more power in the village than other large landowning (*trongpa*) households. In fact, there is some intermarriage between them. This classification also recognizes that the monastic population does not constitute a separate rank, but depending on the status of the monk (for most nuns have a fairly ordinary status), may belong to the *skutag* or mimangs category. The only group which in any way may be considered a caste, are the artisans and musicians – the *mon, gara* and *beda*. Most of these families in some villages tend to live somewhat apart from the other ordinary households, and during ritual and other village occasions are seated separately and eat out of different vessels. Most ordinary villagers may not accept food from them, and they tend to be an endogamous group. There is some disagreement about which category among the *rigsnan* (literally, those who have no rank) ranks higher than others. This may probably vary from area to area. But each category tends to marry among themselves, and thus most households (for there are usually only one or two such households in each village) tend to have very widespread *nyen*. The middle ranking peasants tend to be a varied category including among them in the past, the revenue officers, the village headman, the temple guard, the master of the castle, the doctor, the astrologer and the oracle. But this *mimangs*, just as other categories, has undergone modifications in its constitution due to certain processes in contemporary Ladakhi society, such as land reforms, the commercialization of agriculture and new employment opportunities.

After the inclusion of Ladakh within the Indian state, the abolishing of the monarchical system (a process which began after the Dogra wars) and land reforms, the older system of (four) ranks (described above) was altered. Only *gompas* were exempt from land reforms and continue to hold a large amount of land. The socio-economic processes of the Indian state have also created forces which resulted in new forms of social differentiation by creating bureaucratic offices, military positions of power, and a commercial life which far exceeds in volume what existed previous to the closing of the borders and the traffic with Central Asia and Tibet. A person can thus advance himself/herself by state patronage, through education, piety or commerce. Only the starting point of power is land or older systems of power. In the two villages, people tend to identify the following occupational groups: *skutag:* old nobility, the upper strata, generally large landlords; *zingbatpa:* peasants; *imams, lamas* and *chomos* (nuns): religious persons; *mulazzim:* anyone connected with administrative work but generally in the higher echelons; *sepahi:* soldiers in the Indian army; *mon, beda* and *gara:* the lowest category.

The first and sixth form the clearest positions in the social hierarchy, being the highest and the lowest group. In the middle ranges, issues are more complex for this differentiation is largely by occupation, past and present, and in the same household may be combined in a complicated form. It is not just relative wealth which decides, but also, for example, such factors as those with whom one is married or can marry. The monks are usually celibate; only some Drugpa monks marry. The other strata tend to form relatively endogamous groups. The *zingbatpa, mulazzim* and *sepahi* form one such group; the higher positions among the *mulazzim* and *zingbatpa* tend to form another such group with the *skutag;* the *mon, beda* and *gara* tend to be another group. This is less due to a formal rule then due to political, strategic and existential choices.

These broad groups are complicated also by various sources of status and power today. In general, it can be said that there are two systems of role positions currently that combine in a complicated fashion within a household and between households. Given the considerable expansion in population and material resources, especially non-agricultural, it follows that if the classification given earlier is accurate, i.e. comprising of the royalty, the nobility, the middle-ranking peasantry and the out-castes (though we must include in this classification also the clergy who rank with the nobility or the peasants depending on the rank of the monk), then this earlier role system has been replaced by one that is far more complicated. This is indicated in Figures 3A and 3B in the earlier chapter which gave the occupational differentiation for each household.

THE WORK GROUP

The work group is situated in the agricultural landscape described in chapter three. The conception of land which emerges from the practice of agriculture, the dominant economic practice, is common to both villages. Within the limits of this agricultural space and ecological time, the village households organize themselves into fairly stable units for work. The smallest kind of work group is the household which I defined as the unit of restricted simple exchange and cooperation. The household is the locus of consumption and production and revolves around the axis of the hearth and the field, made available by the joint efforts of its members.

But there are tasks in the field for which these do not suffice. Larger tools are pooled together by a stable group of various households composed of kin and neighbours or in the case of landlords, including their tenants. These tools include the plough, and the large winnowing plate used by the group of extended simple exchange or cooperation. This group of cooperation also harvests, ploughs and sows fields for mustard and barley, takes manure to the fields, and animals to pasture. Women of the simple extended exchange unit weeded the large fields. Again, there are tasks which involve all the households of the village, for example, cleaning of water channels and preparing main canals for irrigation. This involved the group of complex exchange and coopera-tion. Since both groups fall within the territory of the village, they are part of the secondary level of integration. These groups are fairly stable over time although, in the period 1990-1, the Muslims had organized themselves into a separate group and had disassociated themselves from their Buddhist kin and neighbours due to the anti-Muslim boycott.

The Phaspun

All major life-crisis events – birth, marriage, death – are marked by rituals which accompany the shifts in household structure brought about by these events. Deaths, for example, involve both emotional and economic expenditure, as do marriages. At such occasions in Nubra, it is a group of families who are not related by genealogical ties called the *phaspun*, who are the main officiants and helpers in rituals. These families provide mutual assistance for the performance of the main rites of passage as well as in such tasks as choosing the marriage partner, and escorting the bride from her home during marriage. The *phaspun* includes kin groups that are not related by affinity since there is a custom that one cannot marry a *phaspun* member. They share a deity in common, the *pha–lha*. Membership of a *phaspun* is mutually exclusive and the group becomes visible in its corporate form during life-crisis rituals of various sorts – birth, marriage, or death. *Phaspuns* may belong to the same village or to adjoining villages although the importance of their presence makes it necessary that they do not belong to far-flung ones.

Some writers have emphasized the common ancestor within a *phaspun* and assume that its members are blood relations; it has been argued that the *phaspun* is essentially a kinship association in the form of a patriarchal clan.[4] In Zanskar, all children belong to their father's lineage, called the *ruspa*, on birth. In each family, however, the mother belongs to a *ruspa* which is different from her husband's and children's although through marriage, she has become part of her husband's *phaspun* and is no longer part of her father's. The *phaspun*, therefore, amounts to a patrilineal clan with genealogical relationships determined through the patrilocal *ruspa* of which married women and *magpa* (in-marrying) husbands, are members.[5] This stress is, however, absent in the *phaspun* in the Indus valley region where kinship links through a mythical ancestor are purely symbolic. The *phaspun* is not literally a clan although the kinship idiom is used. [6] In my view, a clan is not an accurate description of the *phaspun* in Nubra. Firstly, society here does not have strong patrilineal or matrilineal tendencies in the practice of kinship and functions on a bilateral basis. Secondly, in terms of practice, it can be observed that it is not consanguinity that is the decisive criteria. The idiom of fictive siblingship through the *pha-lha* is decisive in defining membership. The support of the *pha-lha* is sought for prosperity and well-being; it is either a god or goddess, and usually a locally converted spirit-being. In general, the Nubra-*pa* are in agreement that inter-marriage is rare within the *phaspun* and there was no evidence of it in Tegar.

In Tegar, being a member was not bequeathed through males only. All children succeed to their father's *phaspun* or, in the case of uxorilocal (*magpa*) marriages, to that of their mother. Change in residence can also lead to a different membership. Thus blood relations can belong to different *phaspun*. The fact that at funerals it is the *phaspun* that takes care of all the funerary arrangements which are taboo to the blood relations proves that it is not descent and blood that is a decisive criteria, either patrilineal or matrilineal. Although, in the same way as the household members of the dead, the *phaspun* are under a certain state of pollution, the pollution is not as direct as in the case of the members of the household who must avoid contact with the hearth and the altar as well. During the pollution period of birth and death, the rules of which are prescribed by the *phaspun*, the members of the *phaspun* take over tasks in the house and the field for the household members. The *phaspun* also has a commonly owned furnace for the dead or a site for cremation.

Phaspun duties in Tegar primarily included assistance in life-crisis rituals since it is the *phaspun* who are supposed to stand by you in 'sorrow and happiness'. Mutual support is expected in political disputes and, very occasionally, though it is not a rule, in agricultural work. There was some disagreement about whether Muslim households were also *phaspun* members. In Tegar, there were seven *phaspuns* comprising between two to five kin groups each, and it is said that in the past the *Arghun* household used to be a member of a *phaspun* as well. At this point it must be stated that the *phaspun* is a local level association in many ways and does not have the same religious and extra-local connotations as the monastery or the mosque. In many areas of Nubra, Muslim households are held to have been members of *phaspuns*, though this is a dying practice, and the cleavages that have developed between Muslims and Buddhists in the recent past have led the *phaspun* to be regarded as a 'Buddhist' institution rather than a village-level support group.

The *phaspun* meet at a feast twice a year. Each *khangchen* of a kin group calls every other kin group of the *phaspun* for a grand meal by turns. The first occasion when this happens is during *shrupla*, when the sickle is removed from the house for cutting grass in the fields. This usually occurs during the month *Dawa Tukpa* (roughly, mid-July to mid-August). On the twelfth or thirteenth day of this month, all households in the village go to the main sluice of their fields and pour *chang* into it in an act of consecration. They then cut a basket full of grass from the fringes of the field and bring it to the house. A ring of grass or corn is made and tied to the main pillar of the house, usually in the kitchen, the *axis mundi* and the dwelling of the god of the house. This cutting is only symbolic and the main work of grass cutting begins on a day fixed by the village headman. The *phaspun* affirm their solidarity at feasts in the nights of *shrupla*. All the *khutus* and *khangchens* of a *phaspun* meet in various *khangchens*. An elaborate meal is prepared and *chang*, meat, rice and other food are served. Men and women are seated on separate sides of the main room of the house or the kitchen, indicating their age and status. The tone of the meeting is merry, gossip and news are exchanged, and songs are sung.

The second time that the *phaspun* meets is at *Losar*, part of a cycle of festivities described in a later section of this chapter.

THE IFTARSPUN

The Sunni Muslims in Hundar also have a group based on siblingship. I was given to believe the Nurbakshias too have such groups. This group consists of a set of households related by ties of marriage and consanguinity, i.e., *khutus* of a given *khangchen*, who meet primarily during *iftar* (the daily evening meal that breaks the *Ramzan* fast). It is my understanding that this group, which I call the *iftarspun*, also assists in the main rites of passage. It appears to be equivalent to the kin group, and is not fictive as in the case of the *phaspun*.

On the fourth day after the death of a person, the *Koran* is read, and five or seven pieces of *tagi* (bread) and 150 gms. of meat are said to be distributed to all the village households. Between the first and the fourth day, people in the area visit bringing a small quantity of barley flour and some money with them. Till the fourth day, food and water in the house of death are not ingested because of pollution. On the fortieth day, the *Koran* is read again because the *ruh* (spirit) is said to inhabit the house until then. After a year, about fifteen people gather and read the *Koran* to 'give peace to the *ruh*'; food is distributed to all those gathered and those who have prayed for the dead are paid a small monetary compensation.

On the occasion of the birth of a child, the *azan* (prayer call) is spoken into the child's ear. On the seventh day the child is named, an occasion called *akhikat*. The naming takes place by a sort of lottery where pieces of paper holding various names are put into a container and a child is asked to pick one piece. A goat is slaughtered on this occasion and a part given to the mother to replace the 'milk and blood' she has given to the baby. The rest is distributed to the poor and others.

On the day of the *sunnat* (circumcision), which is usually performed before a boy is eleven or twelve years old, relatives and friends, both men and women, go with *kalchor* (sign of good omen – generally milk or curd carried by women), eggs and other gifts, to give *mubarak* or good wishes. Ritual scarves are also exchanged.

On the occasion of marriage as well, the *iftarspun* is present. A 'lawyer' is appointed to speak for the girl and two witnesses vouch for the proceedings. In a separate room, the *imam* verifies the girl's acceptance of the proposal. The boy also gives his acceptance before a congregation. The *imam* reads out the appropriate prayers and ascertains the dower. The nuptial ceremony takes place in the groom's house, or if it is a *magpa* marriage, in the bride's.

The *iftarspun* is usually a family consisting of brothers, father's brothers, sisters, etc. i.e. the branches of a *khangchen*. It is my under-standing that given the number of virilocal marriages among the Sunni Muslims in Hundar (for the Nurbakshias appear to have a greater incidence of uxorilocal marriages), the *iftarspun* is usually an agnatic group. There were eleven such groups that met by turns at *Ramzan* in Hundar.

During *Ramzan*, the *iftarspun* are visible in their corporate existence (although of course, they are also visible in life-crisis rites). They participate in the greater body of Islam even as their local character is visible. In the period of my residence in Hundar, *Ramzan* began in the night of 19 March 1991. The *imam* explained that the fast should be kept because it allowed everyone to experience how the poor lived. It also forced people to observe certain moral codes strictly, for example, not to steal or lie, for it was a sacred period. Since the Muslim ritual year is lunar, it meant that people experienced the fast in all seasons. Finally, the giving of *fitr*, i.e. a tithe of two kgs. of grain or its equivalent in cash by each member of the household to his poor brethren, created a sense of solidarity among all Muslims. Three days were important during *Ramzan*. The third day of the month is observed as *Namroz* by the Shias but this day was also considered to be sacred for all women because it was Fatima's, the favourite daughter of the prophet and wife of Ali's, birthday. The day was generally auspicious and the morning and evening meal (the *sar* and the *iftar*) were better than usual. The twenty-sixth day was also auspicious since it was Ali the fourth Muslim caliph's birthday and sacred for men. Both the sexes maintained an all night vigil in the *masjid* during this period.

The men go to the mosque to do the *namaaz* (the five times prayer) but the women do it in their homes in the night since they have to prepare for the *sar* the next morning. The *imam* rings the gong at his house at 3 a.m. for the beginning of the fasting period. This is rung twice a day, once for the *fagir namaaz* and once for the *magrib namaaz* (the dawn and dusk prayers). By 4.50 a.m., the gong is struck again by which time the *sar* has to be completed ('before it is light to see the lines on one's palm', I was told). Work proceeds as usual, although in 1991, work in the field was minimal since the ploughing had not yet begun. The first morning after the *sar*, everyone went to the mosque. It had snowed in the night and the snow still lay on the ground. Candles were lit in the *masjid* and about twenty men and women prayed in sonorous voices.

The gong for the *iftar* is struck at about 6.30 p.m.; the people complete the *magrib namaaz* and then break their fast. After the *iftar*, some people go to the mosque for the remaining two *namaaz* of the day. On most days, the women do not go since there are duties in the kitchen to complete.

Most of the days are spent finishing tasks about the field and the house. This is also a time of increased frequency of talk and gossip because groups of relatives meet at the *iftar* in the evening. Each household of a family invites all the others for a meal at least once during *Ramzan*. Men and women sit in separate rooms, the women at the kitchen and the men in the guest room. Both conduct their *magrib namaaz* separately and eat separately as well. The meal is very rich and composed of many courses – dates or fruit to break the fast, rice, meat, a vegetable curry, a sweet, etc. but no *chang*. The sons move back and forth between the kitchen and the guest room. The men go to the *masjid* after the *iftar* while the women remain behind. Such occasions not only express the corporate unity of the *iftarspun* but also bring to the fore competition between households to outdo each other at the *iftar* meal. Differences of status between households also become visible during this period.

Before the *Aakhri Jumma* (the last Friday prayer at the mosque at the end of *Ramzan*), the houses are scenes of great activity. They are cleaned completely and the preparation of food for *Id* begins. Migrant sons, daughters and sons-in-law return to their parental or affinal homes. At the *masjid*, a partition between the two sexes is raised and the *Jumma* is led by the *imam*. At night after the *iftar*, the *Shab*, an all night vigil of prayer and recitation, takes place. The *imam* gives a sermon and families bring tea, biscuits and bread. These are distributed among those gathered. By about 2 a.m., the strict lines degenerate somewhat and people can be seen talking.

Three days later, in the year of my residence, it was *Id-ul-fitr*. On the first day, only the men attended the *namaaz* at about 10.30 a.m. in the *masjid*. All the Muslim men in the village and those passing by such as drivers, soldiers and other strangers, also attended. After the *namaaz*, the men greeted each other with '*Id mubarak*' and then went collectively to the house of the *imam* to greet him. They were seated in the living room and served tea, biscuits, fried meat and a variety of delicacies. Then all the other houses were visited in order of seniority of their male heads. On the second day, the women did the visiting and greeting. On both days, children moved around in small groups and were given gifts of food and money called *idi*. There was, of course, in every house, the ritual killing of the goat and the preparation of a feast which the household members partook of.

The *iftar* cycle and the period of *Ramzan* separate the domains of men and women both in the house and the *masjid*. This is in contrast to the situation in everyday life where such sharp separations do not occur. The structure of the *masjid* and the house replicate each other but there are also certain reversals. For example, the central orientation in the *masjid* is towards the *Kaaba* for both the sexes which lies in the male space, while at *iftar*, the orientation is towards the stove and the female space.

In the period 1990-1, the *iftarspun* collapsed into the work group in the context of the boycott of Muslims by Buddhists. This coalescence is described below.

The calendar of work for a Muslim household is similar to the Buddhist one for the area. The ritual calendar is different but periodically at the completion of a cycle of festivity, the cycle of work provides a space and time of convergence in the ways of life of Buddhists and Muslims. Earlier, the festive and ritual period also accommodated Buddhist neighbours and kin for a Muslim household. In the period prior to 1990-1, there was an exchange of food, gifts and visits during occasions such as *Id* which suddenly ceased. This was reflected in the work process as well. Hundar is divided into five geographical areas for the purpose of certain agricultural activities such as the cleaning of the canals or taking manure to the fields. This is similar to the division of labour involved in Tegar. During 1990-1, this division ceased in all but the basic necessity, i.e. the cleaning of the main canal.

One informant, *Abba* Ali, told me about the grand reception given to the Dalai Lama on his visit to Nubra a few years ago. Villagers met him at the Khardung pass and held a meeting for him at the *masjid* in Diskit. 'Inspite of this, the Buddhists have not heeded his call for peace and amity during the boycott', he said. It appeared that Muslims and Buddhists had moved apart in work by stages. For some time, the Sunni Muslims borrowed the grinding mills of the Buddhists via the Shia groups in the village during the boycott, till one day the LBA youth seized and broke it. So *Abba* Ali fixed a mill of his own and began to lend it to Muslims, even from as far as Sumur village. 'Our relations used to be so good. Our cemeteries used to be visited by the Buddhists and we also used to go to them to give condolences. I am a teacher but now even my former students do not recognize me. When Hassan's father died, he had to go to Leh and I helped him and even looked after his camels. But his Buddhist son does not remember that. What can one say of those who know nothing about *duniya* (the world) or *qayamat* (the day of judgment)?'

At the time of the agitation and the social boycott, largely between 1990 and 1991, the Muslims split into three groups in the village: Nurbakshias, who sided with the Buddhists since they were excluded from the boycott; Sunnis, who were intimidated by the threats of the LBA and said they would support it in its demands, and Sunnis who opposed the LBA and were boycotted. This was in the period late-1989 onwards. But in late 1990, two movements occurred to change this configuration. All Sunnis came together as the LBA became more extreme in its approach and the Nurbakshias began to oscillate between the two groups. Towards mid-1991, when there was a possibility of elections being organized in Jammu and Kashmir, the LBA realized that it would not win the Congress-I ticket unless it attempted a rapprochement with the Muslims. Some Buddhist families began to borrow tools and animals from Muslims for work purposes and also began to buy goods from their shops or travel in their vehicles which hitherto had ceased. In the meantime, Muslims had begun to assist each other in work, meet for the Friday congregation and form themselves into smaller work units for mutual assistance. When questioned, the Sunnis claimed that they formed one group with all Muslims since they were a cohesive ritual and work unit, although, clearly, in terms of origin and social and religious factors, there were differences. The Sunnis were descendants of Ladakhi Buddhist women and Kashmiri men (usually traders or officials). The Nurbakshias were mainly tenants and servants of wealthy Buddhist families in Hundar who received land after the reforms, descendants of men from Purig and other parts of Kargil, many of whom had married Buddhist women.

The *iftarspun* and the work group for a Muslim household in 1990-1, thus, tended to become unified and it was linked to its Buddhist neighbours only in the most formal sense. That is, for the purpose of cleaning and regulating the water canals for which the labour and cooperation of the area's households was unavoidable. Prior to the boycott, the ritual and the work group were not identified. I do not know if the current political reconciliation between Buddhists and Muslims from the end of 1992 has altered this situation.

THE VILLAGE

The minimal and customary locus of political power in the valley is the village. From a height, a village is usually a triangular patch fanning out towards the river. The only ecological constraint here for the founding of a village is that there must be water in the form of a glacier-fed stream since Ladakh is a cold desert. Villages are usually found by the side of a major channel sometimes sharing water with a neighbouring settlement. In the case of Hundar, water was shared between three villages, while in the case of Tegar, it was shared with two others, the times of receiving water being fixed by custom and need. A village usually has a *manekhang* with a priest, a *Zimskang* and sometimes branches of a noble family from Leh such as the *Kharpon*. In a purely spatial sense again, territories of villages are separated by large distances, especially in a region where the population is extremely thin and the inhabited area, small, making a village easily identifiable. A number of villages also have 'gateways' to them (hollow entrances standing in the middle of the road).

In general, one may say that there are three components which constitute political power in Tegar or Hundar. Firstly the village headman and his council. The representatives of a village's political unity are the village headman (*goba*) and the village council. In the past, the position of the village headman may have been hereditary, the families of the nobles and the *Zimskang* also having de-jure political powers in addition to their being large landlords. This was largely customary and power as such was not centralized. Rather, nobles and petty chiefs had a great deal of autonomy, sending some gifts of tribute to the king in Leh and occasionally raising an army for him. The nobles and the *Zimskang* owned a large amount of land in the villages in the area, as did the monastery, with a number of tenants, this itself being a source of great power. While relations within a village may have been oppressive, between the king and the local landlords, chiefs, ministers and monasteries, power seems to have been a site of centrifugal and centripetal forces rather than a clear-cut centralized system in which the clergy and the nobility were allied. In the present period, the power of such nobles and monasteries within the village is considerably diminished both economically and politically and the *goba* is chosen by rotation among the households for a period of two years. A male member of a household (it was rare that women became *gobas*) is chosen to be a *goba* for two years at *Sakha*, the day ritually marking the beginning of an agricultural calendar. A village council with about six or eight members is also chosen by rotation every year. The village council and *goba* maintain authority for the period of their office by agreement on the part of the people. The process is democratic and fair and every household has a chance to assume authority for a defined period. The political power of the *goba* includes: a) the settlement of disputes in the village, b) control over the fair distribution of water along with another person, the *churspon*, appointed for that purpose for a year, c) mediation between the district authorities and the village, and d) assumption of a leading role in some rites like *Losar*. (Some of these functions are described in the cases presented in the next chapter).

The symbolic unity of the village seen in the relationships between Gods and men, and between people significant 'others' such as kin, neighbours, ancestors and spirits. The field of power in the territory of the village is constituted by the gods whose blessings must be invoked, and by the thoughts, actions and words of its members. All of these form the 'life-force', (*la*) of the community, embodied in the *yul-lha* (the god of the village or settlement) which is affected and affects the life-force of individual villagers. Thus a rise in the disputes in the village, a decline of morality, or a lack of participation in work and ritual by some members, is felt to affect this power, whether it be that of the village council, the *goba* or the *yul-lha*. This is from the Buddhist point of view, although there exists an analogy between the concepts of the *ruh* and the *la* used by Muslims and Buddhists, respec-tively. I do not know if all Muslim households subscribe to a belief of a community spirit; I was, however, told that at Turtuk, near the cease-fire line, a nearly completely Muslim village, the *yul-lha* is also propitiated by Muslims.

The symbolic unity of the village as opposed to other villages, the internal field of power and well-being, is affirmed in the presence of the god of the village settlement. Each settlement has a stone-cairn or *lhato* where the *lha* is felt to dwell. Every year at *Jipa Chukshik*, the eleventh day of the fourth Buddhist month, the *yul-lha* of Tegar, called the *Yultsa lhato*, has its annual *lapsang*. The 'waist band' of the *lhato* is replaced with a fresh one during the cleansing, and *shukpa* (juniper) burned, with organizers providing these items and *chang* to the praying monks. These organizers belong to the entire village and two families take turns every year to be the officiants. Both men and women may be present. The *pumpa* (sacred little pots containing seeds) are removed from the body of the *lhato* and replaced. There is a direct relationship between these seeds, the agricultural crop for that year, and the well-being of the village. If that year the seeds are not depleted in the pot then it is read as an omen of good fortune and auspiciousness; otherwise some danger is felt to be augured for the village community. The *Yultsa lhato* is also felt to be a protector of the community and propitiated if need be.

The second time that the symbolic unity of the village becomes visible is during the ritual called *Bumskor* (*bum* meaning kernel, and *skora* meaning circle) in *Dawa Tukpa*, the sixth month of the Buddhist calendar, this occurs on a full-moon day. On this day, scriptures are taken out of the monastery or the *manekhang* after dawn and all the men, women, and children of the village carry the holy books on their backs through the village on a designated route with the monks. Since, the Buddha was enlightened on a full moon day, this day, the texts of the Dharma also confer benediction within the boundaries of the village, the community, and the habitat. At various places, people bend down to let the books pass over them, the focal point being the head. A circum-ambulation is done before the scriptures return to the monastery. This is a time when the crops are mid-point between sowing and reaping and the monastery and the village, the mountain and the earth meet.

The third time when the boundaries of the village as a locus of power become visible is during *Losar*. This time, the community of persons in the village is acknowledged by all groups in the village, though again in the context of the boycott, Muslims did not participate in the festivities as they had done in the past. A detailed description of the festival is provided below. The boundedness and unity of the village are affirmed by participation of the households in village events, the exchange of gifts and visits, and the assembly of the village men at a bonfire to burn the evil, of the past year.

Losar, the Ladakhi New Year festival, occurs in the tenth month of the Tibetan Buddhist calendar. A number of stories were told to me about why this festival occurs in the tenth month and not in the first as in the Tibetan case. A long time ago, the king of Ladakh wished to wage war against the ruler of Baltistan. He was told by the astrologer that if war was waged before the New Year, it would prove disastrous. The king then decided to advance the New Year festival to the tenth month and went to war. He lost. The other tale goes that there lived a tyrannical king called Chobongskang at a place in Nubra near Tegar called Lakjung. He had the legs of a donkey and the horns of a goat. Drunk on his power, he decided that the first rays of the sun would fall on his palace and nowhere else. This desire was obstructed by the steep mountain which rose behind his palace. So he organized the people to work at levelling it. The subjects were tired of this tyrant and wished to rid themselves of him but could find no means to do so. Finally, an old woman in the village gave them a clue. She said: 'Just as a wax-seal is melted by fire, so will the king be destroyed.' A blacksmith gathered courage, picked up a torch of fire and led men into the palace where the king was burnt to death.

On *namgang* (the twenty-ninth day of the tenth month), a bonfire occurs in the villages surrounding Lakjung. Men carry torches from the *Zimskang* in Tegar to the crossroads of the village accompanied by drummers. Before the men leave their houses with their torches, a ball of dough is rolled in the left hand by each member of the family, symbolically wiped all over the body, spat on and handed to the men and boys. The evil of the past year, the sins of speech, thought and deed are thrown into the bonfire in the body of the dough. A dance takes place with the men-folk circling the fire seven times while old food is thrown into it and fire-crackers go off. When the men and boys return to their houses, a woman stands in the doorway to throw water over them to ward off any residual evil. They return carrying pieces of ice or stone – 'gold', goodness, prosperity and luck. A male of the blacksmith's house, who torched Chobongskang still leads the dance at *Losar* in Charasa village.[7]

Losar has a complex ritual structure which is detailed below drawn from my field work in Tegar. Some of the events attest to older religious influences, for example, the Bon, in the enacting of the cosmogonic myths of creation, or the recitation of the Kesar epic in some parts of Nubra.

(A) THE TWENTY-FIFTH DAY OF THE TENTH MONTH

Galdan Namchot is Tsong Khapa, the Buddhist Reformer's, birthday. Some days previous to it, the Samstanling *gompa* prepares for its rite of offering, the *skangsol*, which begins on the twenty-fifth day and ends on the twenty-ninth. On the day previous to *Galdan Namchot,* all the households begin to make their lamps for placing on the windows and balcony of the house. These are made out of a red soil from the mountain by baking in a stove and are lit on *Galdan Namchot.* In the evening, a drummer beats his drum at the three most important houses in the village – of the *Kharpon, Zimskang* and the *goba.* At night, all the household members cook food made especially for that event. The next morning, the drummer again beats his drum at the three houses, an event which goes on till the end of *Losar.*

(B) THE TWENTY-NINTH DAY

The deities at the *gompa* are unveiled from *Galdan Namchot* till the end of the twenty-ninth day. People of the village go with butter, tea and greetings for the monks, oil for the lamps of the deities, and *khataks* for the idols. The monks are engaged in making a dough effigy out of barley flour and butter. This is the *linga* kept in a three cornered box at the *gustor,* the calendrical festival of the monastery. During this time, the *Zimskang* also has its *skangsol.* Its effigy is brought to the crossroads near the house for the people to view. On this day, there are ritual prayers at the *gompa* which are witnessed by all the villagers. To the beating of drums, cymbals and gongs, monks emerge from the monastery carrying the *linga* which is taken, after prayers, to the orchard outside to be burnt. A large *thanka* (cloth painting) is unfurled along the side wall of the *gompa* depicting Tsong Khapa to whom the Gelugpa owe their allegiance. On this and the next day, prayers and food, an event called *Shimi*, are offered to the ancestors by the *khangchens*. The offerings are kept at the shrines which house ashes, or on rocks. That night there is the bonfire at the crossroads which was described earlier.

(c) The thirtieth day

In the early hours of this day, the families who are or were the tenants of the *Zimskang*, *Kharpon* or the *gompa*, go with tea and *khataks* to greet their landlords. *Phetik* (a white design made of flour) is made on the central pillar of every house signifying a connection between this world and the other one. The pillar houses the *lhas* of the house: the *khyim-lha* is considered to be the *lha* of women just as the *po-lha* is associated with men (and household defense) who offer incense to it every morning at a niche or on the wall outside the house. The design is composed of representations of the sun, the moon and the crops of that year. *Phetik* also symbolizes the seal of wax that is a metaphor for the burnt Chobongskang. From this day for the next few days, all the *khangchens* of a *phaspun* feast the *pha-lha* by turns. The *phaspun* members gather in each others *khangchens* to feast and drink.

(d) The first day to the third day of the eleventh month

On *tsespachik*, the first day of the eleventh month, household heads offer cake, *kura* (fried and sweet crisps) and *khataks* to the *lhas* of the house at the *choskhang*. They then come and greet the *thap-lha* and in the order of seniority, pay their respects to the older members of the house. On the first three days, families move back and forth with *khataks*, gifts of food, and greetings for their neighbours and kin. Muslims also come to offer greetings, at least, they used to before the boycott and it is said that *kura* is made chiefly for them. On the third day, all the households go to the *Zimskang* to greet them and lamps are again lit in the house. People go to their roof tops and throw away a blackened piece of bread over their shoulder symbolizing the removal of the dark forces. The moon is sighted that day.

(E) THE FOURTH DAY

There is a horse race (*sangrak*) at the large meadow near the crossroads of the village; this is participated in by all the men of the village although the entire village congregates there in their best clothes. To the beating of drums, the organizers of *Losar* for that year come riding on horses to the meadow accompanied by three 'Masked People' (*Bag-pa*). These *Bag-pa* are village males who play the roles of characters whose nature is part comic and part sacred. There are many races up and down the meadow. Towards the end of the festivities, a *maryak* (a butter effigy of a yak) is placed in the middle of the field. It is supposed to be felled by an organizer galloping past it on a horse with his whip. If he is unsuccessful, one of the *Bag-pa* fells it with clownish antics.

After this, people congregate in the *chulda* (orchard) of the *Zimskang*. There, two of the *Bag-pa* do a *lhashun* (the dance of the *lhas*) and then go to one of the *khangchens* in the village where they are feasted that night. After the feast, they return to the *chulda* and there is another *lhashun*, this time with five *Bag-pa*. For the next six days, except for the seventh day of the eleventh month, a *lhashun* takes place every night in the *chulda*, till, on the eleventh day, there are eleven players. On one of the days after the *lhashun* (which involves a race around a tree by the *Bag-pa* on sticks and the felling of a pile of stones, similar to the events of the *sangrak*), there occurs a farcical play. This is about a reluctant but pregnant wife, her husband and a crazy oracle who delivers the baby. The antics of the trio are greeted with screams of laughter from the villagers. I was unable to discover any explanation for the *lhashun* apart from the fact that the *Bag-pa* were *lhas* or *paris* (angels) who descended every night from the heavens during this period to drive away evil forces. Some villagers said that they were also the first men who came to Ladakh and, thus, it was a story about ancestors. The play, though farcical, could have symbolized the process of creation. Similar events are described for other parts of Ladakh and Tibet: figures called *Babas* appear at Khalaste village in Ladakh on the thirtieth day of the tenth month. They dance in the village, are invited to various people's houses, and go to the *yul-lha* to make an offering. They are smeared with ashes, wear straw hats and after a horse race and a dance, are expelled from the village. Later they return for a village feast and boys and girls dance while the *Babas* carry away a scapegoat. After this, the villagers wash and welcome the New Year. In

Tibet, similar specialists appear in masks singing about creation, chanting wishes of good omen and help in crossing from the old to a new year.[8] Each night in Tegar, the *Bag-pa* are invited to various *khangchens* and are feasted. They dance around the central pillar of the house, the axis mundi, conferring a blessing on the inhabitants. On the eleventh day, there is a mock wedding in the *chulda* and the entire village is invited for a feast at the *Zimskang*.

(F) OTHER EVENTS

There are two other characters who appear at the *Losar* festivities; these are the beggar *Baltis*. They are a ragged pair who carry bags for collecting raw items like meat, flour, etc. from various households that they visit everyday. These items are given to the organizers of *Losar* who use it to cook the meal for the *Bag-pa* and the musicians after the day's ritual events are over. The *Balti* are a pair who traipse about the village parodying themselves and others followed by a pack of excited children. In each house they visit, they make importunate demands and are given a meal and drink.

The last in the series of events is *Pichokchok* which occurs on the fifteenth day of the eleventh month. On that day and the next, groups of children wander through the streets and visit people's houses. They are temporarily endowed with power as they sing ditties at the doors of houses parodying this grandfather's pigtail and that lady's cooking. It is a sort of 'trick or treat' and they can only be sent away with gifts like food, sweets or money. During this event, the theme of *Losar* continues: a series of inversions when the society is turned upside-down and roles inverted. Thus the New Year shifts backward in its dates; the tyrant king is defeated by a wily old woman and a lowly blacksmith; gods and angels appear before men; the secrets of a process like creation are revealed; beggars and children are momentarily powerful. The entire village is in a liminal period the signs of which are excessive speech, feasting, singing, and drinking. This inversion can also be explained according to the theme of death pollution and exorcism. The old year dies and the community, as in any death ritual, has to be cleansed of pollution through a scapegoat figure. In Nubra, the scapegoat, which represents demonic forces as well as the pollution of the old year, is disaggregated into a number of related rites and events: *Losar* as a whole recalls the burning of Chobongskang; the *skangsol* of the monastery and the *Zimskang* involve the burning of an effigy of dark forces; so also, the pieces of dough burnt in the bonfire after having been moved over people's bodies, the felling of the *maryak*, the ransom demanded by the beggar Baltis, and the children play out the scapegoat complex of 'offering - effigy - ransom' as well.[9]

These symbolic aspects of the village's boundedness are complex in nature. It can happen that a certain rite can come to be perceived as a rite of a particular group, as was the case on the three occasions cited above, i.e. *Bumskor, Losar,* and the rituals around the *Yultsa lhato.* It was felt by the Muslims in Tegar and Hundar that these were specifically Buddhist rites. Although *Losar* has achieved the status of a Buddhist festival in recent years, this idea of a festival to mark the winter solstice and to view it as a rite of transition to a new period, is common to a number of agricultural communities. Certainly, there are a number of elements in the festival which are neither Buddhist nor Muslim but merely those of peasants.[10] Even if it is assumed that it is a Buddhist festival, the exchange of gifts and counter-gifts ensured that the Muslims were also part of festivities marking the New Year. They visited the houses of their Buddhist neighbours to give greetings and *khataks* and in turn were visited and greeted during such festivals as *Id.* It is possible that such exchange has been resumed since the boycott has been called off.

In Part Two of this book, this component of the symbolic unity of the village and the manner in which it affects power in the community is described and analysed.

Finally, political power in Tegar or Hundar finds expression in the material culture of the village. For both Muslims and Buddhists, this is most evident during the constitution of the complex unit of exchange. This involves the labour of everyone within the bounds of the community for the purpose of the very basis of their existence – channelling of water through the canals for agriculture. As explained in an earlier section, when the village community was under threat by the anti-Muslim boycott, its material unity nevertheless continued in a very basic sense due to the system of water management in Ladakhi villages. (I did not hear of any instance during the boycott when water was denied to Muslim farmers although there was one case in Hargam village when pasture was denied). In most villages in Ladakh, water systems encompass more than one village, their usage fixed by ancient custom it more or less continued during Dogra rule and after 1947.

It has been suggested that the analysis of water systems in various societies of the Tibetan ecological zone provide clues as to the practice of politics in these societies.[11] Thus, in Tibet, water rights were adjudicated by a district official responsible to the Dalai Lama of Lhasa and relatively centralized. In Ladakh and Zanskar, they were less centralized and managed by a village official in the former and an intra-household consensus in the latter. Disputes were also decided at the village level, rarely reaching higher authorities and one may presume that this was true of most other conflicts. Power is not concentrated in Ladakh and Zanskar. Water has to be channelled to every field by a strict system of rotation and equality, with everyone in the village keeping a strict watch on the usage of water and on each other.

The field of power in the village is cross-cut and affected by other forces from outside its boundaries. This will be apparent in the next chapter which describes how groups such as the LBA and the LMA affect local life and intervene in disputes; this is also a description of the way in which political institutions such as the army and the district administration affect power situations in the village.

Notes

1. This is the classification assumed, for instance, by Gokhale-Chatterjee 1987 and Mann 1986.
2. See Jaeschke 1975 [1881]:527.
3. See, for instance, Crook and Osmaston 1994; Gokhale-Chatterjee 1987; Grist 1990a; Kaplanian 1981; Phylactou 1989.
4. This argument is used by Peter 1963.
5. Crook 1994:501-15 et passim.
6. This is attested for the Indus valley by Brauen 1980 and Phylactou 1989.
7. Vohra cites a more or less similar account of 'Cho Bongskang' for Nubra; several features of lore about the ruler—oppressiveness, death by fire, the secret of his vulnerability being known to women etc.—are similar to the myths of Sri Badat (11th-12th century), the ruler of Gilgit (Vohhra 1996: 226-229).
8. Stein 1972 [1962]:218-20.
9. This kind of offering of a ransom and a scapegoat is mentioned by Ortner (1979 [1978]:91-127 et passim) and Tucci (1980 [1970]:146-56 et passim). Ortner (ibid.p.121) mentions that the unitary scapegoat figure of the Tibetan case is polarized in the Sherpa case.

10. The disappearance of 'fuzzy' boundaries between religious groups in border areas due to factors associated with nation-state formation is visible in groups such as the Meos of Mewat cited by Aggarwal 1971.
11. c.f. Gutschow 1993.

Chapter 6

The Tertiary Level of Integration

The Kindred

There are two social categories which relate a household to other households in a territory which is larger than the village. The first is the kindred category.

Some writers point out the existence of a lineage in Ladakh. In the Leh area of the Indus valley, the *gyut* has been defined as a group of people who trace an ancestor in common.[1] It is based on a blood tie and although there are no names for *gyuts*, they are recognized for upto five or six generations. The son and daughter inherit their father's *gyut* and cannot marry into their mother's. People of different *phaspun* can belong to the same *gyut* and a common stock is recognized. Similarly, for the Suru-Karste areas of Kargil, mainly with Shias and some Sunnis, a group of families sharing a common ancestor or a patrilineal group called a *phaspun* or *zat* has been categorized as the effective kinship category. Marriage can occur in the category of relatives. Among the Shias, the marriages are mainly virilocal and one-third of them occur with relatives (parallel or cross cousins) and with parallel cousins among the Sunnis. Though divorce rates are high and there are many unmarried men at a time both among Sunnis and Shias, marriages seem to occur mainly in the village and *zat*, and few between Sunnis and Shias.[2] The patrilineage has been reported as the effective kinship category in Zanskar; officially, no marriage is allowed between members of the same patrilineal generation for nine generations. The *phaspun* in Zanskar is largely a group of families denoted by patrilineal descent and, therefore, a form of kinship organization. The inheritance of estates between the *khangchens* and *khutus*, or *khangchungs* as they are called in Zanskar, also seems geared towards the preservation of the patrilineage.[3]

Taking a wider sample, a comparative analysis done of the terms *ru* and *tag* (bone and blood) among Tibetan-speaking populations, shows that the terms are multi-vocal. Among the Nyimba of N.W. Nepal, the term *ru* signifies along with *tag*, a basis for reproductive theory among the people. It implies the transmission of the main formative substance from the parents (*ru* in the case of the father and *tag* in the case of the mother) to the offspring. *Ru* refers to the patrilineage or clan while *tag* refers to matrilateral links and complimentary filiation. The former also refers to commensality because those of similar bone have similar 'mouths', while through the latter, stratum endogamy is implied because those of similar status usually intermarry.[4]

In Tegar and Hundar, customary prohibitions created a 'field' of consanguinity. During *Losar*, although households of kin groups could be identified as work groups, and as making up a *phaspun*, kin groups were constituted according to both patri- and matrifiliation. A lineage as such could not be identified as a significant or effective kinship category either in the Buddhist or Muslim sample. If one derives an understanding of the nature of kinship in the valley not according to the system of prescriptive rules or models of kinship which replicate ideas of linguistic syntax (such as in the works of Claude Levi-Strauss), but according to the nature of practice and regularity, the effective kinship category is not the lineage or the descent group but the kindred. I make the qualification here that the links that are being examined are those of a broad majority of peasant households (*trongpa*) who, apart from the two extremes of the nobility (*skutag*) and the outcastes (*mon, beda* and *gara*), tended to intermarry rather than to form closed marriage groups. It is possible that stratum endogamy and an emphasis on descent make marriage patterns among the extreme groups of the social hierarchy very different from others. But in the absence of historical data for these strata in Nubra, it is difficult to speculate and not particularly useful to consider whether they conform to Levi-Strauss's categories of generalized and restricted exchange for nobility and commoners, respectively.

In Nubra, at least in the two villages of my fieldwork, marriages were arranged for a variety of reasons, descent being less significant than a host of existential and economic factors. To the extent that *gyut* was an idea impinging on marriage and kinship, it conveyed the idea of parentage and family background of both parents rather than a lineage. In most cases, it referred to the kin group in the absence of genealogies and memories of generations beyond the grandparents' generation. The kinship terminology is identical among the two groups of Buddhists and Muslims in the two villages of the valley except for two terms.[5] Kinship terms are applied to whoever the ego is in contact with depending on the nature of the relationship and the kind of distance/proximity that is felt to exist between the two speakers. Any old man will be referred to as *abba* (father) or *meme* (father's or mother's father) while someone one's own age but to whom one wishes to indicate respect, will become *ajang* (mother's brother) or *ani* (father's sister or mother's brother's wife) and so on. The kinship terminology used in the two villages is shown in Figure 4.

Figure 4 : Kinship Terminology

+2	Father's mother *Abbe*	Mother's mother *Abbe*	Father's father *Meme*	Mother's father *Meme*	
Mother's younger sister, Father's younger brother's wife +1 *Machung*	Mother's brother (elder and younger), Father's sister's husband *Ajang*	Mother, Mother's elder sister, Father's elder brother's wife *Amma*	Father, Mother's elder sister's husband, Father's elder brother's wife *Abba (Appa)*	Father's sister (elder and younger), Mother's brother's wife *Nene* or *Ani*	Father's younger brother, Mother's younger sister's husband *Agu (Chacha)*
Elder sister 0 *Ache*	Younger sister *Nomo*	EGO (male or female)	EGO (male or female)	Younger brother *Nono*	Elder brother *Acho*
-1	Elder daughter *Nomo*	Younger daughter *Nomo*	Younger son *Nono*	Elder son *Nono*	
-2	Daughter's daughter, Sister's daughter *Tsomo*	Son's daughter, Brother's daughter *Tsomo*	Daughter's son, Sister's son *Tsao*	Brother's son, Son's son *Tsao*	

1. Terms in the brackets indicate Muslim terms for the same word.
2. Only in the -1 and -2 generations are terms of address and terms of reference different.
3. In the -1, +2 and -2 generations, there are only two kinship terms distinguished by gender.
4. In the +1 generation, there are six terms distinguished by gender and age, and whether the relationship for the ego is through the father or the mother.
5. No distinction is made between male and female speaking ego or when referring to the husband's or wife's family in the 1, -2 and +2 generations. This also means that siblings of husbands or wives, or husbands and wives of siblings will be referred to as if the ego were equivalent to the person through whom the relationship is established; or the person being addressed is equivalent to the age group of the person through whom the relationship is established. Thus, the husband's elder brother will be called *acho*, the younger sister's husband will be addressed as *nono*, and so on.
6. The 0 generation is distinguished according to age and gender. No distinction is made between cousins and siblings in terminology. Among Buddhists, the customary practice is that marriages with cross and parallel cousins are not approved of though it is possible that it is common among the *skutag* strata who have been largely endogamous. Among the commoner strata it is very rare. Muslims do allow cousin marriage, but it was equally uncommon in my sample.[6]
7. No distinctions are made beyond the -2 and +2 generations.

Although these terms have a form when applied to those in the ranges indicated by the diagram, as applied to those outside the range of these sixteen terms, they are ego-focused and not according to any strict rules. There is a bilateral reckoning of the kin which is not a fixed category, given the custom and practice of marriage which is largely village exoga-mous and includes both virilocal and uxorilocal residence on marriage. It is not the lineage or the descent group that is the effective kinship category but the kindred. This is similar to the connotation of the local term, *nyen*, described in chapter four. This kind of bilaterality, with its attendant features such as the non-existence of extended families as the principal

An *Ihaba* is consulted in a case of illness.

The older *imam* of the Sunni mosque in Hundar.

Bactrian camels in Hundar.

Ploughing against the backdrop of Burma mountain.

The possessed *manekhang* priest adjudicates and heals cases in Tegar.

norm, the equality of inheritance, prominent female roles in social and economic life, the non-transmission of surnames for women, etc. has also been seen for some other societies such as Burma. The kinship system in these areas can be seen as a form lying between the joint family system reported for large parts of India and the extended family of China. [7]

It may be useful to briefly review the properties and functions of the kindred in order to understand how it operates in this area.[8] It has been pointed out, firstly, that the kindred of any ego are the cognates known to this individual. The personal kindred consists of people who have a relative in common. They are not a group but are a category for it never happens that all the members of a personal kindred emerge in group action. But theoretically, at any given time, the social universe can be separated into kindred groupings recognized in practice as distinct.

Secondly, in some societies, there is a moral obligation for cognates to support each other and temporary action-groups to form from the kindred category. Friends and affines may also be included and, therefore, for an understanding of the role of the bilateral kindred, a distinction must be made between the kindred as a cognatic category and kindred-based action groups formed from time to time for specific reasons. In Nubra, various kindred-based groups can be identified from the larger category: Firstly, there is the kin group including *khutus* and *khangchens*, which is largely a cognatic group; secondly, there are kindred-based action groups involved in such tasks such as work in the field; and, finally, there is the 'pseudo-cognation' of the *phaspun*, members of which are significant in ritual and the real cognation of the *iftarspun*.

Thirdly, it has been pointed out that for societies in which the kindred is a significant group, the only important corporate group is the family. The continuity of the family and the estate is maintained by 'utrolateral filiation', i.e. at each generation level, at least one of the children of the family, male or female, maintain residential membership.

Fourthly, the kindred may or may not be exogamous. Where marriage of cousins is continued generation after generation, there is a consolidation of stocks. A closer cognatic network results, thus, in those societies in which there are marriages of close cognates. In the villages in which I did my fieldwork, the practice of marriage showed the cognatic network not to be so cohesive and the range of the kindred to be decided by such factors as memory, domicile, or social utility. Thus, the rights and obligations of the kindred are not so sharply drawn on the ground. Kindred relations may be contrasted with relations with strangers but in the absence of precise boundaries, it is social intercourse which revives a relationship from dormancy or terminates it. A village may comprise of households that can trace their connection upto three generations from the head of the household. *Khangchens* and *khutus* are related both by matrifiliation and patrifiliation – this was true both of the Muslim and the Buddhist sample. The custom of avoiding marriages with anyone with whom a connection can be traced back to seven generations on the father's side and three on the mother's, the fact that residence after marriage can be uxorilocal or virilocal, and the transmission of property through sons and daughters, tend to disperse kindred links.

The nature of present marriage patterns in Tegar and Hundar is shown in Figure 5. In Tegar, taking only the Buddhist households, the number of males was 217 and the number of females was 191. The number of households were eighty-nine and the average household size, 4.58. The number of in-marriages, i.e. occurring within the village, was twenty, and the number of out-marriages, i.e. occurring with other villages, was sixty-five (approximately 23 percent and 77 percent respectively). The number of virilocal marriages was fifty-nine and uxorilocal marriages were twenty-six (approximately 70 percent and 30 percent respectively). All the marriages contracted outside the village occurred in Nubra except for three, all of which belonged to the *skutag* strata (except for one) and all three were with women. Among the Muslim households in Tegar (including the *Arghun* and the Nurbakshia households), all three marriages which existed were virilocal, out-marriages. One of these included an alliance between a Nurbakshia male and a Buddhist woman (who converted).

In Hundar, among the Muslims, kin groups of households two to three generations deep, descended from a remembered ancestor, existed but were not necessarily constituted by patrifiliation. There were 118 women and 121 men and the average size of the household was 4.35, there being fifty-five households. The total number of in-marriages was twenty and out-marriages were thirty-nine (approximately 34 percent and 66 percent respectively). The out-marriages included twenty-seven within Nubra and twelve outside (eight with Leh [one with a man and seven with women], two with men from Kargil, one with a man from

Figure 5 : Marriages in Tegar and Hundar

	In-marriages	Out-marriages	Viriolocal marriages	Uxorilocal marriages
Tegar	20 (23%)	65 (77%)	59 (70%)	26 (30%)
Hundar	20 (34%)	39 (66%)	38 (64%)	21 (36%)

Dras and one with a Nepali man). Most of these marriages outside Nubra were to be found among Sunni Muslim households. There were thirty-eight virilocal marriages and twenty-one uxorilocal ones (approximately 64 percent and 36 percent respectively). Among the Sunni Muslim households, there are three marriages with Buddhist women (all of whom converted) and none between Nurbakshias and Buddhists in this generation. Among the Nurbakshia households, there were three alliances with Yarkandis (one was female) from Hargam in the same valley, but most of the out-marriages occurred with the next village; two alliances were contracted with Chushot in the Indus valley. The percentage of marriages with Buddhist women has dropped since the time of the *Bandobast* by 75 percent. From Leh, the movement into the village is that of women, while from Kargil and Dras, of men.

The network of effective consanguinity and affinity within which each household moves is nowhere more than three to four generations deep. Traces of kindred links which forbears have created are forgotten (except among the nobility) in the absence of genealogies unless they have any practical function and each generation makes choices according to demographic and socio-economic fortunes. The kindred category tends to be shallow in depth though it is wide in spread, since the tendency of affinity is dispersal rather than the separation of the population into marriage classes. Nearly all the cross-cutting ties that occur across different religious groups are through women: in the past, from the genealogical data that was collected, it appears that not only were there alliances between Sunni Muslims and Buddhists, but also between Nurbakshias and Buddhists, and Sunni Muslims and Nurbakshias.

Networks of kindred and kindred-based groups have been shown to be significant in various activities such as travelling and trading, warfare, local-level political organizations such as sports clubs, producers cooperatives, parish councils, etc.[9] Under border conditions, as in Nubra, the kindred may have a further function apart from the ones described above. Because of the growth of the cash economy, the changed occupational structure, and the forces of nation-state formation (described in the next section in detail), the boundaries of the kindred may alter to exclude certain persons from the kindred category. The idea of the kindred can also accommodate the notion, of 'cognatio naturalis', i.e. the view that men may be seen as being descended from a common stock in the past and therefore there exists a blood tie between them by which they are kindred, and a 'race'. This kind of pseudo-kindredship may be politically relevant as the basis for identity-formation of ethnic groups, nations, linguistic families, and so on. In Ladakh, it is this idea of a Buddhist people, a race, or in local terms, a *quom*, that during the period of the agitation for Union Territory Status and the boycott against Sunni Muslims between 1989-1991 led to the exclusion and non-recognition of certain persons – the *Arghuns* – from the category of the kindred. There was a movement, initiated by certain political organizations, away from the essentially bilateral nature of the kindred groupings towards what may be termed 'political patriliny'.

POLITICAL PATRILINY

At the tertiary level of integration, a household is related to other households in political organizations, the most significant of which during my fieldwork period were the Ladakh Buddhist Association (LBA) and the Ladakh Muslim Association (LMA). These, I call politically patrilineal groups.[10] They were political organizations dominated by a male leadership, the perception of ethnic differences between the religious groups of Buddhists and Muslims, the reckoning of 'descent' through males as a criteria for membership of religious communities, and an implicit policy geared towards limiting inter-religious marriages (which occurred in the past chiefly through women). These two organizations have been working towards regional autonomy and developmental benefits for Ladakh, separately and together. The demand for Scheduled Tribe status has been granted since the period of my fieldwork and the foundation laid for the creation of an Autonomous Hill Council for Leh district. The boycott has also been called off. Thus, this construction of political patriliny is to be seen as belonging to a specific moment in Ladakhi politics. But the effects of such constructions may continue through other forms. For instance, at the time of granting of Scheduled Tribe status for Ladakhis, recommendations made stressed genealogical links through males. In the case of inter-religious marriages, for instance, between a Buddhist woman with a Sunni man, the offspring was to be regarded as a Sunni *Arghun* by origin and therefore denied Scheduled Tribe status which was being offered only to eight 'ethnic tribes' of Ladakh, *Arghuns* being deemed non-natives of Ladakh. The Indian state, therefore, has participated in the creation of such patrilineal tendencies even in regions which were customarily bilateral in their kinship reckoning.[11]

The emergence of these groups has occurred in a particular historical conjuncture. In chapter two, a chronology of these events was given. In the context of this chapter, it needs to be emphasized that the political organizations of the LBA and the LMA (although the latter is an ad-hoc body convened at specific times, as for instance was the case during the 1989 agitation and afterwards, during the boycott) have been active at different stages of Ladakhi politics. They are not necessarily monolithic bodies. When the LBA was founded in 1934, it was chiefly at the instance of Kashmiri Pandit neo-Buddhists. Earlier in 1931, in order that the Buddhists in the state of Jammu and Kashmir were given representation in government, an organization called the Kashmir Raj Bodhi Maha Sabha approached the Glancy Commission with a memorandum listing the grievances of the Buddhists of Ladakh. This was the first time that there was an 'official' attempt at establishing the separateness of Buddhists of Ladakh. There was only one member of the delegation who was Ladakhi – Sonam Norbu. The list of grievances included economic exploitation through the backwardness of educational facilities, lack of share in public services, neglect of the religious needs of Buddhists, etc. At this time, there was no local Ladakhi organization. It was a group of Kashmiri Pandits who were the force behind the formation of the Young Men's Buddhist Association in 1934, the drafters of the Abolition of Polyandrous Marriages Act (1941), and other such reform campaigns. Such a representation of Buddhist identity appeared later again at the agitations of

1969 and 1989, but there were other agitations where a collective Ladakhi identity was emphasized. For instance, during the All Ladakh Action Committee for the Declaration of Ladakh as a Scheduled Tribe area and the various memos and demands that were put forth before the State Cabinet after a visit to Ladakh in 1982 and to the Sikri Commission. Again, after the 1993 negotiations with the Centre and the State, delegations and negotiations for the working-out of the details of the Hill Council for Ladakh included all communities. Demands for a separation of Ladakh from Kashmir certainly also went back to the immediate post-1947 period. Leaving aside for the moment the 1969 agitation, the events that occurred at the time of the 1989 agitation show that it was a specific group among Ladakhis who stressed the distinct Buddhist nature of Ladakh. After the initial clashes between Muslim and Buddhist youths, the Ladakh People's Movement for Union Territory Status drafted a memorandum that bears striking similarities to the 1931 document.[12] Later in the course of the agitation, the LBA became the leaders of the agitation, and a boycott was enforced on the Muslim Ladakhis, especially the Sunni *Arghuns*. The leaders of the agitation were those whose role derived from their literacy and bilingualism.[13] They were younger men from Leh district who had been educated at Delhi, Chandigarh or Jammu, with modern degrees. This younger group, chief among whom were Rigzin Jora, Rigzin Spalbar, Tsering Lagruk and Thubstan Tshewang, also stood opposed to the older LBA leaders. They organized the LBA into a relatively centralized structure with a network of branches spread out in different villages and carried out propaganda against customary practices among Buddhists. One cannot say, however, that the support for them was unanimous even in Leh. Certainly, in many villages, dissent continued and consensus had to enforced, often by violence. Equally, during the boycott, surreptitious exchanges between Buddhists and the *Arghuns* continued. But what the 1989 agitation showed, as with other agitations, was that political organizations in Ladakh contain various kinds of cleavages and coalitions. In this particular case in 1989 – between younger people and the old guard, between Buddhists and Sunni Muslims, and between the town and the village.

The LBA saw Ladakh as heterogeneous from Kashmir. Based on a number of interviews with LBA leaders, members in Tegar village, as well as speeches during LBA rallies between 1989-91, it is my understanding that the LBA policy was basically premised on the view that except for Dogra rule as a commonality, Ladakh was fundamentally heterogeneous from Kashmir. At a large rally in October 1989, LBA leaders expressed the concern that Ladakh was a vulnerable region for 'Islamic zealots' from the valley to indulge in proselytization. Pamphlets stated that the Union government should be concerned about the state government's design to transplant the valley-based separatist and secessionist culture, especially through the *Arghuns*.[14] The discrimination of 'Buddhist' Ladakh by 'Muslim' Kashmir was listed by the LBA under the following categories: the neglect of the Bodhi language, Buddhist art and culture; conversion; discrimination in the allotment of state land, services and recruitment against Buddhists; and discrimination against Ladakh in state programs.

There is obviously a relationship between the ideological content of the LBA and the parallel reactions of the LMA at that conjuncture. But it is not enough to merely see it as a competition for scarce resources such as land, women and office. Formal symmetries and asymmetries can be seen between different groups in Ladakh which find their way into the political unconscious. Ladakhi Buddhists and Tibetans could be seen as conjoint because of a general Buddhist unity symbolized in the figure of the Dalai Lama although they can also be distinguished by the fact that the Ladakhi Buddhists are related to other groups such as Kashmiris, Central Asians and Baltis. (Ladakhi Buddhists will often emphasize this as they did after a fracas with Tibetan Buddhist refugee youth in 1989). Similarly, the relationship between *Arghuns* and Buddhists, historically one of proximity, has become a contentious one, especially with direct state rule by Kashmir. The Sunni *Arghuns* of Ladakh, products of inter-marriages between Kashmiris (and Central Asians) and Ladakhi Buddhists, came to be viewed as a symbol of domination and difference. This process had it inception much earlier but was reinforced after the 1989 agitation by the giving of Scheduled Tribe status to Ladakhi Buddhists and Shias while excluding the Sunni *Arghuns*. This parallels the earlier decision to divide Ladakh into two districts in 1979, Kargil and Leh, with a majority Muslim population in the former from a district-in which the two were balanced. All these factors allowed a conceptual-ization of Kargil and Kashmir as the 'Other' and the conception of the new Leh district as a primordial Buddhist region by the LBA.[15]

This situation created groups that I have called politically patrilineal, such as the LBA and LMA. The distinction between political and domestic patriliny is: domestic patriliny refers to the action of a number of households *vis-à-vis* other households linked by genealogical ties brought about by marriage, residence, and networks of economic and ritual obligations. Without political patriliny, a village or region would consist of a number of domestic patronymic groups linked together by overlapping and cross-cutting ties mainly through the exchange of women. In Ladakh, such patrilineality is rare. Pseudo-patriliny has developed under specific historical conditions in political arenas through groups such as the LBA and the LMA who consider themselves distinct units on the notion of separate 'blood' and descent. The *Arghuns* are a focal point of contention as they symbolize the marriage of Ladakhi Buddhist women to Muslim 'others' thereby weakening the 'racial' cohesiveness of each group.

What has not been dealt with by other authors writing about this period is the way in which such organizations functioned in the villages and the nature of their effects. Most newspaper reports and other analyses restrict themselves to Leh or Kargil town, and the Indus valley area in general. I will look at the nature of the functioning of the LBA in Tegar village in the period 1989-91, in order to understand the cultural consequences and complexity of political patriliny. The LBA had branches in nearly every village composed of all the adult males in the village, the participation of the female population being tacitly assumed. The organization in Tegar was called the *Tsokspa* and grew out of a cultural group which had existed in the village for putting up plays, restoring *chortens*, and so on. It was very influential in the day-to-day functioning of the village community – carrying out welfare work, performing religious services, and holding cultural programs – and finally, in village politics. Since the agitation began in Ladakh from 1989, the *Tsokspa* had been intervening in disputes over land, marital conflicts, inter-village disputes, assisting the *goba* in his daily tasks, and finally, negotiating with the army and the local authorities. In neither Tegar nor Hundar was there a LMA subsidiary and my general impression is that the LMA was not as well organized as the LBA in the area of Nubra.

In the cases described below are a series of events in which the *Tsokspa* of Tegar intervened. They also provide a description of how two components of power, one local and the other supra-local, i.e. the *goba* and the village council, and the army and the administration, affect village politics. The *Tsokspa* was involved in mediating a series of conflicts in Tegar and acting as a proto-judicial means of redressal. These conflicts occurred at the various levels of integration analysed in the last few chapters.

CASE ONE

The daughter-in-law of the Gompa-*pa* had been married to the elder brother of the household and had lived in the neighbouring hamlet of Tegar with her husband. The latter had been adopted by his father's brother. The husband and wife did not get along, so the woman was 'brought' as a wife for the younger brother to the hamlet in which the Gompa-*pa* lived. The family divided into a *khangchen* and a *khutu* in 1988, the younger brother and his wife forming the new *khangchen* while the old couple moved into a *khutu*. The quarrel brought to the *Tsokspa* involved the daughter-in-law and the owner of the field neighbouring hers. They had quarrelled about who should receive water that morning from the channel for the field and the daughter-in-law had resorted to physically assaulting the other woman. The woman belonged to the Neyo-*pa*. Some evenings later, the Neyo-*pa khangchen* (comprising the woman's husband, his father and his brother) came and beat up the old couple of the Gompa-*pa*. The *Tsokspa* and the *goba* decided that the Neyo-*pa* must pay a fine to the Gompa-*pa* to replace the 'blood' lost by the old couple while the daughter-in-law of the Gompa-*pa* was warned and fined heavily for her belligerence. The quarrel between two households was thus resolved.

CASE TWO

Tsewang, a resident of Tegar, was earlier married to a woman in another village. After his wife died, he had children by her sister. Later, he came to reside in Tegar with a woman there abandoning his wife's sister and the children. She complained to the *Tsokspa* and it was decided, after mutual consultations between the *Tsokspas* of the two villages that the children of Tsewang by his dead wife would be raised by his wife's father till they grew older and then they would come and reside with Tsewang; he would gift some clothing for the children by his wife's sister and also pay her a lump sum of Rs.3000; and the land he owned in the other village would be leased out till his children by his dead wife were old enough to farm it. The conflict within the same household required the intervention of the *Tsokspas* of two villages because it was spread across both villages.

CASE THREE

Angmo's son had to be married and his wife-to-be had to be brought from the village across the river where she was temporarily residing. Sensing there might be opposition from the *phaspun* to this marriage, Wangdus was deputed to go and bring the bride as he was Angmo's mother's brother's son. When he returned, he found that the entire kin group of the Gyan-*pa*, of which Angmo's was a *khutu*, was gathered at the entrance of the village with slings and sticks to accost him. Angmo and her son lived with her mother's sister who had been married into the kin group of the Gyan-*pa*. The old lady was childless and her land was going to be inherited by Angmo and her son since they had toiled on it; the Gyan-*pa* wished to prevent the marriage. Wangdus took a circuitous route into the village, entered the house through a back window and in the presence of two witnesses, the couple were married by nightfall. The next morning, when the Gyan-*pa* opened the front door of the house which they had locked, the deed was done. Three men of the group then attacked Angmo and her son. The *goba* and the *Tsokspa* intervened at this point. It was decided that the Gyan-*pa* had no case because the land rightfully belonged to Angmo and her son as they had been farming on it for more than twenty years. A heavy fine and a penalty of a goat was imposed on the Gyan-*pa* ('to make Angmo's and her son's health').

CASE FOUR

In the winter of 1990, a Buddhist bus driver from Tegar apprehended an *Arghun* man belonging to a village across the river and a Buddhist man of the neighbouring village, Lakjung, loading wood from the jungle into a truck. Lakjung shares a brush jungle with Tegar near the Nubra river. In recent times, vast amounts of wood, normally meant for consumption locally, have been cut and carried to Leh for sale. The driver informed the *Tsokspa* members about the incident and they went to Lakjung in a truck and prevented the wood from being lifted. Meanwhile the *Arghun*, an employee of the Public Works Department (PWD), complained of harassment to the head of the police station in Diskit, a Kashmiri Muslim, and claimed that the wood was actually being procured for the PWD and was, therefore, for official purposes. The bus driver was taken to the police station and beaten up and it was claimed that Rs.2000 were extracted from him. A meeting was then held by all the *gobas* and the *Tsokspa* members of villages along the river and it was decided that inter-village encroachments on the jungle area would be prevented. Any unlawful cutting, i.e. without the permission of the village, would be punished. It was decided that members from every *Tsokspa* would be appointed to police certain areas of the jungle which belonged to the village in concern. A great deal of jungle wood is lifted by Buddhists as well, but in the context of the present agitation, a decision was taken to guard village boundaries against 'strangers' due to the triggering fact that and *Arghun* had been found guilty of the crime.

Case Five

Canals which supply water to villages have to be shared between them and cause at times, inter-village disputes. One such incident occurred between Tegar and its neighbour, Sumur. Customarily, it has been agreed upon that Sumur would use water from the main channel uninterruptedly from September/October to July when it is no longer essential to have water for crops. Then two feeder channels to Tegar would be used by the villagers there depending on the flow of water. Tegar also shares a canal with Chamshen village on the other side; water from the canal collects in a pond daily at night for the fields of Tegar and is let out every morning from the early hours onwards. During the day, water from the canal feeds Chamshen. However, in August 1988, when the people of Tegar went to divert water from the main canal that is shared with Sumur towards their village by way of the monastery, they found that the people of Sumur had gathered on top of the mountain near the entrance of the canal. They began to pelt the villagers of Tegar with stones from their slings. The villagers of Tegar escaped with some injuries.

The next day, an elaborate strategy of counter attack was prepared by the *Tsokspa*. All the men from the village divided into three groups. One group was supposed to use the main link road past the *manekhang* towards Sumur. The second was to travel up the mountain by the road that went by the *gompa*. The third was to use the road above the *gompa* to the source of the channel. The three groups were supposed to support each other depending on the region of attack by the people of Sumur. The villagers of Sumur made their way to the top seeking to cut off water flowing to Tegar but before they could reach, they saw standing all along the ridge of the mountains, the men of Tegar. A leader of the group said: 'This was like the Hindi film, 'Sholay'!' Stones were pelted on both sides with slings and two or three people were seriously injured. A *beda* of Sumur, who used to play at festivals and other rituals, was hit and died. It was said : 'Although he ate our salt, during the fight he was on the side of Sumur; naturally he got hurt.'

The fighting went on for a long time. Neither the Assistant Commissioner nor the police could stop the quarrel. Two trucks of the Central Reserve Police Force had to be brought from Leh across the pass, their presence an unheard of event in the valley and a high official in the tehsil had to be deputed from Leh to mediate.

The villagers of Tegar gathered near an orchard near the *gompa* while the villagers of Sumur assembled at a *chorten* on the other side. The monks themselves were divided, some of whom were said to have sheltered the men of Sumur and even beaten up a few villagers from Tegar. On a site in between, the district officials and the tehsil officer with two representatives on either side, including *Tsokspa* members, held discussions. These efforts resulted in the decision that both villages would honour the customary system of division of water from the canal. The incident was the talk of Nubra for several months and songs were even composed about it, lampooning and lauding villagers, although most were forgotten by the time that I arrived there.

CASE SIX

Around the same time as Case four, the Military Police raided the shops of Tegar. There is a lot of trade between the villages along the roads on which the army plies and the military population. Products of barter between the army and the civilians find their way into village shops which have sprung up along the highway. The district authorities have set up ration shops to supply essential commodities for the villagers such as rice, wheat, oil, sugar and salt. Three or four times a year, villagers can be seen making their way to the ration shops with their animals to carry their goods. A great deal of goods are also procured from village shops, which in turn receive their products from army sources, often because their supply is more regular, their products more diverse. These include urban and processed products like tinned food stuffs, Amul butter, condensed milk, Maggi noodles and kerosene. Their prices are directly related to the distance from the scene of armed conflict.

The military raid prompted a certain amount of panic. The house of a Buddhist shopkeeper was raided but before the Military Police could reach, the shopkeeper transferred his goods to the house of his *Arghun* neighbour. The circumstances were altogether curious. It was suspected that the policeman living in the house of the *Arghun* was an informer (he had been appointed by the local administration for protection to this Muslim family in Tegar since the agitation began in 1989 when the crops in the field of Muslims of the neighbouring village were burnt by Buddhists). In fact, this *Arghun* family was under a social boycott by the villagers, although clearly, relations did exist between Muslim and Buddhist neighbours, albeit surreptitiously, as this case demonstrated. The suspicion about the policeman, a Sunni from the next village, proved to be unfounded, but there was a tense moment when the suspicion could have fallen on me especially since, like this policeman, I had some relations with the army and district authorities, as well as the villagers. The villagers, however, pressed me to intervene as a mediator. The *Tsokspa* was also galvanized into action. They barred the doors of the shops and prevented the goods from being confiscated and also appealed to the Assistant Commissioner. On his intervention, no case was registered against the shopkeeper.

The case brought into focus the complex set of circumstances under-lying the tertiary level of integration. In particular, the relations of the village with the army and the state in the domain of cash exchange and illegal trade, as well as the situation of political patriliny. These exchanges of goods are widely prevalent, especially in the context of the closure of borders which has cut off trade across the borders with other communi-ties. This has made certain essential and luxury items unavailable, including the supply of items like salt, tea, butter, barley and textiles. which were procured subject to their availability in government and civilian shops. This domain of exchange is open to the vagaries of supply and demand in the market, to illegal transactions, and is a source of conflict and cooperation between the civilian population and the army. At another level is the situation of conflict between Muslims and Buddhists which directs suspicion in cases such as those against *Arghuns* but allows this context to be used, depending on the circumstances, in subterfuge against other sorts of 'outsiders'. In this case, the shopkeeper could very well hide his goods in the house of the Sunni villager because army personnel would not, under the conditions of the boycott, suspect that it would be hidden there.

CONCLUSION–THE TWO SYSTEMS OF EXCHANGE IN THE VALLEY

It has been pointed out that although Ladakhi society is divided into a number of *rigs* or statuses, the vast majority belong to commoner households. Among them, interesting contrasts can be observed in terms of their connection with land tax, labour requirements and household organization. In the period before 1947, there were four types of households.[16]

These were, firstly, village households who were government tax payers, mainly *khangchens*, who made annual payments in terms of grain and money. They also had to provide provisions such as butter and wood to the king and other officials and visitors in Leh. The grain tax was usually put in the state granaries to be sold to traders and travellers as supplies. Each *khangchen* also had to supply men and animals to fulfill the *begar*, carriage requirements. These were in order to carry official and private traders to the next staging post, a heavy drain on labour because most often than not, it occurred during the summer months when labour was needed for agriculture as well. They also sometimes provided labour for irrigation works or roads. and also gave an annual donation called the *soniyam* to the *gompas*. This was probably the reason that *khangchens* of this sort tried to conserve land and labour by marrying polyandrously.

Secondly, villages or households who were attached to *gompas* had to provide labour and provisions in return for land owned from it. About half the yield of their crops went as rent and in addition, they sometimes took care of *gompa* cattle and flocks, collected incense and wood for them, and also had a to act as servants when the *gompa* went on trade missions. People could also become tenants by moving to a village and leasing land from the *gompas*, terms of tenancy being lower than those in other tenancy relationships. Most of these households were *khangchuns* (or *khutus* as they are called in Nubra).

Thirdly, households attached to royal or noble estates acted in much the same manner as those in a tenancy relationship to the *gompa*. They acted as servants, goatherds, retainers when the nobles went on trading missions, and even watered their land in return for some loans and leases on bits of land. If the households in the categories of households attached to noble estates and *gompas* were not *khangchens*, in which case they tended to marry polyandrously or sometimes polygynously, they were *khangchuns* of younger brothers or new households who were recent immigrants or those who had separated from their original households and were now considered to be new households. Most of these were monogamous couples.

Finally, there was yet another type of household that was formed of single women, women with illegitimate children, a *chomo* (nun), or a man and his offspring. These were given a small piece of land and also worked as servants for wealthier households.

Low caste *mons* and *bedas* as well as *skutags* tended to marry monogamously for different reasons: the low castes because there was a shortage of marriage partners in any given area and the former (who also married other *skutags* and wealthy families who were Christians, Muslims, etc.) because they had land and responsibilities in various places and marriages were often political alliances.

What were the types of household in Tegar and Hundar? In Tegar, about 1908, there were seventeen *khangchens*, and eight *khutus*, with six tenants among the latter. Only one of the *khangchens* was Muslim. In 1990-1, the number had increased to twenty-three *khangchens* and seventy *khutus*, with eleven tenant families among the latter, many of them also owning their own small pieces of land. Most of the *khangchens* had been government tax payers but since I did not find that there were many polyandrous marriages at the turn of the century (only two among the Buddhist families), one may presume that the tax and labour burdens were lower in Nubra than those in the Leh valley. The *begar* obligations, however, did exist between the Khardung and the Karakoram passes. The Samstanling *gompa* is a fairly recent institution and in Tegar at least, most of the families leasing land from it seem to be poorer households and those of low castes, about six or seven families by all accounts. Diskit monastery also owns land in Tegar but most of its tenants belong to the third hamlet.

In Hundar, most of the households attached to Diskit monastery were Buddhist although there were five poor Nurbakshia households in Hundar who also worked on *gompa* land, just as they leased land or worked as servants of the *Zimskang*. Two wealthy Sunni *khangchens*, out of a total of eight *khangchens* in 1908, were originally traders or officials of the government and I was told that they were exempt from taxes. In Hundar today, the total number of Muslim *khangchens* are thirteen and *khutus*, forty-two. The *khutus* include tenant families whose number has increased to nineteen. Nobles, such as the *Zimskang* or the *Kharpon*, owned a great deal of land and entered into arrangements with commoner households in quite the same fashion described earlier although land reforms have diminished their requirements for tenants and servants. Most of the changes that have occurred in this century seem to have been the same for Muslim and Buddhist households. That is, they include the subdivision of land among family members, the tendency to marry monogamously and the diversification into cash occupations with the abolishing of tax burdens, *begar* requirements and land reforms.[17]

In this and the previous three chapters, the basic articulating principles of social structure in the two villages of Tegar and Hundar have been described. The community is organized in terms of social fields as a result of two inter-related principles of social organization – levels of integration and various kinds of practices and exchanges. Three levels of integration were identified depending on the territory – the space of the household, the village, and the region. Each unit within these levels is constituted by a particular practice relating to food, work, ritual, power, and kinship. Two kinds of systems of exchange may be demarcated: I use the term 'symmetrical exchange' to connote balanced reciprocity (the direct exchange of the same types of goods of the same amounts with returns occurring in a finite and narrow time period), a stress on horizon-tal links in social relations, and non-cash exchange. 'Asymmetrical exchange' is used to connote negative reciprocity (transactions conducted towards a net utilitarian advantage, practically a negation of reciprocity), a stress on vertical links in social relations, and cash exchange.[18]

At the primary level, a commoner household stands in its individuated aspect as unit of consumption and production. The exchange here is largely symmetrical though in the recent past, some of the members of a household have also entered the sphere of cash exchange and vertical relations with the state. In the secondary level of integration, it is related to other households in groupings which are based on ties of work, ritual, or political office. In the past, there were also vertical ties such as those of rents to village landlords and the monastery, labour duties for landlords and political allegiance to certain nobles. Some of these were extra-local and thus belonged to the tertiary level of integration. The tertiary level also includes kinship relations in the form of the kindred which creates ties which cross-cut a household's and a village's unity.

Before 1947, the strata of nobles were linked to those in Leh and to the king by similar ties. Nobles and the king were in turn linked by relations of trade, politics or affinity, to other regions such as Baltistan, Tibet, Kashmir or Central Asia. Similarly, the ritual power of the monks and the *imams* was also related to other centres, each centre being a nodal point of dispersion and combination of ties. The entire set of transactions in the pre-1947 situation, one may presume, was largely in kind and partly in terms of symmetrical exchange.[19]

Figure 6 : Symmetrical and Asymmetrical Exchange

Domain	Symmetrical Exchange		Asymmetrical Exchange
Domestic domain / primary level of integration	i)	Households of men and women exchange food, work, etc.	i) Nepali labourers sell services to household for cash.
	ii)	*Chospun* exchange food, rituals, help etc. with household.	ii) Households sell labour, produce etc. to army for cash.
	iii)	*Lama/imam* exchange ritual services with household.	
	iv)	*Larje, beda, gara, onpo* etc. exchange services with household.	
Local domain/ secondary level of integration	i)	Extended group of co-operation for threshing etc.	i) Occupational differentiation which includes cash and non-cash exchange.
	ii)	Complex group of co-operation for clearing channels.	
	iii)	*Phaspun* exchange services at life-crisis rituals.	
	iv)	*Iftarspun* exchange services at life-crisis rituals.	
	v)	Practice of power in village through *goba* etc.	
Extra-local domain / tertiary level of integration	i)	Kindred category.	i) Politically patrilineal groups.

With the inclusion of Ladakh in the Indian state and the closure of borders, the upper levels of the cross-cutting networks, i.e. the king and the nobles, have been replaced with the Indian state and the army. The land reforms have also reduced the power of the large landlords and nobles and have done away with the system of rents and corvee tax. Thus for a household, some of the lateral and vertical links in kind, remain in the village, but at the tertiary level, the entire set of ties of political allegiance, military duty, or trade have been transformed. Within the secondary level, one may assume that with the removal of certain relations of power, tax, and so on, the relations are fairly symmetrical. In the tertiary level, two kinds of relations exist: kindred relations which are part of non-cash exchange, and labour and political relations which are established with the state and the army. There are two forces acting at the tertiary level – one centralizing and the other decentralizing – one derived from the state apparatus and the other from customary forms of life. It is within the tertiary level with its centralizing tendencies that the LBA and the LMA also function. This sphere is one of cash exchange – involving labour for the state and the army, as well as forms of employment made available by the forces of the state such as in bureaucracy, tourism, commerce, and so on.

There are thus two systems of exchange underlying these levels of integration: the first is customary and the second is a result of the transformed nature of Ladakh. The two are also organized according to different principles. The first system includes the primary and secondary levels of integration while only the kindred at the tertiary level is part of this system. All five categories – the household, the work group, the ritual group, the village, and the kindred, form part of the domain of symmetrical, balanced and non-cash exchange. The second system includes political patriliny at the tertiary level and social differentiation in the village at the secondary level as a result of forces such as the role of the nation-state and cash exchange. These two systems of exchange are depicted diagrammatically in Figure 6.

Notes

1. c.f. Mann 1986.
2. c.f. Grist 1990.
3. See Crook 1994:501-15 et passim; Gutschow 1996.
4. See Levine 1981:52-78 et passim.
5. This paralleling of the structure between two coexisting groups seems to be

common to other areas as well. The case studies in Ahmad 1976 show that in general, Muslim family norms in India correspond closely to their non-Muslim counterparts; while the majority live in nuclear families, there is an incidence of joint families which corresponds fairly closely to the average for India. There is an elaborate web of extra-familial groupings though its function and importance among the Muslims and Hindus in India underscores religious differences. There is no evidence to show that among the former, divorce, polygamy or preferential cousin marriage is as widespread as is believed.

6. Murdock (1968:235-53 et passim) distinguishes between three types of cognatic social organizations, one of which is similar to that existing in Nubra. 'Bilateral cognatic descent groups' are described as those which do not have unilineal descent groups; in which the small domestic family is the main corporate unit; extended families do not occur; residence is neolocal or ambilocal; the kindred is an important social category though the range of the category may vary; and the domestic group is exogamous while the kindred may not be. Some of the other characteristics described for this type do not occur in Nubra. Cousin marriages (first) are forbidden among Buddhists and though allowed among Muslims did not usually occur among the peasants. Second cousin marriage is also rare. Parallel and cross cousins are not distinguished in terminology.

7. See, for instance, Brant and Khaing 1951:437-54.

8. My understanding of the kindred in the valley is derived mainly from Freeman (1961:192-220).

9. See Freeman 1961.

10. I owe the concept of 'political patriliny' to Cohen 1965 as used in his work on Arab villages within the Israel border. The paradox that Cohen analyses is that while the villages ceased to be self-contained entities and were drawn by the processes of industrialization and integration into the Israeli state, an old form of political organization which had been disintegrating in the period before 1949, the 'hamula', reemerged. The resurrection of the 'hamula' was due to certain conditions which Cohen terms the 'border situation'. These are villages which lie literally on the most strategically sensitive part of the border, and are cut off by that border from close associate villages only a few miles away within Jordan. They are also in intense interaction with the Jews in Israel with whom they have great economic interests, and are seriously caught up in the strife between the Israel and Arab world. The 'Triangle villages' studied by Cohen demonstrate how in the border situation, social continuities from the past in the form of 'hamula' organization, i.e. through patri-local, in-'hamula' marriages and the redistribution of power and prestige through the ballot system and the industrial economy of Israel, allowed the revival of 'political patriliny'.

11. See Srinivas 1991 for details of the basis on which Scheduled Tribe status was con-ferred on certain groups in Ladakh. Also refer to Srinivas 1994 for the incompatible principles of political and civil society in Ladakh today as evident in the different styles of integration through the kindred and political patriliny.

12. See Van Beek and Bertelsen 1995 for a detailed analysis of these shifts and

formations leading to the 1989 agitation.

13. Anderson (1983:104-28 et passim) points out that movements for self-rule often draw their cadres from those who have undertaken the colonial- bureaucratic 'pilgrimage' which led them to an imagining of 'nation-ness' and a perception of unity; 'the intelligentsia's vanguard role is derived from its bilingual literacy, or rather its literacy and bilingualism' (ibid.p.107). This puts them in a key position as mediators and initiators of certain unified ethnic identities, for example, as in the case of Burma. In a region such as Ladakh, these characteristics have been important at particular moments, though not all.

14. One such pamphlet was titled 'Ladakh Agitation: People's Movement for Union Territory Status in Ladakh'.

15. Similarly, Goldberg 1977 describing the pogrom against the Jews in Tripolitania in 1945, states that the relations between Muslims and Jews combine both conjunction and disjunction. At the level of myth, Jews and Muslims are similar being descendants of Abraham but are separate since they recognize different rightful heirs. Given this symbolic ambiguity, the riots which occurred in the period of the festival of *Id* and the end of Italian rule reversed the status of the Jews from that of symmetry to asymmetry and emphasized the disjunctive aspects of myth and custom.

16. The description of the four main types of households is a summary of Grist 1990a.

17. Grist 1990 points out from studies done in the 1970's in Leh tehsil that the average family size is 4.1-6 and in Kargil tehsil (Suru-Karste), about 4.8. Goldstein and Tsarong (1987:443-55 et passim) point out that for a village near Leh, the fraternal polyandrous family was the basic unit which served to overcome such contradictions as the feudal corvee tax system, the inelasticity of the environment with respect to land, the need for male labour to fulfill tax obligations in the past, etc. It served to reduce aggregate fertility but because of it, a number of Buddhist women remained unmarried and had to marry non-Buddhists. Muslims in that region did not have polyandrous families but usually a patrilineal joint family and married from the pool of unmarried Buddhist women. The changes after 1947 – the abolishing of corvee tax, land reforms and the creation of new opportunities for freed labour, led to a breakdown of polyandry and the fragmentation of land. According to the authors, a hundred years ago, there were sixty-four *khangchens* who held land and were basic tax payers in the village. Today, there are 143 households, all small houses, an increase of 123 percent in three decades. But because Muslim and Buddhist family structures were different, Buddhist families increased 1.3 times and Muslim families increased seven to eight times.

18. I use the terms balanced and negative reciprocity in the way outlined by Sahlins (1972:191-6 et passim).

19. A description of these traditional modes is provided by Samuel 1994 for a range of societies in the Tibetan-speaking area and substantiates my observations.

PART TWO

Chapter 7

Speaking in Tongues

'If there is faith, one can see light even in a dog's teeth.'

– a Nubra proverb

The existence of two systems of exchange in the villages of Nubra valley give rise, in the life of persons and groups, to stresses and conflicts. In order to understand their effects on cultural processes within the community, I use the frame of the 'social drama' to descriptively show how these conflicting tendencies operate in practice.[1] Each case described here is a separate one which occurred in Tegar, but it also refers to groups and forces outside the boundaries of the village. It is, therefore, inaccurate to treat each case as a purely discrete cultural situation, although the cases taken together are in no way a concatenated series of phases and a 'narrative'. The events described in various cases refer to the different levels of integration analysed in the earlier chapters and show, therefore, how these social categories – the household, the *phaspun,* the village community, or the kindred – become operative. They are frames which rest on a dramaturgical model of community existence; they present the ways in which individuals and groups represent and reflexively act on themselves, and the sense of crisis, pain and healing, that occurs in a community.

CASE I: DEATH IN THE VILLAGE

On the first day of my arrival in the Nubra valley (6 August, 1990), I heard that a twelve or thirteen year old boy had died in the village. He had been tending goats with his friends at Tirit village nearby when he was overcome by pain in his chest. He managed to get home but could not be saved. The local nurse was away in Diskit attending a medical camp (Tegar has a little clinic with one or two medical attendants, no doctor and few medicines). The nearest well-stocked and functioning medical centre belongs to the army and is some distance away. The entire village visited the house of the deceased by turns before the fourth day when the body was burnt. Every visitor brought the customary gift of flour, bread, biscuits, butter, tea or *chang* and some money. *Chang* and tea are con-sumed continuously by visitors and the other items are given to the family of the deceased. In return, guests are served food (usually rice, vegetables and a curry) which they take home. The household members do not perform any tasks such as the cooking of food, tending animals, or working in the fields. All work is in the hands of the *phaspun* members.

The boy belonged to the house of Mutup-*pa* in Hasara, one of the village hamlets. We walked to the place bearing bread, butter, and tea. Inside the house in a room were the praying *lamas* wearing their ritual head dresses with bells in the left hand and little drums in the right. In another room were the visiting villagers and the kinspeople of the household. The cooking was being done by the *phaspun* women. The chief mourners appeared to be the mother of the deceased and her sisters.

During a death ritual, the space of a house is transformed. Everyday tasks are suspended or taken over by the *phaspun* members. All the mourners and those offering their condolences were seated in the kitchen. The father and mother of the dead boy and the mother's sisters were seated on one side of the stove near which various 'gifts' of barley flour, biscuits, and so on were placed. On the other side were the visitors. In the guest room, an elaborate shrine was set up and *lamas* were praying around the coffin. Outside, below the steps under a white parachute serving as a tent, were *phaspun* women cooking around fires created for the occasion. In the courtyard were the men (chiefly of the *phaspun*) who later carried out the coffin. In the courtyard, separate benches were laid for men and women who stayed on for the funeral meal.

The *phaspun* men carried the body in a coffin, with *lamas* leading the way, to the *phaspun* cremation site near the mountain where, after prayers, the body was burnt. At the time of the removal of the body, there was much wailing by women in the courtyard and everyone threw their *khataks* into the coffin. The women (mother and mother's sisters) fell unconscious and had to be carried upstairs and revived. The bones of a dead person's body are broken and the body is usually rolled up into a ball and, except for the feet and face, bound by a rope. The elder brother of the dead boy could not bear to see this done and it was avoided. When the *phaspun* men returned from the cremation, they were given water from a bucket to wash their hands and mouth at the entrance.

Three days after the body is burnt, another set of prayers occurs. Then the ashes are taken and scattered on the mountain and in the river. For seven weeks, prayers are conducted. On the thirtieth day of the death, a preparation of barley flour, *chang* or butter milk, and butter is made. This is called the *tsogs* and is conical in shape with a red peak. It is distributed to every house in the village. In the forty-nine day period, the spirit is in the intermediate realm between this world and the other world, *Bardo*, and hovers around the house. The spirit has to be persuaded not to return to the land of the living. During the first four days, the *lamas* also read to the deceased the description of the road after death, and the sights on the way so he or she may recognize it.[2]

During the forty-nine day period when the spirit is in *Bardo*, it can either return and occupy the body (the *onpo* is in a position to say whether this will happen or not) or reincarnate in a different body. If the spirit returns and occupies the body, then, in the initial period, it must be offered *sur* (barley flour sprinkled on hot coals/embers in a container usually offered everyday to dead ancestors, spirits and *idak*) or incense.

The day following the funeral, I was invited to the house of Chuli-*pa* in the village for a meal. Apart from feasts of the *phaspun* or village gatherings, members of the same social strata have their own dinners and meetings. Four such families used to meet regularly: the first two were old landed families; the third received a great deal of land after the land reforms and had also diversified into politics, contracting, and administrative work; the fourth had aspirations to a higher social status and had the means to do so because they owned agricultural machinery. Dinner was served very late. All the attention of the house was diverted to the courtyard where various family members were sleeping. In August, it is warm enough to sleep outside in the moonlight. The daughter-in-law of the household, Yangchen, had become possessed by a demon (*dre*). She was laughing and talking in the hoarse voice of a man, sometimes hissing and spitting at people around her, her ire directed especially against her brother-in-law's daughter. Her disconnected speech seemed to refer to the events of the previous day when she was returning from the funeral. She had become afflicted by a spirit-being which had taken possession of her body. She was the dead boy's father's younger sister. It was difficult to ascertain who was speaking – Yangchen or the person in whose voice she spoke. The *ruh* (spirit-being), as they referred to it, seemed to be in a great hurry to leave because he said he had a great distance to cover, yet anxious because some work was not complete. Someone sitting close to Yangchen hit her shadow repeatedly with a stick to threaten the *ruh* and make it speak. The *ruh* is said to inhere in the shadow. After a while, Yangchen fell into a kind of slumber.

Local beliefs accept the relationship between *lus* (the body) and the *la* (life-force). Lassitude, weariness of the body, emotional distress, and illness are explained as a consequence of the weakening of the *la* or even the loss of it. There were two kinds of explanations in the village about Yangchen's possession. One set of people said that the absence of her brothers and male members of the family at the time of the boy's death made its burden fall on the women and therefore Yangchen became 'mad'. Others said it was because of *mikha* (literally, 'people's mouths', but generally, their talk) connected with her husband who was an intermediary between the villagers and the army for agricultural sales and was subject to a great deal of gossip and criticism (about favouritism and corruption) by the villagers. He was also not present in the village at the time of the boy's death. Yangchen, thus, seemed subject to the pressures of men leaving the village (for jobs outside as truck drivers, labourers for building roads, soldiers in the Ladakh Scouts, etc.) in a dual capacity – as a substitute for her husband and as a substitute for her brothers. It was generally accepted that she had suffered a loss of her soul or life force and was, therefore, vulnerable to demons and spirits of all kinds.

CASE II: THE MONASTERY DRAMA

On the first few days of the eighth month of the Buddhist calendar, *Dawa Gyatpa*, a festival is held by the monastery to mark the completion of one and a half months of restriction and prayer by the monks in the Samstanling monastery. On the first day, about fifteen monks headed by the abbot of the *gompa* go around to all the *yultaks* (threshing grounds) accompanied by drummers, the *goba*, and other members of the village council. By this time, all the barley in the field has been harvested and brought to the *yultaks*. The period of isolation, *Gay*, which began at *Tukpe Chonga* (i.e., the fifteenth day of the sixth Buddhist month) is over. During that period, the monks have to observe certain restrictions. They are not to cross water, grass, and so on; they cannot leave the monastery for more than six days even for urgent business. The head monk explained that these injunctions were laid down by the Buddha for his *lamas* when demons taunted him that his followers could not stay in a place for more than a day when even the birds stayed for more than a few months in their nests. The feast given by the monastery to the village coincided with the end of *Gay*. The prayers and ritual performed at the *yultak* are to ward away or satisfy those beings to whom something is owed from this or a previous birth. These debts are claimed at harvest time. The *lamas*, after performing the rite, are given tea in the house. Usually three neighbours combine to host them in one of their homes each year.

In the afternoon of the same day, a feast takes place. In the premises of the *manekhang*, arrangements are made and tents set up for 'guests' (usually the army or other strangers), and for villagers (men sitting towards the left and women towards the right and in the centre, the *skutag, mulazzim*, other village elite and the *lamas*). Food is served to all – tea; *chang; khambir* (roasted bread) with sugar, butter and local cheese on top; rice with cabbage; and radish curry. No meat is served, for this monastery observes strictly the restrictions on meat, egg, and onions. Men and women drink steadily and alternately, tea and *chang* (the latter is served by villagers) and eat food or take it home.

After the feast, people move to the courtyard. There is a raised enclosure there on which the *lamas* and the *skutag* sit; men and women sit in fairly rigidly separated groups, each sex tending towards its own company. In the centre, dances take place. On this particular occasion, only men danced at first, but after some persuasion and a display of appropriate modesty, women joined in. Dances take place in a circle which moves clockwise and anti-clockwise. It is formed in order of seniority by age, though in the formation, differences of rank are also visible. Those of the lowest social strata are at the end of the line. *Skutag* do not dance usually and when they do, a subtle rearrangement takes place so that age and seniority of rank are coordinated to make them head the formation.

People from all the villages neighbouring Tegar were invited for the feast and there was much drinking, shouts of encouragement, and laughter at the dances.

On the next day, a drama was organized by the 'Samstanling Dramatic Club', i.e. by the monastery for the village audience, an event which occurs every two years. The show, 'Nangsa-Udbum', began at 7.30 p.m. and went on till midnight. The tale is about a girl, Nangsa, known for her virtue and piety, who was born to a Tibetan king. She marries a prince but is ill-treated by his sister and father. She bears a child. She is beaten by her in-laws and because of blows received, dies. She goes to *Bardo* where her good deeds, especially her gifts to monks, are found to be abundant and she is sent back to earth to complete her life-span and tasks. By that time, her family has repented and the tale thus ends happily.

The drama is, in its script, entirely in *Bodhi* (literary Ladakhi). Most dialogues and the rendering of rhetorical pieces, which are in classical Tibetan, are not always understood by the village audience. The outline of the plot, however, is known to all and the nuances of script which escape the audience are supplemented by the breaks between 'classical' scenes. These breaks (while costumes are being changed or actors resting briefly) are filled with songs of great originality. These are sung to certain well known folk rhythms – harvesting songs, songs about soldiers, lorry drivers, the state government, and the Ladakh Buddhist Association leadership. One song went:

> Greetings to all men, be united all, be united in words
> and heart,
> be united in words and heart and develop your own
> valley;
> Our hearts are sad because Nubra's villages have not
> developed,
> whatever India has given, the Black Crow, Farooq, has
> taken.
> The Black Crow had fled now with his offspring and
> become a refugee,
> it is good that the Black Crow has gone, and Ladakh's
> fate has brightened,
> the enemy of Buddhist religion has much business
> and many tippers (trucks),

> it is good that dealings with the government are over
> > and the tippers stand abandoned.
> Ladakh Buddhist Association, men and women,
> > O brave people,
> you have led the enemy to great losses and only their
> > noses remain standing.

The audience was convulsed with laughter at the costumes of the monks. They were dressed in jeans, the *gonchas* (robes) of everyday wear of Ladakhis, uniforms, and dressed as women as well. They played the fool not only in the guise of the low musician but also in the guise of a crazy *duba* (hermit). Costumes were identified – this was someone's *goncha*, that someone else's snow goggles – but so were the themes of the song. Couched within the plot of the story, the classical discourse was belied by songs which were sung to the tunes of other festival songs (at village gatherings, calendrical rites, weddings, etc.) and also to the tunes of Hindi films. They alluded, directly or indirectly, to two main issues: the Muslim-Buddhist confrontation and the oppression by the Kashmir government of Buddhists, and the relations between the army and the people:

> Listen people, listen!
> The two of us are going to sing you a song:
> In the three months of summer, Nubra is a garden,
> in the three months of winter, it is very cold;
> It is difficult to get apples and apricots, and only
> > fortunate eyes see them,
> but the mouth is unlucky and does not receive
> > anything.
> In the dream of getting a taxi, he collected money
> > but the money was soon wasted,
> in the dream of becoming a soldier, I left my studies
> > but found myself on the glacier,
> in the dream of getting married, I made *chang* and
> > arrack, but the girl refused to come.

The songs became very popular and were sung for months afterwards in the village, most often by children and youth. The play resembled ambivalent events which previously occurred in mid-summer (the fifth to the seventh months) in Tibet – jousts, jests, amusements, theatrical performances, contests – the sacred, continually verging on fun in order to delight the gods of the soil and ensure a good crop.[3]

The drama at *Gay* bore a spatially metonymic relationship to the domain of the village. From the altar of the *manekhang*, an important focus in the everyday life of the village, the village moved to a half enclosed verandah in an orchard on the first day of the festival, and to the world of the stage, its footlights (made by gas-lanterns enclosed within cut away army milk tins) and curtains.

The social relations most visible in the spatial organization of these events were those between village strata and between the sexes. In everyday life, visits to the *manekhang* do not involve a strict separation of the sexes or a hierarchy where the *skutag* are given any particular preference. Most often, prayers and the journey are individual, though sometimes it is a family outing. The non-everyday life of the feast is to be contrasted with the fast of the monks and the ordinary fare of the laity. Men and women were separated and commonly united and opposed as farmers and villagers to the *skutag* and the monks who sat in the centre. All these categories were collectively opposed to the army and strangers who sat in a separate enclosure. In the dances after the feast, the last category was absent, i.e. 'outsiders', here the army and strangers, and although the position of the monks and the elite had not changed, men and women first separately, then jointly, participated in the dances. The musicians sat on the fringe of the circle of dancing. At the drama at night, the focus was the stage where the monks' roles were reversed. These were non-hierarchical and the opposite of their everyday-life. Men and women and the elite sat randomly organizing themselves according to their everyday life though in their non-individual aspects of it. They sat with their families, their kindred, and their friends, very few according to their status in the village.

Temporally also, the feast contrasted with the fast and alternated with it in time. The drama itself was a 'hybrid' form containing within it two axiologies – one classical/High and the other non-classical/Low; one of piety, suffering and sacrifice, the other of laughter, political rhetoric and work. The contrast between the two unmasked certain sentiments of unity. It demonstrated the tensions in the relationship between the village and the state, and between Buddhists and Muslims.

CASE III: THE ACCIDENT

In January 1991, a Buddhist family in Tegar suffered a serious accident. This was the family of a Tegar *Tsokspa* member, Tsepal. Two of his children were badly injured in an explosion and had to be taken to the hospital. By coincidence, I discovered that the Sunni Muslim family with whom I resided for part of the year in Hundar was related to this Buddhist family in Tegar. Tsepal's father's sister had married a Sunni Muslim in the neighbouring village and had converted to Islam. Her husband's sister was the wife of the head of the Muslim family in Hundar in whose house I lived. In the context of the agitation and the boycott, a sudden erasure of genealogical connections had taken place and no one had thought to tell me that the two were kin.

During *Ramzan*, when I was staying with the Muslim family, the head of the family explained to me that if they had not been subject to the boycott by Buddhists and would not have created an embarrassing situation for the Buddhist family, they would have assisted the latter while they were in hospital near Hundar. They were, after all, kin.[4] When the accident occurred, the children, with the help of the commanding officer of an army camp in the region, were rushed to the hospital where they lay in a critical condition for many days. One child's fingers had to be amputated and both had serious burn injuries. The accident created a lot of speculation in the village: was the blast due to firecrackers (because this accident occurred just after the Ladakhi New Year) or was it dynamite? The latter, in the mood of the agitation and sporadic attacks on Muslim households, could have been available in the village. Some people, including the authorities, felt that the possession of dynamite ('blasting', as it is called in the village) was the most plausible explanation. The accident was, after incidents of harassment of Muslim houses, a kind of harsh justice.

Certain other kinds of explanations were also offered, this time by ritual specialists in the area – the *onpo* and the *lhaba*:

The *onpo* lived in Sumur village. About fifteen days after the accident, he came to perform a ritual of affliction for the children at home. Diskit, the mother of one of them, had consulted him earlier and the date of the ritual had been decided. The diagnosis of any affliction or problem is done by two methods, the *onpo* explained to me: first, by rolling a dice and second, by consulting an astrological calendar with soothsaying possibilities. Accordingly, it was decided that on the thirteenth day of the month, a ritual needed to be performed and the auspicious direction was north. The *onpo* explained that there were four categories of ritual which could be performed:

i. to deal with bad deeds and bad feelings (of self and others); there are eighty kinds of *storma* (representations made from dough) which can be made;

ii. to deal with this life and the securing of merit through good actions in this life; there are ten sub-rituals;

iii. to deal with the other life; there are thirty-five sub-types of rites;

iv. to deal with the safe journey to the other world and to keep those in this one happy; there are eight sub-types of rites.

In general, four types of ritual practitioners can be identified, stated the *onpo*: the *lamas* ensure peace and can help a man's spirit reach heaven; the *onpo* removes evil and assists in securing earthly and other worldly benefits; the *lhaba* sees the spirit of a man and its imaginings as if in a mirror; and the *larje* takes care of the body. The *onpo* from Sumur and his family had been connected with astrology for many generations. All astrologers in Ladakh, I was told, belong to the Nyingmapa sect of Buddhism associated with Tak-tak monastery near Leh. The *onpo* has a shrine at some height from Sumur and on the tenth and eleventh day of each month, he goes there to perform a rite. Initiation to astrologer-hood can be familial or non-familial and is done through penance and the learning of ritual techniques.

Besides Diskit, there were others assisting in the rites. The rites belonged to the first category cited by the *onpo*. Angmo (the *Tsokspa* member, Tsepal's father's sister's daughter) helped with the cooking of food and controlled the store while in the absence of Tsepal, his younger brother assisted the *onpo* in the ritual. The latter made a series of *storma* (effigies of barley flour, *chang* and butter) and chanted prayers to the beat of cymbals and drums which were played by a novice. The priest of the *manekhang*, familiarly known as 'Gelong', was also present to help make the effigies. These were made from a wooden board called *Storme par*. It has two sides: on one side were hollowed 'negatives' of representations of Buddhist calendrical years (twelve in number) and figures of a male and a female. On the other side were representations of *storma* required for various rituals. A combination of these was made. At the end of the ritual, Tsepal's younger brother and a neighbour of another household (also male) took the effigy out, depositing it at the north.

The *onpo* stated that the accident occurred because of *mikha* and therefore required the first category of ritual. The boys, Diskit's son and younger brother, had come from Leh and everyone was talking about them – talk of envy and pleasure, good and bad. The collective life-force of the people was greater than that of the boys and had overpowered them and caused them ill. The *mikha* was also a result of talk about Tsepal (the *Tsokspa* member) which in turn had got displaced onto the children.

The ritual needed two kinds of *storma: Mikha Dolzok* where the *storma* was thrown to get rid of the talk of people, and *Dolma Yudos storma* which was kept in the house to increase the boys' life-forces.

A *lhaba* visited Diskit's house some days after this. He was from Khardung, a village near the pass. During the winter, most people in this village go to lower areas of the valley, partly because of the cold and partly because of the absence of fuel there for cooking and heating purposes. At winter time, the Khardung *lhaba* resides for a few months in Tegar and in neighbouring villages. He attends to various afflictions during this period. When we visited him at a neighbour's, he was drinking *chang*. Gelong of the *manekhang* had just completed his *lapsang* ritual. The *lhaba* then washed his hands and mouth and put on his ritual costume which is thought to represent the dress of the gods – an apron, a cape for his shoulders, a five-piece crown, and a scarf that covers his mouth through which he speaks. A piece of juniper was kept on coals in a container near him. He chanted prayers and invoked his deity. Soon his body started to have convulsions and he was inhabited by the deity. All oracles have a large pantheon. These belong to three classes: *lha* (gods – eight members), *tsen* (spirits of the earth – 360 in number) and *lu* (spirits of the under world – several thousands). Each has its own region, speciality and function and these are acquired by the oracle as gifts from another *lhaba*, by inheritance, or by seeing them in visions.[5]

The first case brought to the *lhaba* was that of Tsewang who was ill. He used to beat the woman he was residing with and the *lhaba* said this was because a *temo* (an evil female spirit) was affecting him. He drew on a piece of paper, the figure of the woman. On a plate containing a cloth and mustard seeds, the name of the *temo* appeared when he threw some grains on it. He kept shaking his little drum, piercing himself occasionally with a dagger, and once or twice hit Tsewang with a whip. Finally, a fire was prepared. Oil was burnt in the pan. The *lhaba* came to the fire holding a drum in his right hand and a *dorje* (a metal thunder bolt) in the left, and dipping the *dorje* into the boiling oil, touched it to his tongue. The *ruh* (spirit) 'appeared' before him and he questioned it. Finally, he pierced the paper (with her figure) with his knife and threw it into the pan. It refused to burn till spoonfuls of *chang* were poured into it. It then burned brightly. He picked up a flame embodying the *ruh* from the pan with his dagger and 'ate' it. The same procedure of burning took place in other houses for *ruhs* causing various afflictions.

There were other problems which required diagnosis. A villager had a sickness of his hand. The *lhaba* asked him: do you dream of dead people? He replied in the affirmative. The *lhaba* then asked him to wear the charm he had given him earlier which lay unused in front of the Dalai Lama's picture in his house. The *goba* complained that there was exudation from his eyes. The *lhaba* said that the figure of Shambala in his house which used to be formerly consecrated with water now lay 'dry'. The exudation of his eyes was a reminder that it should be worshipped again in a similar manner.

Diskit asked about the accident. The *lhaba's* analysis was that the accident occurred because of the conflict between the *lha* of Diskit's brother from Leh and her own. The *lha* of her house in Nubra (her residence by marriage) and her father's house in Leh were at odds with each other. Diskit later told me that in the earlier days of her marriage, when she went home to visit her parents, she would (as was her custom) go into the altar room to light a lamp or pray. She used to fall ill after this. A Leh *lhaba* diagnosed a similar conflict between her two *lhas* and as a sign of her new allegiance on marriage, she does not visit the altar room in her father's house anymore.

Later, at Angmo's house, I engaged the *lhaba* in conversation. Gelong and Angmo's son were also present. The *lhaba* poured himself a glass of rum. He told me that there were 360 *lhas* and many *tsen* against whom people had to guard themselves. Houses, therefore, have a patch of red paint at the entrance which works against these *tsen*. He said that with the Chinese occupation of Tibet, the *lhatos*, where *lhas* dwelt, were destroyed. Hence they fled to Ladakh to seek their residence in people's bodies. Seventy-five *lhas* would come to reside in Nubra (at the moment there are twenty-one), exiled from their former homes.

He also told me how he came to be possessed. He said that he was an ex-serviceman and had retired from the Ladakh Scouts regiment nearly ten years ago. A *lha* would visit him and at first, he would be found doing strange things. He was found walking at night in the countryside far away from his home and he fell repeatedly ill. Finally, he consulted a monk who diagnosed his affliction as possession and said he must seek a teacher. He was given *lhapchok* (initiation) under the *lhamo* (female oracle) of Sabu village near Leh. In those years, he learnt how to remove illnesses from the bodies of both men and animals. He initiated six other people after he became a *lhaba*. He gave up cigarettes and now drinks in moderation. He said his ritual purity was like a monk's cleanliness but 'we are civil (i.e. civilian) people and therefore do not give up these habits completely'. He claimed that during a recent incident on Khardung pass when two men were buried under a snowdrift, he had divined the exact spot where their dead bodies lay.

The Khardung *lhaba's* selection and life career bear some similarities and differences with others that I have heard of. It is said in the Leh area, practising oracles sometimes inherit their gods and belong to shallow oracle lineages including parent and grandparents.[6] But most cases of oracles in Nubra, to my knowledge, are 'achieved' statuses. All such oracles are selected by a kind of madness in which there is a loss of self control (because the person's life-force is weak, among other things) and for many months and years, novices wander in a sort of spiritual wilderness. After a diagnosis is made by senior oracles and monks, two courses of action may follow: the person afflicted by the spirit may not chose to keep it and returns to his quotidian existence; or, following a life-crisis ritual, the *lhapchok*, the person moves to a new social position by being recognized as an oracle. Various skills are learnt before he can follow his calling – sucking out poison, exorcising demons, and so on – usually with a senior oracle. Everyday life usually continues, whether it is work on the farm or government work.[7]

CASE IV: THE SPIRIT POSSESSION OF THE MANEKHANG PRIEST

In January 1991, the priest of the *manekhang* who also performed the *lapsang* for various households in the village – Gelong, as we referred to him – came to be possessed by Chamshing, a *lha* whose idol stood in the *manekhang*. I was told Chamshing's idols are found in no other place in the Nubra valley except in Tegar. It is the *lha* of one *phaspun* in Leh, but I found none in my village or the ones in the neighbourhood which had Chamshing as a *phaspun-lha*. Tegar is known for this particular idol and villagers treat Chamshing as a fierce *lha*, one who is a *dharmapala* – a defender of Dharma. Villagers believe that a long while ago, Chamshing was the leader of the Hor (Turks). When Kesar, the epic hero whose stories are recited by bards in Ladakh even today and from whom the kings of Ladakh claim descent, defeated the Hor, Chamshing was also 'converted' from being the enemy to being a *dharmapala*.[8] He passed through several rebirths in which, among other things, he 'conquered his anger' and finally achieved the status of a *lha*. His status in the local pantheon is extremely high but it has not been heard of till date that any oracle has been possessed by Chamshing. Chamshing's last 'appearance' in Nubra was during the 1948 war with Pakistan just after the Partition. The Pakistani troops had advanced from the north-west practically till Skuru village in Nubra and many villagers from Tegar had fled. Reinforcements of the Indian army were still to arrive. At this point, the monks from Samstanling *gompa* prayed to Chamshing to save them and it is said that a ray of light shot out from the roof of the *manekhang*, moved across the sky, and fell behind the Burma hill towards the spot where the enemy forces were. After this, the enemy receded and the war was won. The Ladakh Scouts troops from the village stationed at the border also speak of seeing a light move across the mountains and of miraculous interventions, which they associate with Chamshing, when their lives were in danger.

I give below a descriptive account of various moments of Gelong's possession by Chamshing before undertaking to analyse its symbolism and historic significance in the next chapter.

The possession

Rigzin, the sister of Diskit in Case III, had hurt her thumb while trying to chop meat. The neighbours said it was *mikha* which had afflicted her brother as well and caused him to lose several fingers. Gelong was present and I asked him if he had ever been affected by *mikha*. He said that for the past few days he had been ill and thought it was *mikha* (in his opinion, because he was learning English from me). He wished to see the *onpo* before he began his *Tangpo* fast. The fast occurs after the *gustor* (the festival of the monastery) at Diskit. The monks at Samstanling observe silence and a fast every alternate day. On the thirteenth day of the month, they come for a three day stay to the Tegār *manekhang*. Batches of other monks also go to villages affiliated to the monastery in the valley. On *chonga* (the fifteenth day), the villagers visit the *gompa*. Some other *gompas* such as Diskit, do not observe the fast strictly and it is left to a monk's initiative to do so.

On 26th January 1991, many people (monks, Nepali labourers and villagers) went to the army camp nearby to watch the Republic Day parade held in Delhi on television. Gelong and I set off to the *onpo's* house on a road that went past the *gompa*. The *onpo* had just returned from the jungle after cutting wood. He stated that Gelong would need to be branded for his affliction.

On the second day of February, we heard that Gelong had been possessed by Chamshing. Angmo brought us the news as the declaration of the *lhas* identity had occurred in her house: Gelong had stood up suddenly and declared who He was.[9] Then Chamshing said he could see, in a vision, people from the village waiting at the airfield to return from *Gyagar* (the area south of *Kache-yul* or Kashmir, used generally to refer to the Indian sub-continent). Villagers had gone to Banaras for the Dalai Lama's 'Kalachakra' rites. On the next day, one of the families in the village returned. Again, on the day of the *Tsokspa* drama (24th February), He saw some more villagers returning and on the next morning, another family returned. At a *lapsang* in Pinchimik (a hamlet of Tegar), He asked the *abba* of the house, a soldier on the Siachen glacier, had he seen a light at night on a particular day? *Abba* agreed that he had. That was I, said Chamshing. The third occasion of possession, Angmo told us, was at Gelong's own house in the next village. He suddenly rushed into Gelong's sister's house where she was drinking soup and said that a letter and money from her husband, a soldier, would arrive the next day. They did.

Gelong told me that when the *lha* descended, he yawned a great deal; he also saw strange sights – scenes from the Kesar epic, visions of horses and other animals entering his body – then a period of darkness when he had no recall. Ordinary sounds and sights seemed to be at a great distance away. The abbot of the monastery explained to me that *lhas* possess people who are pure or clean with weak life-forces. One night, Gelong visited by Chamshing, walked up the road to the *gompa* from the village. The monks were very perturbed by this and made Him promise not to come again till the Shras *rinpoche* (the incarnate head of the chief monastery of this sect) came to visit Nubra, whenever that was. He said He knew the exact date of the Shras' arrival from *Gyagar* but did not have the mandate to reveal it just yet.

The Yarma festival

On 18th and 19th February 1991, the annual festival at Yarma monastery took place. Going there involves a journey up the Nubra river and at a certain point, the river has to be crossed to reach the monastery on the other side. Vehicles can go halfway across the river where, in deep winter, the bed is wide and dry. There were two parts of the river which had not frozen over and the villagers had put bridges across it – first, nettles and dry brush on rocks, next, two long poles placed in a parallel fashion across the fast-flowing water and last, flattened tin sheets on top of it. These kind of bridges are common in Nubra and withstand pressure very well. The river bed was extremely cold in the central portion because of the chilly winds blowing down from the glacier.

Yarma village itself was small, with twenty-odd houses all belonging to Drugpa monks and their families. These monks can lead a family life, drink *chang*, and so on, in contrast to the Gelugpa. The *gompa* itself was very old, certainly over five hundred years old. At least three hundred people from the neighbourhood had come for the festival: soldiers, villagers, and government officials. They wandered around the fair at the foot of the *gompa* where stalls with clothes, shoes, toys, food items, and games of chance had been put up. Others fixed little tents for themselves on the commons of the village, unrolled their bedding and made tea. Still others circled the *gompa* ritually on their right and went into the *dukhang* (room where the idols are kept) to pay their obeisances. The walls of the altar room, where the scripture and the Gonbo deity are placed, are covered with paintings whose representations are found on the hills around the monastery. Groups of ten and fifteen pilgrims were led there by the *onpo* of another village, a rotund, cherubic man. He pointed out the likenesses of Gonbo, Paldan Lhamo (a female deity), Kesar's horse's hoof prints, a flame, and so on, for the eyes of the faithful. It is said that once upon a time, a veil of stones covered Gonbo and no one could see the deity. One day, the head monk of the monastery called the people together and told them to expect a visitor. On the morrow, the veil of stones had fallen and Gonbo's likeness became visible.

The monk's dances – the *chams* (monastic drama or mime) – began at 4.00 p.m. The monks were dressed in brightly coloured costumes and masks specific to the monastery's *chams*. The head monk was from Hemis and was the only completely initiated monk in Yarma monastery. He presided over the events while the other monks executed the steps of the *chams* unique to Yarma. After the performance, people crossed the river again to make their way to neighbouring villages for the night if they had not already found a place in Yarma.

The next morning, events at the *dukhang* were chaotic: we saw people running out of it in part panic, part awe. It seemed that at least half a dozen people had been possessed by *lhas*. Two of them came to the steps of the monastery brandishing an axe and a dagger, both of which lay with idols in the *dukhang*; cuts were made on the tongue by one breathing fiercely, while the other had blood on his forehead. Suddenly, they ran into the courtyard and marked a spot on the ground with a sword to indicate the ritual space for the placing of the *linga*. At 2.00 p.m., the monks descended from the *dukhang* after the prayers were over to the blowing of pipes and the clash of cymbals. A triangular black box was kept in the marked spot. An *onpo* offered prayers while the *lhabas* who had accompanied the monks and the players whirled round and round the *linga*. The *lhabas'* movements were unsynchronized compared to those of the dancing monks, weaving in and out of the latter, sometimes whipping them with their whips. They also moved to the crowd where people offered them *khataks* (placing it on their shoulders) and asked them for solutions to their various afflictions. By the time of the last dance of the *chams*, about nine *lhabas* (men and women) were present. They had decided that no one present at the festival would leave till the effigy was carried out of the monastery and, indeed, none of the pilgrims dared to leave.

The *linga* was taken out when the sun's rays had finally disappeared, accompanied by the blowing of trumpets and the beating of drums. It was taken to the ground outside the *gompa* where a wide circle of people stood around in the snow to watch the last portion of the ritual. The nine *lhabas* also gathered in their bare feet or socks. The monks threw the *linga* into the bonfire amidst a flourish of instruments, ridding the monastery of the old and the evil, and ushering in the new and the good. The *lhabas* by this time seemed to have exhausted their frenzy; no more attempts were made to slice their tongues or their arms though one of them put his foot into the fire. The pilgrims finally dispersed, having to make their way back barefoot across portions of the ice-cold river where the bridges had suddenly been washed away.

The group from Tegar returned to the village late at night. It appeared that simultaneously with the first day of the Yarma festival, Gelong had become possessed. Diskit had gone to light a prayer lamp at the *manekhang* for her husband's illness and Gelong had told her that at the *lapsang* at a neighbour's house, he had gone into a trance while performing the ritual.

The old *abbe* (grandmother) of the family lay ill but at the end of his trance, she was cured and got up from her bed.

The Tangpo fast

On *Tuk* (the sixth day) of *Tangpo* (22nd February, 1991), considered particularly auspicious, villagers undergo a fast. They eat only one meal the whole day although butter tea is drunk throughout; the *chos* (scripture) are read continuously, all of which are in classical Tibetan, while people turn their rosaries. In the day, they do their *skora* (circumambulation) of the *manekhang*. We met Gelong in the *manekhang*. It was the day he observed silence and so only spoke through signs. He pointed out barley grains scattered on the floor (used during a divination) and the sword of the idol of Chamshing which had been used to cut his (Gelong's) forearm during a possession the day before.

On 24th and 25th February, the Tegar *Tsokspa* held its play, 'Timet-Kundan', which was enacted in two parts. The drama was held in the *manekhang* courtyard on the stage used by the earlier drama, only this time it was put up by the village and not the monastery. The tale is about a charitable prince, Timet-Kundan (the Buddha in one of his earlier births). He is generous hearted and gives away many of his royal possessions as gifts. Among these is a priceless jewel. This act of charity so angers his father, the king, that he is banished from the kingdom. On the way, wandering through the jungle in exile, he is asked for further gifts: a *duba* (hermit) asks for his wife, another for his children, and finally, a blind one for his eyes. He returns to the kingdom after the period of exile, completely destitute and blind. The gods are all gathered there to reward him for his gifts – he gets back his eyes, his family and his kingdom.

Behind the stage, parachutes had been used to make tents for players, musicians, and announcers. Gas lamps were kept in them to be replaced at need, with others on the stage. The drama proceeded after an announcement was made by a *Tsokspa* member. It appeared that Chamshing had once again possessed Gelong. He had summoned the *Tsokspa* member to the *manekhang* stating that He had arrived just then from the glacier. He asked the member to watch out for a villager who wished to begin a quarrel on the day of the drama and not to permit anyone to drink *chang* on the premises of the *manekhang*. Chamshing possessed Gelong eight times that day and in one of the possessions, He said He would visit again on the *chonga* of *Tangpo* (fifteenth day of the first month).

After the announcement, the first scene began with a *duba* being called to rid the afflicted king of *mikha* so that he may have a child. The static demeanours of the king and his ministers speaking the Central Tibetan dialect contrasted with the *dubas*, blind, deaf and lame, the *tamzeys* (mendicants) speaking colloquial Ladakhi, and the songs of the chorus which were a mixture of the colloquial and the 'High'. Announcers frequently began with an explanation of the scene in the classical language and ended in a sort of a mixed code.

On the fourteenth and fifteenth day of *Tangpo* (27th and 28th February), the monks from the monastery, having distributed themselves among the *manekhang* of the various villages of their flock on the night of the thirteenth day, maintained a fast and prayers. Early on the morning of the fourteenth day before dawn, a conch sounded from the *manekhang*. Thereafter, villagers intending to keep the fast went to the *manekhang* where, after the head *lama's* prayers, all those who had resolved to keep the fast for a day and to affirm the teaching of the Buddha, chanted a 'promise' after him. This festival is called the *Mon Lam* (the vow). They did a *skora* of the *dukhang* and returned home. In the afternoon, the entire village seemed to be outside doing a *skora* of the *manekhang, chortens,* and the *lhatos* in front of the old *Zimskang* house on the hill. Inside the *dukhang,* monks of the *gompa* were continuing their prayers with cymbals and gongs. After the rite was over, people gathered in the courtyard. *Meme* (grandfather) Wangchuk, one of the older men in the village who had been a monk at the monastery earlier but had been subsequently derobed, was reading out the text of 'Dowazangmo' (a tale of a journey by a woman to Bardo). A fraction of people seemed to be listening to the text; they were whispering among themselves, were turning their prayer beads or looking over the wall at the highway to see which vehicles were passing by. Once in a while, they joined in the chorus of '*Om Mane Padme Hum*'. Tea was served in the break.

There was a general sense of expectancy in the gathering which was fulfilled when Chamshing suddenly appeared in the courtyard. Gelong had been possessed by Chamshing inside the *dukhang* and He berated the monks inside for thinking that He was a *dre* and not a *lha*. He said that if they persisted in their disbelief, He would throw *Luyar* (the containing vessel of the spirit, i.e. Gelong) down from a great height and kill him. When he emerged outside, there was a strange glow on *Luyar's* face. He announced that He was Chamshing and He had ridden on the rays of the sun from the glacier. Chamshing was angry because of the spiritual laxity of the villagers: toilets had been built near the *manekhang* and people were desecrating its premises by drinking *chang* and rum there. He also berated the *goba* for raising sheep only to be sold for slaughter to the army – wolves would be set loose in the jungle to eat them, He threatened.

The theft

The pronouncement which caused the greatest furore among the villagers was about a theft in the village. A village woman had lost her pearl earring on the night of the drama and it was not to be found anywhere on the premises. Chamshing announced that one of the women sitting in the courtyard had found the earring but had not returned it. Instead, it had been wrapped up in a red cloth and kept in a chest in her house. He threatened to go and fetch it unless by noon the next day, it was placed at the foot of the Dalai Lama's chair in the *manekhang*. *Meme* Wangchuk again continued the reading of 'Dowazangmo' in the late evening and villagers sat around the enormous heater in the *manekhang*. Chamshing had stated He would come again at night and the villagers gathered there expectantly. At about 9.00 p.m., in the rooms near the balcony of the *manekhang*, Gelong was possessed by Chamshing again. *Luyar* was on his knees, hands clasped, eyes rolled upwards, his head at an odd angle. He began to speak, making at times gurgling sounds, to the monks and villagers gathered there. Various queries from villagers were attended to. By 10.30 p.m., the possession was over and Gelong was moving about clearing up tea cups, looking a bit worn, but otherwise with no recollection of the events past.

After the completion of the reading and hearing of 'Dowazangmo', villagers wandered up to the *gompa* in the afternoon in their best clothes. Long lines of people from the villages adjoining the *gompa* could be seen winding their way up the hill. At the *gompa*, the deities in all the *dukhangs* were unveiled. Men and women were going in and out of rooms carrying bottles of apricot oil for the lamps there. Some people stayed back to chant their prayers at the *gompa* while others went back to their villages. In Tegar's *manekhang*, people were gathered waiting for rituals to be completed and to do their obeisances to the gods. Gelong was possessed for the third time that day: His main injunction was about the stolen earring. He said that He would give one more chance for it to be replaced before punishing the person who had taken the earring. Everyone begged for forgiveness on behalf of the thief.

On the first day of March, *churuk* (the sixteenth day) of *Tangpo*, there was a feast for all those who had died in the village in the past year. Inside the *manekhang*, monks were engaged in prayers before the gathered villagers. In front of the *dukhang* before the Dalai Lama's seat, were three trays of *tsogs* made from flour taken from each household in the village on the previous day. This is made by an officer called the *kotwal* appointed for that year. It was a large, conical-shaped structure with biscuits and sweets stuck into it. On other trays were *khambir* brought by villagers and a clay pot filled with *chang*. At an auspicious moment, to the beating of drums by the village musicians, the trays were carried aloft by young men and monks and offered to Chamshing and other idols. It was then distributed to everyone. Inside, meanwhile, Gelong had gone into a trance. He asked again about the earring. It was decided ingeniously that a bag would be passed around, everyone would thrust their fist inside, so the one who had taken the earring could replace it without shame (*thelba*).

Everyone made their way to the courtyard. *Meme* Wangchuk led the chanting of prayers for the dead while the bag went around. Offerings of households who had lost a member in the past one year – roasted barley grains mixed with dried apple, walnuts, peas, *chang*, etc. – were distributed in the courtyard. *Churuk* is a break in the *Tangpo* fast when meat and *chang* may be consumed. *Luyar* appeared, meanwhile, on the roof of the *manekhang* with the *goba* and some *Tsokspa* members. The earring had still not been replaced. He stated that the woman who had taken the earring would be given an illness as a warning; her husband, similarly, would have a fall. Chamsing pointed out the direction of their house.

The villagers clearly believed that a certain couple were in possession of the earring and His pronouncements confirmed it for them in time as events – illness and an accident for the couple and finally the returning of the earring by the woman – occurred as predicted.

Other redressals

Many other events occurred. On the eighth day of the third month (22nd April), Gelong was again possessed. He caught some mischiefmakers who had left cigarette stubs in the *manekhang*. Also on the same day, He scolded some boys of the village who had broken the twirling prayer wheels on the *manekhang* balcony while hitting birds with their slings. Chamshing said that He had come riding on the wind from the glacier and a stone had hit Him in the eye. He threatened to send Chogyal (His animal-helper) to punish them. As it happened, one of the children of a house near the *manekhang* was injured when his cheek was bitten by a bull. He also predicted that by the end of the month, an old person in the village would die. On 5th May, Gelong was possessed by one of the lesser deities, Chamshing's *mulazzim*, as the villagers called it, and 'flew' over the wall of a villager's house. There a cow lay ill, harmed, He said, by a serpent and advised a remedy for it. Suddenly, the *lha* in *Luyar* was replaced by the *lha* of the wind; doors and windows began to rattle, their latches burst and windows and doors flew open. On other occasions, He recovered lost objects, cured afflictions by removing black and other coloured mucus from bodies, and rid houses of *temos* (afflicting spirits/witches). Chamshing went to surrounding villages as well. In Khalsar village, some items stolen from the *gompa* were recovered by Him. There was an altercation between two houses in Sumur village and the *gompa* about water; in anger, He went to the *gompa* and swallowed all kinds of objects – a nail, a watch strap, etc. When villagers petitioned Him that all this would hurt *Luyar*, He removed them by sucking them out from *Luyar's* elbow. He even drove a truck for nearly 5 kms. though Gelong does not know how to drive.

On *chonga* (15th day) of the third month, the *lhaba* from Hundar also arrived at the *manekhang*. The two *lhabas* were welcomed to the village from the *gompa* to the sounds of drums beating and the scent of incense. It was said that three ibex had accompanied them down for a distance from the *gompa*, an auspicious sign. The procession circled the *manekhang* ritually on their right and went in. For first time, *Luyar* put on the ritual costume of a *lhaba* and villagers gathered there to be healed of back trouble, sore eyes, *temos*, etc. There was one dramatic moment when Wangdus, a villager who claimed that Gelong's possession was fraudulent, was berated by Him: He picked up a sword and began to pierce *Luyar's* body. The villagers forced Wangdus into hurriedly doing twenty obeisances for forgiveness. Mutual consultations took place between the two *lhabas*, talking to each other in a language full of honorifics as meant for those to whom great respect is due; they attended to people's ailments separately and together by touching afflicted parts of the body with a whip or dagger, blowing into people's eyes, and so on. The session got over when *Luyar* fell senseless to the ground. The Hundar *lhaba's lha* left him in a gentler fashion – he began to wheeze and dropped his head onto the carpet.

On 27th May (*chupji*), when the monks from the *gompa* arrived for the unveiling of Chamshing's idol in the *dukhang* of the *manekhang*, the two *lhabas* were once again in a trance. Again there was a session of healing; the possessed woman in Case I was rid of the *dre* which had continued to afflict her; an old woman was summoned because she had not paid the monastery's rent for many years, and so on.

On the next day, a session was held in the courtyard of the *manekhang*. There were, at this point, three *lhabas* (including one from Charasa village who was not allowed to speak by *Luyar* and the Hundar *lhaba* because his *lhapchok* (initiation) had not been completed). Chamshing was in a very angry mood: He said that some people wanted to transfer *Luyar* out of the *manekhang* and would not beg His forgiveness for having cast suspicion on the truth of the possession. He cut *Luyar's* tongue with a sword (the two other *lhabas* did the same) and drew blood. All three spat blood into a container which was sent to the *gompa* as a 'sacrifice'. He stated that it should be placed before the deities there and ordered that the veils of the idols be removed for fifteen days. This act roused great fear among the villagers because a blood sacrifice of this nature, as well as an untimely removal of the veils of the gods, boded ill for the people. On the way to the *gompa*, the priest taking the container up said that he had seen a figure riding on a whirlwind. It circled him three times before vanishing. He said it was His spirit accompanying the priest. The detractors, in fear and trembling, were forced to beg Chamshing for forgiveness.

The shakspa ritual

Jipe Chonga (the fifteenth day of the fourth month) is the day on which the Buddha was born, enlightened, and died. On that day, there is an early morning rite called the *lung* in the *manekhang*. Later in the evening, after a prayer by the priest of the *manekhang*, people offer obeisances and ask for *shakspa* (forgiveness/atonement) for their wrongs. *Zatpa* (acts of the Buddha, usually the twelve central events in his life) are chanted/read out.

There were events of high drama on *chonga*. Some weeks earlier, a theft had occurred in Pinchimik. A *mon* in the hamlet had been accused of theft from a shop, tied, and beaten by a group of shopkeepers. He came to plead his case to Chamshing on the grounds that he had been wrongly condemned. Chamshing told the victim that the real offender would be revealed on *chonga* and the ones who had wrongly accused him would be punished. The shopkeepers and their allies came to threaten Gelong in Tegar – they closed the *manekhang* doors, locked him in to intimidate him and even broke some windows. Gelong became possessed, picked up Chamshing's sword from the altar room and brandished it at them. The shopkeepers left hurriedly.

The next day when people came to the *manekhang*, *Luyar* was throwing his possessions out of it. He threatened to leave the *manekhang* unless the offenders accepted that they had done wrong. The scene in the *manekhang* was tumultous – women weeping and begging Chamshing not to leave, monks trying to calm people down, and men shouting angrily. The *Tsokspa* men went to Pinchimik and hauled the shopkeepers back in a truck. *Luyar* was throwing out various instruments of ritual from the *dukhang*. The shopkeepers and the village men nearly came to blows in the premises of the *manekhang*, the latter demanding that the former ask for forgiveness. Finally, a sort of tribunal was set up with the Hundar *lhaba* and *Luyar* sitting in judgment and the victim and the shopkeepers putting their case before them. The shopkeepers confessed that their evidence was slender when they had beaten up the *mon*. They were persuaded, as an act of contrition and reconciliation, to offer butter tea to the monks of the *gompa, khataks* to the two *lhabas*, ten obeisances each to the deity, a prayer flag for the *gompa, manekhang* and the *Yultsa-lhato* (the shrine where the *lha* of the community dwells), and a veil for Chamshing. Their offer of *chang* to the villagers of Tegar was refused. He also produced two *srungas* (a scarf with a knot in it to 'bind' good spirits, a blessing) and conferred it on the *gobas* of the two hamlets. They exchanged it between themselves to ensure that in future, amity prevailed between the two hamlets.

After these events, the *shakspa* ritual proceeded as usual: *tsogs* was offered by two monks to the deities. One was an offering from the men who had completed the whitewashing of the *chortens* in the village; the other was from the villagers, and was distributed among them. In the afternoon, there was an archery contest (in which only men participate) in the courtyard of the *manekhang*. The participants were led by the two *lhabas* who also, in a trance, played archery.[10] On the next night, there were dances and songs by the villagers which continued late into the night. The monks left before midnight, but the villagers danced on.

On 6th June, *Meme* Phunstog died (a death of an aged person had been predicted by Chamshing by the month end). The custom in Nubra is that as many prayers/rites and have to be conducted as the deceased has children. Normally, the priest of the *manekhang* would have been present at the various rites, for the instruction given to the wandering spirit of the dead person about *Bardo* and the journey ahead, and so on. But Chamshing had ordered that *Luyar* was not to go to the site of death because of *tib* (pollution). Gelong had also been relieved of his duties at the *manekhang* by the abbot. He was to return to the *gompa* and was asked not to perform rituals in the village any longer. He was given a private cell in the monastery to spend the rest of his days in prayer and divination. The monastery had claimed Gelong for itself after his sojourn in the village.

The day after *Meme* Phunstog's death (he belonged to the same *phaspun* as the household in which I lived), I left Nubra.

Notes

1. This concept is used by Turner (1957) in his study of Ndembu village life; the social drama shows how latent interests become manifest, how persons and groups oppose each other, and how conflicts are resolved. It is an analytical tool along with others such as genealogies, censuses and diagrams.

2. I was told the story of Skarma Wangzen, a Tibetan girl who died and reached the other world. There, the God of Justice told her that her time on earth was not complete and sent her back to earth to finish her allotted tasks. All that she saw in *Bardo* is set down in a text which is read along with others in the first month of the Buddhist calendar, *Dawa Tangpo*. For instance, it is told how after her death, she returned to her home not realizing that she had died. Her cup of tea was not filled and no one greeted her at her mother's house. She went up to the roof of the house to look at the full moon and saw, with shock, that she cast no shadow. She then realized that she was dead.

3. See Stein 1972 [1962]:219.

4. The boycott and closure of borders have not only erased genealogical links but have also created a genre of stories. One I heard quite often was: The Prince of Khapulu (in Baltistan) married a noble lady in Nubra. The marriage procession returned to Baltistan leaving behind the Prince's *Koran* (he was Muslim and she, Buddhist). Meanwhile, hostilities broke out on the border in 1948 and the boundaries were sealed. The *Koran,* thus, remained with the Buddhist family. They kept it under a pile of their own prayer books but it would mysteriously appear on top. They tried again and again to get rid of it, throw it into the river, burn it, but to no avail. It drove two sons of two generations of the family to insanity.

5. There are a great variety of approaches to oracles and their presence in the Tibetan-speaking areas. Nebesky-Wojkowitz (1993 [1956]) is a classical reference and there are early references to Ladakhi oracles in Ribbach (1986 [1940]). Day (1989 and 1990) examines the symbolism of initiation and other practices among village oracles in Ladakh, chiefly in the Indus valley. There are references to equivalent phenomena in the Himalayan belt (David-Neel 1931; Furer-Haimendorf 1964; Hitchcock and Jones 1976; Holmberg 1989; Peter 1979).

6. See Day 1990:208

7. Oracles in Nubra were generally Buddhist but this need not be so. Day (1990:208) mentions that she met a musician oracle and a beggar oracle in the Leh area. She also mentions a Hindu soldier, a Muslim and a Christian practising as oracles. In my own fieldwork, the previous *imam* of the Hundar mosque used to practise divination and was popularly referred to as a practising *lhaba*. The practices described in this case – preparation for a trance, the setting up of an altar, ritual equipment of an oracle, singing by the oracles, healing activity, and drum divination are fairly similar to most descriptions of oracles/spirit mediums in the Himalayan area. The experience prior to becoming a *lhaba*, i.e. seeing visions, roaming in the wilderness, and psychological stresses during the period of election till their identity is explained by a traditional authority like an abbot or a *lhaba* (and they are trained), is also fairly standard.

8. See Day 1990 and Samuel et al 1994 for some reflections on Kesar and shamanic power.

9. I use the capitalized 'He' to indicate the speaker is the deity Chamshing and not the *Luyar*, the vessel of the deity i.e. Gelong, who is indicated by 'he'.

10. The arrow is a multivocal symbol in Ladakh. It is associated with hunting, ploughing, male sexuality and also marriage. It is used in weddings when it is taken to the bride's house. There are three sections to this shaft which could represent three worlds, three generations, or the unity and mediation of two polarities. In the initiation rite of an oracle, a wedding arrow is converted into a ritual arrow symbolizing the union of god and person in the teacher, the union of teacher and student, or the capture of a god for the novice. The arrow is planted in a nourishing pot of barley signifying also the tree of life and fertility (Day 1990:214-5).

Chapter 8

Cultural Processes in a Frontier Community

'MIKHA'– PEOPLE'S MOUTHS

The language of Ladakh is generally considered to be divided into five regional varieties depending on the culturo-geographic region to which they belong.[1] Areas of mutual intelligibility and difference exist between these varieties – *Shamskat, Stotskat*, Zanskari, Central and Nubra Ladakhi. The Ladakhi speech community has been described as a 'diglossic' situation where languages are used in separate and hierarchically related domains for performing specialized functions. The 'high' language has a written and literary tradition while the 'low' is used in colloquial speech. The diglossic situation is seen further in the fact that folk songs and tales are usually in the local variety of the region.[2] The religious writings, literary compositions, plays, religious education of Buddhists, etc. are done in Classical Tibetan which attests to the links between Tibet and Ladakh in the past through monasteries and scholars. This literary language is taught in schools today as a subject called *Bodhi*. By contrast, the Ladakhi Muslims, although they too can use Bodhi, show a tendency to use the Arabic script for writing. Ladakhi is written in the Tibetan script which is syllabic in nature combining a Chinese phonetic system with an Indic script. A similar hybridization occurs when groups other than monks and scholars use the Urdu script, the language which is the medium of instruction in state schools, for writing letters, and everyday correspondence. Standard, colloquial Ladakhi is the language of the All India Radio, the newspaper, election speeches, and posters. There are also other kinds of media – the Hindi film; news broadcasts from Srinagar and Karachi; pidgins for speaking with tourists, Bihari and Nepali labourers, the army; and so on.

A broad variety of relationships between 'standard' languages and 'dialects' can be described according to traditional socio-linguistic perspectives for multilingual situations;[3] or as a preparatory exercise towards a description of the standard Ladakhi language which is largely the language of the town, Leh.[4] But in practice, there exist a number of codes in communities in Ladakh, written and oral, primary (part of everyday rejoinders, letters, etc.) and secondary (folk tales, plays or essays), and complex relationships exist between these codes and the way in which they make up the character of the standard and literary languages. These codes also partake of stylistics differentially according to their functional use, their theme, composition or enabling conditions. *Mikha* (people's mouths) is a term used to describe the speech used by a community's members among themselves. This may be gossip, praise or censure. It may be good or malevolent. It is regarded as having the power to affect people's bodies insofar as envy or gossip can overpower people and cause them illness, possession, and so on. *Mikha* can be considered to be a sort of 'life-force' of the community.

But the mouths of people are also associated with eating, hospitality, gluttony, and the exchange of food in general.

For example, during manuring, which occurs in Tegar at the beginning of the agricultural season, groups of kin and neighbours carry manure on their animals from the animal sheds and the dry toilets to the fields, placing it there in a designated number of heaps. The household head, normally treated deferentially, is placed forcibly on the manure amidst laughter, his normal social status inverted. The speech style used in this situation is a joking one and it is associated with the mouth and orality from 'below', i.e. with the waste products of men and animals. Similarly, during this period, strangers are subjected to joking though in this region they are usually addressed in honorific speech reflecting hierarchy, distance or formality. A ransom is also extracted from any passing stranger, his hierarchical status being reversed temporarily.

Linguistic exchanges can be seen to be a part of other types of exchanges in a community – labour, work, property, marriage, or food.[5] In chapter six, the sphere of symmetrical exchange was described as one that produces and distributes goods (barley, mustard oil, vegetables, etc.) meant for household consumption, a sphere that does not involve cash. The sphere of asymmetrical exchange was said to involve commerce, work for the army and the administration, employment of Nepali labourers, etc., for cash. The two spheres are also divided linguistically between the domain of the vernacular and 'sacred' codes (of Classical Tibetan and Arabic); and the domain of the vernacular and non-sacred languages (such as Hindi, Urdu and Standard Ladakhi). The linguistic and economic markets are, therefore, far from integrated.

Figure 7 : Codes and Markets in Tegar and Hundar

	Non-Cash exchange, Vernacular, Sacred Languages		Cash exchange, Vernacular, Non-Sacred languages	
	Adult Men	Adult Women	Adult Men	Adult Women
Tegar (all households)	93 (65%)	113 (89%)	55 (35%)	13 (11%)
Tegar (Buddhists only)	87 (62%)	109 (90%)	53 (38%)	12 (10%)
Hundar (all Muslim households)	40 (57%)	66 (94%)	29 (43%)	4 (6%)

Certain statistics can be given to reflect this differential distribution of codes and markets which is shown in Figure 7. Among the Muslims of Hundar, out of a total adult population of sixty-nine males and seventy females, forty males and sixty-six females (about 57 percent of the men and 94 percent of the women) worked in the sphere of non-cash exchange, and the vernacular and High, sacred languages as farmers, musicians, shepherds, and so on. Twenty-nine males and four females (about 43 percent of the men and 6 percent of the women) worked in the sphere of cash exchange and the vernacular and non-sacred High languages as soldiers, drivers, teachers, shopkeepers, labourers, etc. The total population was composed of 121 males and 118 females, school-going children being largely bilingual. Correspondingly, for the households in Tegar, out of a total adult population of 148 males and 126 females, ninety-three males (including monks) and 113 females (about 65 percent of the men and 89 percent of the women) worked in the sphere of the vernacular and High, sacred languages, and non-cash exchange, while fifty-five males and thirteen females (about 35 percent of the men and 11 percent of the women) worked in the sphere of cash exchange and the vernacular and non-sacred, High languages. The total population was composed of 228 males and 197 females, school-going children being normally bilingual. If the Muslim families are excluded, then the corresponding figures of males and females working in the non-cash sphere are eighty-seven and 109 (62 percent of the men and 90 percent of the women) and the number in the cash sphere are fifty-three and twelve (38 percent of the men and 10 percent of the women) respectively, the total population being 217 males and 191 females. The two religious groups thus show a parallelism in their involvement with the economic and linguistic market.

Linguistic exchanges are also related to wider processes of nation-state formation and certain forms of language reflect struggle and crisis in culture and society as a result of these processes.

BODY, LANGUAGE AND THE STRUCTURE OF FEELING

What is the relationship between the inner and the outer, between social relationships and the individual psyche? The oracle in chapter seven, as well as some of the other ritual specialists, employed redressive rituals to deal with certain pressures in social life. These rituals, unlike life-crisis rites which have affinities to the life-cycle of individuals and social regularities, are particularly sensitive to changes and breakages in the web of social relations.[6] The function of these rituals is to reveal what has been masked by society, or is the source of affliction in the individual – spirits, secret malice, ill intentions and impure actions. Divination is followed by a remedial action which involves healing, destruction, or propitiation of spirits. Each of the cases reflected dramatically certain conflicts at the various levels of integration. Due to the presence of two systems of exchange in the villages of Nubra, several structural cleavages run through the community which were stressed in different social situations as described in the various cases. In certain historical moments, some individuals become the site of societal antagonisms by virtue of their intercalary position in the community. They are usually mobile persons who occupy positions, or occupy such positions at particular moments, which expose them to social contradictions. Rituals of a redressive kind involve a close scrutiny of conflicts in social relationships in the community and conflicts of loyalties in the psyche of the victim who occasions the ritual arising from competing social principles: 'The resolution of the conflicts within proceeding *pari passu* with the resolution of conflicts without.'[7] If, however, the victim of social conflict is the weakest link in the social order and the 'acid test' of the community's basis and its moral order, the opposite is also true: the ritual specialist or the diviner embodies the unity of the social relationships of the community and the unity of the loyalties within the individual's psyche.

Within the psyche, the conscious and the unconscious are not different ontologically. The unconscious 'is only another form of consciousness, only an ideologically different expression of it.'[8] In this sense, the unconscious can be called the 'unofficial conscious' and verbal utterances (along with jokes, wit, songs, or dreams) which make this unofficial conscious accessible are a product of the interaction between speakers and of the whole, complex social situation in which they occur. 'Inner speech is the same kind of product and expression of social intercourse as is outward speech.'[9] The official conscious expresses the well formulated fully-fledged ideology of the dominant groups in question, their law, morality and world view, while the unofficial conscious speaks of all those centrifugal forces reflecting the disintegration of the unity and integrity of the system. In a society without conflict and contradiction, there is no discrepancy between the official and the unofficial conscious. But to the extent that conflict exists, the inner speech of persons and the unofficial conscious is censored and only emerges through certain linguistic forms. In this sense, the possession of the oracle and the other cases described in the last chapter are the unofficial conscious using oblique strategies to express the split of the psyche, the divergence of social roles, and the conflict in custom and morality brought about by social transformation in the frontier villages of Ladakh. They are signs of the linguistic, social, and discursive asymmetries in the community.

Gelong, during his oracular utterances, switched between colloquial Ladakhi and what was perceived to be Classical Tibetan. Similarly, some of the other cases also involved a shift in codes.[10] But in this study, rather than analyse the 'text' of those codes, their use in boundary maintenance in conversation or specific social contexts, these cases will be analysed as indices of struggle in the community. There are two aspects to these instances of shifts in codes.

Firstly, language use is intrinsically related to structures of feeling and an attempt has to be made to understand the somatic coding of linguistic forms. Laughter, heartache, longing, pain, or madness are registered on the body as much as they are expressed through certain culturally accepted codes. For instance, in Nubra, as in some other parts of Ladakh, at least three linguistic categories of 'pain' can be identified. *Dug* is the most general term used to express sorrow, a publicly validated condition that accompanies death or some instance of suffering that is common to all persons. *Tsherka* is pain that is felt as heartache, that accompanies some distress, or loss. *Sunpa* is associated with melancholia or nostalgia. Each of these kinds of pain may lead to a loss of vitality, illness, or possession, as one falls prey to hostile forces and beings, and sometimes leads to death.

Secondly, language use is also embedded in the network of social relationships and can be seen as having specific effects: displacement, inversion, substitution or condensation. It is possible to say that in the case of the dead boy's father's younger sister, Yangchen, in Case I, her female identity was temporarily displaced by a male persona, interpreted by the community as a demon possessing her body. In the *gompa* carnival in Case II, there was a breach of social hierarchy and decorum and the roles of the monks were inverted. The children became scape-goats or sacrificial substitutes for their parents in Case III. And finally, in Case IV, the key cultural values of the community were condensed in the figure of Chamshing for whom Gelong became a vessel (all these cases have been discussed in chapter seven). All these shifts imply a struggle that takes place on the boundaries of the social and personal body. An individual's body, as well as the social one, can be filled with deities, spirits, ghosts, and memories of dead or lost persons. It has been stated that houses are inhabited by at least three kinds of *lhas*: the *thap lha*, the god of the hearth, the *pha lha*, the god of one's *phaspun*, and the *khyim lha*, the god who inhabits the central pillar of the house. But boundaries of the house are not static and forces may enter it. Therefore, most Buddhist households have a patch of red paint on the walls of the house, flags with sacred words and magical formulae inked on it are tied to the roof, *lapsang* is performed, *idak* and other spirits are fed outside the house in an earthernware container, and so on. Otherwise, ill luck and danger may befall the inhabitants of the house. The body is also similarly permeable. *Mikha* or a person's ill intentions may cause affliction, one has to be careful from whom one receives food, and even the breath of a person is a force. Thus the *lhaba* breathes on people to cure them in certain cases, and deities may enter one 'like a breath'. The body, like the house, and society, has to be strengthened. One may wear a protective amulet, be cleansed of impurities and afflictions by the *lhaba* sucking them out of one's body, and be careful of having one's *naksha* (photograph) taken in case the life-force is captured by the picture.

All the effects of language use occur within the frame of social processes and categories.

The social unit which was the locus of the events of the death of the boy and the possession of his father's younger sister, Yangchen, (Case I, chapter seven) was the household, affinal and consanguineal. In local explanation, a demon was said to have possessed her body because of her weak life-force on two accounts. She was a substitute for her husband (i.e. by her status within her affinal household) and a substitute for her brother (i.e. by her status within her consanguineal one). Further, what the possession embodied was the relationship between the household at the primary level of integration and its invasion by the army and the processes of the state. The father's younger sister became an ambivalent person ritually, inasmuch as, her structural ambivalence at the primary level of integration made her a candidate for possession. This possession was also described as 'madness', a result of excessive *dug* connected with the funeral. Oracles also undergo a period of madness before they are identified as mediums, a state when they wander at night, have strange and terrifying dreams, when they are not themselves. They may do bizarre things: laugh at odd times, cry at others, or hiss and spit as in the case of Yangchen. There may be many reasons for this madness. But a restoring to health occurs by ridding the body of the demons which have driven one to madness, by the burning of the picture of spirit beings and the ill intentions of others by the *lhaba*, by exorcisms, or by creating *storma* and effigies which hold the afflictions.

It has been pointed out that social liminality can be linked to ritual ambivalence, such as in possession. Again, in some societies, the adoption of a male persona and the inversion of the woman's role seem to express not only the conflict of roles between men and women (as brothers and sisters and husbands and wives) but also their interdependence.[11] In Nubra valley, the system of exchange in marriage does not involve any significant dowry or bride-wealth. There is movement of both men and women in and out of natal homes and both virilocal and uxorilocal marriages exist, although a greater percentage of them are virilocal. Village exogamy is the usual practise for a household. The system of exchange of work also ensures a fairly symmetrical division of labour between men and women. Through the system of marriage and other practises of exchange, the relationship between the sexes, whether as husbands and wives or as brothers and sisters, is fairly symmetrical. The equivalence and substitutability of husband and wife is indicated by the kinship terminology as well as the division of labour in the household. As mentioned earlier, there are few tasks in a household that only men or women will perform. Husband and wife also use the same kinship terms to address affinal relatives. Again, brother and sister are considered equivalent in terms of work, transmission of property (primogeniture not being strictly followed), and residence after marriage. The incest taboo and rules of marriage for both Muslims and Buddhists, however, ensure that brothers and sisters must establish separate affinal residences creating distance in spite of equivalence.

What this socially acknowledged equivalence and substitutability, however, masks is the peculiar position women occupy between households, natal and affinal, as intermediaries. Many post marital residence are virilocal, and most children are born in the *phaspun* of their father. But the role of the natal family continues, and is seen in a number of cultural forms, for instance the *skyinjug*, which are sung at weddings by brides taking leave of their homes where they have grown up and their neighbourhood. This farewell usually has a deeply personalized form and refers to places and persons dear to the bride. The word which might be used to convey this weariness of the soul, the homesick ache, and the feeling of wandering among strangers is called *sunpa*. Many such songs also express resistance against disinheritance from natal homes. On marriage, a bride must adjust in a new village to the routines and hierarchy of another family. When she enters it, a rite is performed to cleanse her of the influence she brings from another household, and she is seen as potentially polluting. She also loses her rights at her natal family's funeral kiln. Brides who fail to maintain a balance between the two families are seen as destabilizing influences.[12]

But the ties with the natal family continue through a variety of norms. Even if the natal village is not close spatially (though marriage tends to occur within the valley), brothers and sisters play a role in the weddings of their children. The maternal uncle (*ajang*) is central in a wedding and takes charge of many tasks at it. The paternal aunt (*ani*) acts as an escort leading the bride to the groom's house, and so on. At other times, such as at *Losar*, recently married brides return to their natal homes with gifts, and a reciprocal set of offerings from natal hearths are received.

A particular burden as mediators is thus placed on women and this position allows the articulation of pressures and strains in the network of social relationships. In Nubra, with the change in the political conditions of Ladakh as a frontier, the closure of trade routes, the bureaucratization of Leh, and the inclusion of Ladakh in the processes of nation state formation, the gender-based division of labour and roles has altered. This has resulted in three processes: men are moving into the cash economy as soldiers, truck drivers, teachers, tourist guides, etc. while women are less visible in this sector; there is the 'feminization' of agri-culture with a preponderance of women in agriculture and related work; and bilinguality between the vernacular and High, non-sacred languages is a male domain primarily, while women tend to be found in the domain of the vernacular and High, sacred languages.

In the possession case, both the male members of the affinal and consanguineal family were absent at the time of the death ritual. The father's brother worked in the office of the district administration in Leh while Yangchen's husband worked for an agricultural society. As a consequence of the strict taboo on performing household tasks on the mother, mother's sister and father of the dead boy, Yangchen substituted for many tasks that might have been done by her husband and brother. The period between the burning of ashes of a dead person and the end of the forty-nine day period of mourning and pollution is one in which the spirit of the dead person wanders in *Bardo* and is still attached to those living. It is also a period when the loss felt by those living is particularly acute. In the case then, asymmetries and contradictions between the roles of men and women led to a shift in the code employed by Yangchen and was embodied as a possession by a demon. Her substitution during the death ritual, emotional and physical, for her male kin was reflected in the displacement of her female self by a male one through possession; the background of this situation was the growing contradiction in her normal social role. This transformation was made possible by customary social roles that connected men and women as affines and siblings. But in the changed context, her 'male tongue' could be seen either as a symptom of victimhood or an attempt, by adopting a male persona, to reverse the asymmetry of her new social position *vis-à-vis* men and make claims to power, however ambivalent ritually. This, however, is not merely a way of 'coping'. Possession, like *dug*, is a state of deeply felt distress. If households and societies experience disorder at death, bodies also suffer an infringement of their normal balance. There is pain, which like the *ruh*, is a shadow which attaches itself to or inheres in the body.

During the feast at *Gay*, the *gompa* and the village moved into a different position, both temporally and spatially. The feast following the fast depicted another kind of role reversal – that of inversion of the position and daily roles of the monks. A festival or a carnival is usually a ritual of status reversal that accompanies a traditional society's transition from scarcity to plenty, or disease to health and it occurs between 'high', canonical feasts. The most important feature of this reversal is social excess which partakes of communal catharsis. Besides the shifts between the everyday and non-everyday life of men and women during the feast and the drama, the roles of the monks also changed from that of hierarchy and respect to those invoking laughter and familiarity. The festival belonged outside 'high' liturgy and orthodoxy and travestied or inverted its roles, values and customs. It was linked syntagmatically to 'high' feasts and fasts, but in contrast to 'epic' time (formal, reinforcing the order of the past, and hierarchical), its logic lay in the interrogation of this, and it was essentially a subjunctive practice.[13]

It has been pointed out that there exists within the apparently mono-lithic edifice of Tibetan Buddhism, a functional ambiguity which allows alternative tongues to emerge. There is a genre of lampoons, jokes, and songs which parody and reverse canonical themes. This is called *cholok* (joke) which means 'the Dharma reversed'. It articulates the voices of archetypical half-outsiders – women, mad saints, tricksters, bards, and clowns – at carnivals, markets, and other public spaces. The language is a combination of canonical forms, village patois, tantric yoga and vulgarities drawn from the domains of eating and copulation.

This voice is the monastic voice in a different register, a restatement of the normal in terms of its opposite. The other genre, *loze*, is blank verse recounting heroic and tragic tales, celebrating romantic love and the beauty of nature. It represents the voice of lay officials caught between the claims of a disintegrating theocracy and the secular world.[14]

Like *cholok*, the drama at *Gay* inverted the relationship of monks to the villagers. The monks belied the epic code of the play by inserting in its narrative a carnivalesque one composed of harvesting songs, songs of soldiers, the voices and figures of mad hermits and low musicians. This carnivalized code occurred not only at harvest time when the society was in transition from scarcity to plenty, but also at a time of transition from certain canonical rites: the period of fasting and restraint on movement and speech which began on the fifteenth day of the sixth month was over, and the feast given by the monks to the village coincided with the prayers at the threshing grounds after the harvest.

The important feature of this reversal was that there was an infringement of societal taboos, in particular, the parody of sacred norms. The festive situation created a special type of communication which was free and frank and in which norms of etiquette collapsed. Not only was there a transformation of the bodies of the monks through such clothes as *gonchas*, jeans, and women's attire, but there was also a collapsing of the boundaries between sacred, culinary and sexual terms in their speech. There were excessive references to food and waste, puns being employed on numerous occasions. Contrasts appeared together: kings with fools, for instance. While this kind of ritual transgression is to be found in various Tibetan societies, particularly during the New Year, the parody of sacred norms at *Gay* has to be placed in the context of the changing role of monasteries in local life in Ladakh. In the case of Samstanling monastery, for example, there has been an apparent decline in the number of people electing to be monks. These comprised only 3.5 percent of the population of Tegar village in contrast to the traditional practice of at least one son in each household becoming a monk. Also, as can be seen from the statistics given in the first section of this chapter, the clergy belong to the sphere of the vernacular and sacred languages; the domain that they participate in is that of non-cash, symmetrical exchange, but the system of cash and asymmetrical exchange has begun to exert pressures on the monastic system. For many households, a son joining the monastery is considered an unattractive option, especially in the face of the opportunities opened up for cash occupations outside and within the village; this is true even for poor families. It is also clear to villagers that there are few monks who are dedicated to their vocation, and the monks themselves display an ambivalence with respect to their calling. In recent years there has been at least one case of a monk being derobed in the village, and while it is acknowledged that the Samstanling monastery maintains higher standards than others, in the case of other monasteries, many monks are engaged in mundane pursuits.

Besides this parody of sacred and epic themes, there was another theme in the drama which reflected the properties of *loze*, i.e. the conflicts of a secular world and the relationship of the community (and the monastery) to the state. In the context of the social boycott in 1989-91, the play also voiced other relationships that were normally not voiced publicly in the village – the agitation for Union Territory status, and the conflicts with Muslims and the Jammu and Kashmir state. As was stated earlier, Ladakh was added to the dominions of the ruler of Jammu, Gulab Singh, as a result of his incursions into the region and as a consequence of an agreement with the British in 1846. In 1870, it was decided that a Joint Commissioner would be resident in Leh to supple-ment the authority of the Wazir. In 1948, after British withdrawal, there were hostilities in the region and since then, the area has been a key security region. The political history of this area has been detailed earlier; what is significant for our purpose are the following developments: the conversion of Ladakh from an independent region to a periphery of the nation-state; the transformation of its power structure by the removal of the monarchial system, feudal rents, land reforms and the reduction in the authority of the monasteries; the barriers to the cultural and economic ties of Ladakh with other centres – Tibet, Central Asia and Baltistan; and the subjection of Ladakh to centralized administration from Srinagar and the vicissitudes of Kashmiri politics.

All these events have led to a perception in the local community of neglect by the Jammu and Kashmir state, and oppression by Kashmir (also because of the decline in the powers of the king and the *gompas*) and by Islam. It is this idea of difference and domination *vis-à-vis* the state and Muslims that was voiced in the many songs that were sung during the play. There was an attempt to reverse the perceived asymmetry through parody – of Muslim minstrels, the former Chief Minister, Farooq Abdullah, and so on. Parody and laughter were means to decentre their authority and to create the semantic effect of distance.

The situation of the marginalization of the village economy, the effects of the state and the army on the local population, and the growing importance of cash exchange, also became visible in the case of the accident (Case III, chapter seven), but the crisis affected the tertiary level of integration. Although the children who were hurt by the explosion belonged to households linked patrilineally between the village and Leh, the category that was immediately implicated in the case was that of the kindred. The break in the body of kindred relations was signalled by this case. The two children who were injured in the explosion were Tsepal's son and his wife's younger brother. In terms of kinship terminology and attitudes, both the son and younger brother are referred to by both husband and wife as *nono*, i.e. son or younger brother. The explanation of the accident which was given locally by the *onpo* and other villagers was that the children were affected by *mikha*.

What was the *mikha* due to? Tsepal, the father of one of the boys, was an important member of the LBA in the valley. During the agitation, he had played a fairly important role in the crystallization of the *Tsokspa* in the village and in leading the villagers to the giant rally organized in 1989 in Leh when people from all over Ladakh gathered to demonstrate and garner support for their demands, primarily that of Union Territory status. In 1990-1, the social boycott of Muslims was in force in the Nubra valley as elsewhere, although as for so many other villagers in Nubra, Muslims formed members of Tsepal's kindred category. Although in 1991, his position was far less extreme than before and in terms of the leadership itself, he occupied a fairly centrist position, he was a fairly public persona in the village – organizing village plays, helping the *goba* in decision-making, mediating between the administration and the villagers, etc. and therefore subject to a great deal of talk in the village. Also, his household, although part of the middle rank of peasants in the past, with the acquisition of farming machinery and a shift to commercial crops for sale to the army, and a wife who belonged to the large landlord strata, became a key contender for a different social status in the village.

The household was therefore part of the elite in the village with three new sources of power: access to political power through the LBA, the profits of a cash economy, and the benefits of a bilingual education which made members of the household more articulate than the average villager. One can say that this was fairly representative of most local leaders of the LBA. The family was also subject to talk and speculation for this reason.

The rally in Leh organized by the LBA, and the *Tsokspa* activities in the village, including the social boycott, created a rift in the relations between Muslims and Buddhists in the valley; it brought about a shift in the normal code expressing bilaterality in kindred relations and the norms of social intercourse between the two religious groups. The attempt was to emphasize the distinctness in their cultures and also to reverse the asymmetry in their relations as a result of political and economic processes, with Muslims as the perceived beneficiaries of the new dispensation. Simultaneously, there were also LBA members, such as Tsepal, who were seen as attempting to reverse their position in the village *vis-à-vis* others. The accident in this scheme of things was felt by many Buddhists and Muslims to be a tragic and harsh reversal of fortunes, both for aspiring towards a different status and for political acts which the LBA had engaged in including the rupturing of kindred relations through the social boycott. The sins of the father were seen as visited upon the sons who became substitutes for them. The creation of *storma* by the *onpo* after the accident expresses the cultural belief that *mikha* is a force, and can affect the bodies of persons. One variety of *storma* made by the *onpo* were effigies which, after his rites, came to embody the *mikha* of persons about Tsepal, and because of the continuity of generations, its effect on the children. This was thrown outside the house, ridding the inhabitants of its visceral force. The other variety was to strengthen the *la* of the two boys. The *lhaba's* explanation indicated another fracture in the body of the household. He pointed out that there was a conflict between the *pha-lha* of Diskit's father's household (i.e., her natal household) and that of the *pha-lha* of her household by marriage. This kind of tension for many women who marry virilocally has been referred to earlier. Her younger brother who had come from Leh belonged to her natal household's *pha-lha*, and the *lha* of her new household was seen as jealously exacting a price for her conflicting allegiances. On previous occasions, when she visited her parents' house in Leh, she would fall ill, and a *lhaba* in Leh advised her not to visit the *choskhang* of her parents' house. Diskit sometimes longed for the routines and comforts of her earlier life before marriage, and expressed weariness about her life in the village, a condition that was described as *sunpa*. It is probable that this situation created particular burdens, emotional and physical, on her, which the *lhaba* divined. The continuity of generations in the household, therefore, was subjected to two kinds of strains.

THE SENSORY CIRCUIT OF COMMUNICATION

The oracle was the priest of the village temple. It was explained earlier that the household at the primary level of integration is associated with the priest of the *manekhang*. He visits the household for various rituals, both life-crisis rituals, and those connected with the entire household and its inhabitants. This functionary is appointed by the monastery as a caretaker of the village temple and is sometimes assisted by novices in his tasks. If one person can be said to be in contact with every house in the village in this predominantly Buddhist village (apart from the secular authority of the headman), it was Gelong. He visited and knew, in his two year residence in the village, every household, though he himself belonged to another village. He was mainly engaged by them to perform their monthly *lapsang*, sometimes performing upto three or four every morning. Gelong was, therefore, a perfect mediator in the sense that in terms of the basic unit of social life in the valley, i.e. the household, he was an outsider to its membership by virtue of his celibate and ritual status as a monk; but he was also an insider/participant because of his duties. He was able to move between different domains with relative ease, and while his liminal position was a result of his being a ritual specialist, it also exposed him to the conflicts within the community.

Gelong became an oracle, a vessel of the spirit of Chamshing. The practise of spirit mediumship in Ladakh has some elements which, together with his position as the *manekhang* priest, adds to the inter-calary status of Gelong. The life career of the oracle is sometimes a result of inheriting a spirit, but quite often it is an achieved status. The oracle may be a monastic oracle priest (called *shrungma*) who is possessed by major protective deities of the monastery and is consulted by the monastery, or state authorities as in the past, on regular occasions. He appears on stipulated and auspicious days. The other kind are spirit mediums who are lay, both men and women, who divine by vibrating grain on a drum when possessed, heal with the aid of animal spirits, suck illnesses out of a patient, exorcise, and so on. Such oracles, as said earlier, are selected by a period of 'madness' when there is a loss of self-control, a susceptibility to spirits, a diagnosis by another oracle or a monk, and an initiation into oracle-hood, the legitimacy of which is affirmed by a teacher or the head of a monastery. In Gelong's case, he was not only not a traditional monastery oracle consulted periodically, but he was also not a lay medium. He was a *manekhang* priest 'seized up' by Chamshing abruptly, the first case of a possession by that deity in the valley. It was also not an ascribed status making his position more completely that of an outsider. Gelong's was a novel case when compared to other customary specialists, ritual and otherwise, such as the *larje, onpo* and *lhaba*.

This *Luyar* was part of a particular cultural circuit of communication between persons, bodies, gods, and societies that needs to be described in order to understand his significance for the community. In this circuit, linguistic forms are as much a part of the materiality of life – whether these be processes of work, illness and healing, or webs of social relations – as they encode ideas. That is to say, one cannot make the distinction between the ideational and the material if we are to understand the effect of *Luyar's* 'glossolalia' or spirit possession. Like *mikha*, his words are a force which affect bodies and the community. In this sense, the circuit of communication between the divine and humans is a sensory one, felt viscerally. *Luyar* begins to shake and wheeze when the *lha* descends into his body; his words emerge in a form which is felt to be a sacred dialect communicating itself to others. He sucks out poison from the bodies of persons which embodies their illness or others' ill-intentions, and he breathes on them to remove blocks in their vital organs.

The first pole of this circuit of communication is the *lha*. The term *lha* is used by people for all three categories – local deities, gods of the Buddhist heavens and Tantric gods. The distinction between them is not made as strictly as it is by monks, and people believe that causing offense to the gods results in pollution (*tib*), is a source of misfortune to the person(s) concerned, or leads to an attack by malevolent and angered spirits. Inasmuch as these cults and rituals connected with them can be separated into various categories, four groups of *lhas* exist. These are not necessarily perceived by villagers in a hierarchical relationship, for different *lhas* may dominate for the lay person in any community or for a monk. The four groups of *lhas* are Tantric *yidam* (patron deities) and protector deities who are important in popular religious observances and monastic practices; gods of Buddhist heavens; gods of this world – *lu* (aquatic deities), *nyen* (who live on earth, trees, forests and air), *sadag* (lords of the soil), *tsen* (red spirits of rocks), *gyelpo* (king spirits of evil/failed kings and *lamas*), and *lhas* (a class of benevolent white deities or tamed spirits); malevolent spirits such as the *dud* who are beings opposed to Dharma and feed on flesh; *sa*, who are malevolent planetary deities; and other malevolent beings such as dead or living persons, witches and ghosts.

Usually all those in the third category are thought to have an entourage of malevolent and lesser spirits which are kept under control or released for punishment against persons. This category of beings is the most ambiguous because their position varies between being lower level protectors of Buddhist teachings and destructive, powerful forces which have to be tamed by other powers and solicited by offerings. Chamshing belongs to this class. According to local beliefs, he was an enemy hero tamed by Kesar whence he became a *dharmapala* or *choskyong*, a protector of the faith. A description of his qualities also reveals his ambivalent nature. Chamshing was born of a *yaksa* (celestial being) father with 'copper locks' and a goddess mother with 'blood locks'. His place of residence is a leather castle standing in a sea where the blood of enemies has been spilt. Surrounding this is a copper mountain. Chamshing's body is ruby red, his hair yellow red and aflame like meteors, and he wears a copper helmet and a garland of fifty severed heads. He has a pair of consorts, a male and a female, and is surrounded by eight others who hold a sword and a heart symbolizing the heart of the enemy of the faith, with an instrument to cut it out. Thus, Chamshing belongs to the class of fierce *choskyong* or *dharmapalas* brandishing weapons to crush the enemies of the faith.[15]

Much of the local mythology refers to the taming and combating of wildness. Guru Rinpoche, the divinized Indian teacher who visited Tibet in the eigth century, is said to have overcome local gods and the practitioners of the older Bon faith, establishing monasteries and taming men and spirits simultaneously. Similarly, Padma Sambhava is credited with a magical and shamanic role in bringing Buddhism to Tibet. But many of these forces continue to inhabit trees, rocks, and streams, and communication with these through local cults, spirit possessions, divination, propitiation, and charms against their malevolent effects continues. Protector deities of the village or the monastery have to be solicited and listened to. *Yul-lha* sometimes have a *lhato*, a stone cairn, where they dwell. The *lhatos* are not only places of habitation but also serve to 'fix' these gods whose powers are dangerous for humans if unrestrained. Regular offerings are then made to them in return for their restraint. These offerings are usually *sangs* rituals – the cleansing of the *lhas* with the burning of incense and the offering of prayer flags.[16]

The other pole in the circuit of communication is the term *la* or *sparka* – the life force of a region (felt to inhere in lakes, mountains, etc.) or a person. The life forces of individuals are also felt to dwell in trees, animals and other external objects. In some parts of Tibet, it was customary to plant a tree at the birth of a child (*lashing*), the tree of the child's *la*. I was told a story from the Kesar epic where, in one episode, Kesar managed to kill a demon whose *la* had been hidden under a rock by firing an arrow into it. As explained in some of the earlier cases, the *las* of persons are thought to be susceptible to malevolent and benevolent spirits, ghosts and witches, and through wandering, to result in illness. To strengthen the *la* of a person such as the head of a household, a string of prayer flags is tied around the roof of the house. This concept of *la* is associated with the local gods in the form of personal protective deities, *gowe-lha*, who are a set of five protective gods born at the same time as the child. The god of life resides in the heart; the male god resides in the right armpit; the female god resides in the left armpit; the enemy god resides on the right shoulder; and there is the god of the locality.[17] This list is not standardized and varies from region to region. Two of the *lhas* associated with the *la* of the person are also associated with the household – the *po-lha* with the shrine/earthen container where incense is burned daily on the roof or in the courtyard (this *lha* is associated with the men of the house and household defense); and the *mo-lha* or *khyim-lha* who resides in the central pillar of the house (associated with the women and the family's well-being). The *la* of a person can travel at night; if a person is frightened, or if he eats impure foods, his *la* may be weakened. This idea of the *la* is to be separated from the idea of soul (*namshes*) and heartmind (*sems*) which has a technical meaning in Mahayana Buddhism. If the *la* is weakened beyond a certain degree, illness and death and, therefore, the loss of *namshes* will result. But the life-force does not have an effect on one's future life: it is an entity which has an existential force in one's current social being and the system of cultural communication.

There is a continuity between the *lha* of a region and the *la* of a person. The *yul-lha* affects and is affected by the actions, thoughts and words of people in the village. Each becomes a boundary where inner and outer forces, both benevolent and malevolent, meet, and where wildness and power have to be tamed or restrained and brought into some kind of order. It is this continuity which makes protection against malevolent or unrestrained power necessary and requires that the life force of a region or person be strengthened. Relationships of power or social decay and order are never static, however, and have to be constantly negotiated. Thus in Yangchen's possession, a lack of social order and an infringement of customary relations was perceived as one of the reasons for the invasion of her body (through a weakened life-force) by a harmful being. The life-force of a person is weakened by a number of causes. In cases from my fieldwork, it was believed to have occurred through *mikha*; through the neglect of performance of customary rituals thus offending the *lhas*; or the lack of virtuous action especially those central to Buddhism, i.e. the five abstentions – not to kill, not to steal, not to commit adultery, not to become intoxicated, and not to speak falsely. Further, offending spirits by cutting down a tree, ploughing the earth, and so disturbing them; and the overpowering of a person by superior *las* of ghosts, witches, gods, or malevolent spirits also weakened a person. Gelong's *la* was overpowered by the *lha* of Chamshing whose priest Gelong was.

The category of the *lhas* of monastic Buddhism have received more attention by scholars than other categories of *lhas* in Ladakh, the latter being usually considered under the rubric of 'folk' or popular pre-Buddhist practices. It is gradually being recognized that such *lhas* as the *yul-lhas* have a much more complex relationship to both monastic Buddhism and geographical territory. Monastic Buddhism has to contend with *yul-lhas*, for example, through an entire series of rites at different times of the year. These may be *skangsol* ceremonies for particular *yul-lhas* in the region; the annual changing of the clothes of the *lhas* (usually at the New Year); special rites performed as propitiation for various transgressions, for a good agricultural season, etc.; or *skangsol* performed at the time of vow-taking monastic ordinations and the appointment of the acting head of the monastery or the proctor. It would appear from this fact, and the fact that those who are born within the territory of the *yul-*

lha have to contend with their effect on their region and their lives, that monastic Buddhism has to constantly negotiate its relationship with these *lhas*.[18] While it is true that the territory of the *yul-lha* is bounded, and its influence is only on the current productive and reproductive lives of persons in the region (since it has no influence over one's next birth), and that it appears that certain persons such as a reincarnated monk (*rinpoche*) are exempt from its control (even perhaps controlling it), it is nevertheless important to consider that its power is far-reaching and requires constant efforts and vigilance on part of the laity and the monastery to keep the ill-effects of such power within bounds.

Chamshing, in this study, can be seen to possess many of the properties of the *yul-lha* like whom he is a fierce god, 'civilized' through the efforts of Buddhist practioners. In merely looking at *yul-lhas* as having been tamed by a regular system of propitiations, the novelty of Gelong's possession by Chamshing escapes us. It was explained that there are two systems of exchange in the villages. Customary processes of economic and linguistic transactions were described as belonging to the system of symmetrical exchange. Those processes brought about by the commercialization of social life, state formation, etc. giving rise to certain other linguistic and economic transactions were described as occurring within the system of asymmetrical exchange. Both these systems involve the movement of groups, persons, products and words, through social space. These also have effects on bodies and are embodied. This embodiment is particularly evident during moments of conflict, and as I tried to show, the presence of two systems of exchange has created fractures in the fabric of social existence at various levels: the household at the primary level; the village and the monastery at the secondary level; and the kindred at the tertiary level. At each level, the conflict between the two was embodied in the bodies of certain persons – Yangchen through her 'madness', the monks through their parody, and Tsepal's two children through amputation and burns. This is a crisis which is as sensory as it is embedded in the web of social transactions. It is similar with the possession of Gelong by Chamshing. In a society which is based on cross-cutting ties, unity is more a moral unity than a political one. But the moral unity is experienced also sensorily in the circuit of communication.

This connection will become visible when we see what meaning the possession of Gelong had, what were the types of cases in which he

Figure 8 : Classification of Chamshing's Words and Acts and their Significance.

Event	Calendar Dates	Ritual Significance	Person/ Social Unit Addressed	Type of Action and Speech
I. Declaration of Chamshing's identity and divination of the return of villagers from *Gyagar* after Kalachakra	2 February, 1991	2nd half of 12th month: Dark powers are in ascendance and positive ones hidden. Fighting spirit of society must come forth at the critical moment of transition to utmost degree to drive out evil. Faced by uncertainty of coming year, man chooses not to abdicate, but oppose darkness. In Tibet, martial games, overturning of social order by monks and ritual of exorcisms begin. What is evil and hidden and what is good are revealed. Time when agriculture, hunting and pastoralism will begin again.	Village	Declaration and divination
II. At *lapsang* at Pinchimik, declares He was light seen by a soldier on Siachen glacier	Before 15th February 1991 (end of *Dawa Chuknispa*)		Household member	Declaration
III. 'Saw' arrival of a soldier's letter to his wife	Before 15 February 1991		Household member	Divination
IV. Divination of date of Shras Rinpoche's arrival	Before 15 February 1991		Monastery	Divination

Event	Calendar Dates	Ritual Significance	Person/ Social Unit Addressed	Type of Action and Speech
V. Curing of affliction of an old lady at a *lapsang*	18 and 19 February 1991 (same time as Yarma festival - 1st and 2nd day of *Tangpo*)	Tibetan Buddhist calendar begins in 1st month (about 15 February). Religious calendar mimics Buddhist doctrine which divides Buddha's life into 12 acts.	Household member	Healing
VI. Fast/Silence by *Luyar*; showed signs of his possession	22 February (6th day of *Tangpo*)	Calendar reaches its climax in four of these - birth, enlightenment, setting in motion of wheel of law, entry into Nirvana. All 4 are celebrated in 4th month. In addition, there is the famous miracle of Sravasti when Buddha multiplied himself and vanquished heretics. 10-15th day is the anniversary of Sravasti; this follows the *mon lam*, (the Great Vow) to spread the law. The first event of defeating the heretics combines defeating evil and the intransigent enemy forces, while second affirms moral order.	Household member	Declaration
VII. Drama day. Asks Tsokspa member to prevent fights and prohibits drinking in *manekhang*	24th and 25th February		Villagers	Prohibition

Event	Calendar Dates	Ritual Significance	Person/ Social Unit Addressed	Type of Action and Speech
VIII. Keeping of fast and vows by villagers; prayers in *manekhang*; Chamshing angry about moral laxity of villagers - drinking, selling goats/sheep to army, theft	27th and 28th February 1991 (14th and 15th day of *Tangpo*)		Villagers	Prohibition and threats of punishment
IX. Death feast; Chamshing berates people for not replacing stolen earring; threatens punishment for speaking falsely	1 March 1991 (16th day of *Tangpo*)		Villagers	Prohibitions and punishment
X. Berates troublemakers for leaving cigarette stubs, breaking prayer wheels	22 April (8th day of *Sumpa*)		Villagers	Prohibitions and punishment
XI. Cures animals and persons, rids houses and people of *temos*, recovers lost objects	End of April 1991	Around 15th day (*Chonga*) of 3rd month : *Chonga* is sacred to the memory of the preaching of the Kalachakra Tantra for the first time.	Individual households	Healing

Event	Calendar Dates	Ritual Significance	Person/ Social Unit Addressed	Type of Action and Speech
XII. Pierces his body with sword, cuts his tongue and sends blood to monastery as sacrifice. Villagers beg for forgiveness.	27 May 1991	*Chupji* of *Jipa* (14th day of 4th month) is the one that contains the four most important acts of the Buddha, 7th day is festival of his birth.	Villagers	Sacrfice and asking for forgiveness/offering of remorse by villagers
XIII. Prayers for enlightment in *manekhang*, people offer obeisances and 'Shakspa'. Buddha's *Zatpa* (acts and words) are read out. Case of unjust accusation against man by shopkeepers; fight and reconciliation between two village hamlets.		15th day of *Jipa* is the day of Buddha's enlightenment and entry into Nirvana.	Village hamlets	Offering of remorse by villagers

intervened, what was their relationship to the ritual calendar and social crises. The acts of Chamshing fell into a pattern which was in concert with the traditional ritual calendar. These are tabulated in Figure 8.

The Tibetan Buddhist religious calendar in essentials follows the precepts laid down in the Vinaya, texts referring to rules of discipline in Buddhism, along with various celebrations of important events in the life of the Buddha. This is divided into twelve 'acts' (*zatpa*), or sometimes eight, and the calendar reaches its climax in four of these – birth, Enlightenment, setting into motion the Wheel of Law, and entry into nirvana. All these occur in the fourth month. In addition, there are three more events which are added to the principal acts: the festival commemorating his descent from heaven (to which he had ascended to preach the Law to his mother); the Sravasti miracle in which he multiplied himself into an innumerable series of manifestations to defeat the heretics and opponents of the Law; and the preaching of the Kalachakra Tantra, a famous Tantric cycle revealed at Sri Dhanyakataka in India. The main festivals of this calendar are:

First month: the tenth to the fifteenth days celebrate the miracle of Sravasti. This is inserted into the New Year festival (*Losar*) and recalls the defeat of the enemies of the Law and the intransigent forces in the lands in which Buddhism spread.

Fourth month: the seventh day is the festival of the birth of the Buddha; the fifteenth day the festival of his Enlightenment and entry into nirvana.

Sixth month: the fourth day is the feast of the first sermon.

Ninth month: the descent of the Buddha from heaven.

Many of these festivals reveal the incorporation of old local celebrations and rituals; for example in the *Mon Lam* festival, the 'Great Vow', which occurs from the fourth to the twenty-fifth day of the first month. The vow or promise to spread and affirm the Law is tied up with older customs of exorcism and special cult acts to drive out the evil of the old year. The transition from one year to another represents a moment of danger. The community and cults around the expulsion of harmful forces combine with the liturgy and ethics of Buddhism since such actions aimed at driving out evil, result in good karma. In Tibet, the Festival of Good Omen is celebrated to mark the end of one annual cycle and the beginning of another. For two weeks from the thirtieth day of the twelfth month to the fifteenth day of the first month, trumpets and shawms sound to chase away hostile powers and usher in the benevolent ones. In the second half of the last month, rituals also take place to ease the way to Enlightenment for living beings and to destroy demonic forces. It is a time when the monks and lay persons jointly struggle for the good of the community. After a rite of closure and expulsion of evil and old values, there is a fresh period of promise and regeneration. A scapegoat figure is used in these rituals on whom are discarded outworn values and in the interregnum, contests are held and there is a descent of *lhas* onto mediums. In the cult, acts and liturgical practices of the Gelug order of Tsong Khapa, who introduced the *Mon Lam* festivities, the old traditions are carried on in a new guise. The *Mon Lam*, however, does not merely have the task of ensuring a good new year, but also an esoteric meaning given by the Gelug school. The community is situated in a period of decline when evil grows and the teachings of the Buddha are becoming obscure. It is necessary not only that this darkness (also one of personal ignorance and non-knowing) is overcome by burning effigies, making offerings, including the offering of ignorance and defilement in the fire of wisdom, but also that the community helps in the saving activity of the next Buddha, the Maitreya. The calendar, *en toto*, becomes a chain of actions that are undertaken to bring blessings and a renewal of the doctrine, and a way of preparing for the coming of the future Buddha.[19]

If one follows the events of *Luyar's* glossolalia, there are recognizable clusters of cases. His first possession occurred on 1st or 2nd February. 2nd February falls in the latter half of the twelfth month of the Buddhist calendar before the beginning of the Buddhist New Year. This period is considered to be a menacing one when the powers of evil are at their height and the misfortune of the previous year concentrated. The end of the twelfth prior to the New Year, following the possession of Gelong by Chamshing, was a time of declaration and divination.

The first month of the Tibetan Buddhist calendar which begins about the 15th of February (the time of the ancient Sravasti miracle of the Buddha, the affirming of the Law and the destruction of evil), was a period of laying down of moral prohibitions and healing on the part of *Luyar*. This pattern of actions on the part of *Luyar* mimicked the sacred calendar and continued into the fourth month.

The fourth month contains the key episodes in the life of the Buddha. The fifteenth day is the day of his Enlightenment and attainment of nirvana. In the village, around *jipe chonga*, there was the offering of His blood in anger and the offering of remorse by the people. The bodies of persons were sites of affliction in many cases and the body of the community, the site of social malaise: this, Chamshing tried to combat and correct by reverting to a sacred conception of time and calendric events. The *Luyar* became a vessel, body or support of the mobile spirit, and acted by magically recreating the original acts of the Buddha, Padma Sambhava or Guru Rinpoche. This kind of enactment takes place in *mdos* and *gto* rituals of protection against and exorcism of evil powers. In these rituals, offerings of a scapegoat or ransom are made to appease evil powers and an imagined confrontation takes place between the exorcist and these powers. This is also the case when *chams* dancers replay the destruction of the dark Langdarma, a Tibetan king (838-42) who persecuted the Buddhist community and whose reign of terror was explained by the othodox tradition as a result of a demon taking possession of the king.

However, the centrality of *Luyar's* possession and glossolalia was that it reopened the question of the relationship between the spirit and the body, an issue primary to Buddhism. In my understanding, apart from the cultural importance of Padma Sambhava's or an exorcist's taming of wild/evil forces, or the Buddha's vanquishing of heretics or the placating of the *lhas* of a *yul*, there is an epistemic issue within the event of Gelong's possession. It allowed the community to experience in a sensory form the circuit of communication between the *lha* and the *la*. Between the declaration of Chamshing's presence in February 1991, to Gelong's return to the monastery in June 1991, all pathways in the community led to the figure of *Luyar*. Gelong's artless visage was transformed into an almost graven image. Webs of relations in the community converged around him, and reforming themselves, diverged from His presence. Unlike the *Yultsa lhato* who is ritually propitiated once a year and whose mediation is sought for a variety of traditional concerns and afflictions in the village – the health of the children in the village, a good crop, or warding off certain demons – Chamshing's presence was necessary to struggle with demonic forces, both inner and outer, which were radically new. People, words, products, and intentions had suffered displacement from customary styles of living and feeling. 'It is like being in *Bardo*', one villager expressed. It is a region between this world and the next, between one body and the other, and in order that stations on the journey can be recognized, signs are necessary.

How the problem of the word and the flesh, or spirit and matter, humans and God, this world and that world, are resolved depends on the society or religion under consideration. Docetism is a term associated generally with the second century Christian heresy that the Saviour's body was only a semblance or an ethereal substance.[20] There is, by this standard, a strong docetist tendency in Buddhism. It is sometimes a question of emphasis because the stress on the historical Buddha, metaphysical speculations about his personality as a Tathagatha and its relationship with the truth he revealed, as well as the practical moral teachings of the Master and obedience to the rules of the community, make docetism less in Theravada Buddhism. In Mahayana Buddhism, by contrast, the tendency to idealize the Buddha and see his historicity in connection with the universal Buddha (*Dharmakaya*), the creation of multiple Buddhas, etc. makes docetism prevalent in later Mahayana schools.[21] Among the first Buddhists, the belief was that the Buddha, in the course of numberless lives, accumulated the necessary conditions for the realization of the unreality of the phenomenal being of the world and thus 'awoke' in human condition. The earliest Buddhists were not docetists. Those who believed in docetism were those who identified the Buddha with the Dharma and therefore stated that men only saw his 'fabricated body', the *nirmanakaya*.[22] Again, the conceptualization in Vajrayana Buddhism of the *trikaya* (three bodies) scheme allows reality to be experienced in terms of Tantric deities as well as mediated through shamanic practitioners, healers or diviners.[23]

In the case of Gelong's possession and glossolalia, this issue of docetism was enacted in a visceral way. In the first period (declaration and divination), what was established was the separation of the person into two parts – the body, present in the case of *Luyar* and the life-force which was absent in his case. The word *la* has been dealt with earlier. If someone is ill, his *la* is said to have become weak; if someone is dying, his *la* is said to be wandering from his body; if someone is possessed, his *la* is said to be overpowered by another one; and so on. Rituals exist to deal with these circumstances. This *la* is mobile and can take up residence in any object. Although the *Luyar's* body functioned as a support, his life-force was replaced by that of Chamshing, a supernatural power. In general, these powers can be said to be of two kinds – good/white and evil/black, locally divided into the *lha* and *dre*, respectively. During the period of divination and declaration, what was established was the dual nature of man and of supernatural powers.

The second period dealing with afflictions and prohibitions signalled the relationship between the *la* and the body. A person's affliction was related to the weakening of the *la* certainly, but this weakening was through impurities and pollution of certain kinds. Illness has a physical basis but its cause is also to be sought for in an impurity, a shadow or a defilement. These impurities or shadows can originate in sinful actions, in eating impure foods, burnt foods, substances used in the house producing bad smells, destroying spaces where the spirits dwell, and so forth. The prohibitions that Chamshing pronounced for the village as a whole in this period of healing of afflictions also point to the relationship between the body and the *la* because all the afflictions were the result of contravening certain prohibitions and the resulting impurity. This also points to the relationship between the social and the individual body. Not only were the *las* of persons weakened, but also the *la* of the region by the collective actions of the villagers – the use of intoxicants like rum and *chang*, smoking, the desecration of sacred spaces, the sale of goats and sheep to the army, speaking falsely, and stealing. Some of these are traditional Buddhist prohibitions, but according to Chamshing, it was a sign of a decline in moral standards, a symptom of the current social malaise brought about by new cultural forces.

The third period of offering blood as sacrifice to the *lhas* of the monastery on the part of *Luyar* and the offering of repentance on the part of the villagers establishes a link, both symbolic and real, between the inner and the outer realms. The *lha*, a protector of Dharma and a symbol of collective well-being as opposed to the forces threatening it, had a correspondence in the local belief that each man has in him two spirits which exist simultaneously – one, the embodiment of the good and the other of evil. At the moment of death, these two become concrete and before the the god of death, Shinje, become a counsel for his defense and an avenger, respectively. In these eschatological represen-tations, the dividing of the conscience into two and its embodiment in a defending god and avenging demon, are ethical preoccupations.[24] This idea is conveyed through the image of a mirror, a balance, a register, and so on. In this phase, a correspondence was set up between inner *la/lha/dre* and outer *la/lha/dre*. If the sacrifice or the offering of blood was intended to be a mediation on the part of the oracle, there was also an attempted mediation by the people for their actions in a number of ways: gifting prayer flags, *khataks*, etc. and also non-materially by the offering of remorse. The possession of the priest not only dramatized but also embodied the relationship between the spirit and the body, society and the individual, humans and gods, inner and outer spheres, and good and evil.

CONCLUSION – CODES AND MEDIUMS

Studies on spirit possession in the Tibetan-speaking area make the distinction between High and Low, clerical and shamanistic, and new and archaic religions. Oracles are seen as belonging to the latter category. Tibetan oracles are sometimes related to the older 'base' of the Bon faith onto which Lamaism was grafted. Some authors separate it from Siberian or Central Asian shamans because the latter engage in a journey of the soul to another realm while the Tibetan oracles are mediums. There is no unity of terminology – they may be called mediums, oracles, or shamans. In general, the anthropological writing on spirit possession is part of a general theory of magical belief and practice where the ritual agent mediates between this world and the other world. Spirit possession is generally held to be a collective representation which addresses social conflicts, ritual uncleanliness, and the transgression of social norms.

While spirit possession is usually viewed within a dramaturgical frame in the Himalayan region, most authors have not addressed the issue of the linguistic form that the utterance takes during possession. There are two broad schools of thinking on glossolalia or spirit possession in this regard. The first is the behavioural approach which sees 'speaking in tongues' as a non-communicative form of vocalization and, therefore, essentially, non-linguistic. Although the utterance is accompanied by kinetic and sensory indices like somnambulism, hysteria or hypnotism, the utterance itself is held not to be a language reproducing syntax or semantics as understood by linguistics.[25] The second approach is based on the *oeuvre* inaugurated by M.M. Bakhtin's work.[26] This conceives of society as a contradictory, polysemic world where different 'voices' speak different tongues. In religious discourse, there might be all kinds of voices speaking the holy word – deity, demon, shaman, or astrologer. In treating spirit possesssion in this second manner, the basic assumption is that society is not separable from language. But language has to be seen not only as a symbolic system, whether this is based on a dramaturgical or dialogical model, but also as a 'material segment' of reality, along with physical bodies, instruments of production and forms of consciousness. There is a connection between language and the body, and the body politic, which is a relationship perceived and felt by communities in Nubra.[27] It is not that the oracle merely uses words and creates symbols that the afflicted employs to translate his or her distress and then undergoes some ideational catharsis which exhibits the struggle between two 'voices'. Rather, in the healing and mediation process, the actual sensory basis of the illness is altered and a substantive change occurs. Forces are removed from bodies, and others are instilled in it. Possession and healing, therefore, are not merely ways of acting, or symbolic systems, but tactile, experiential and embodied communications. The same is true of processes of struggle and renewal in the community. Dark forces (brought about by speech or deed) are expelled, and offerings of blood and remorse staunch the spread of the social malaise.

The emphasis on transactional behaviour, based on ethnocentric assumptions, has led to explanations of exchanges of various kinds – marriage, work or products – within utilitarian and economistic frames. For the initial purposes of analysis, I described two systems of exchanges in the valley, composed of work processes and marriage alliances, linking households together at different levels of integration. These systems of exchange were also shown to be related to language use in the villages. But the sphere of language and other exchanges are not connected merely in some layered form, but as the case studies in chapter seven show, they are linked viscerally. Linguistic forms, like the exchange and the ingestion of food, or any other product, come to inhere in people's bodies and act on them like a force. In this sense, language, the body and the community are not organized 'architecturally', one above the other, but interpenetrate each other. The field of linguistic force lies both within and in between bodies, households and goods. Again, ritual processes like possession, or social events like feasts and dramas in the villages, are sensorily linked to laughter, fear, tears, and pain. In the villagers' own reckoning, a real alleviation of distress or any other feeling arising out of social processes takes place. To capture the nature of this kind of sensibility, the language of social description being generally ill-equipped to deal with the 'sense' of a culture, requires new modes of analyses. Through the various chapters, I have tried to show that exchange and meaning are part of a sensory circuit of communication, and languages, like bodies and products, have a real presence.

The cases described and analysed in this and the previous chapters are an attempt to convey a particular sensibility that is voiced and embodied in the life of persons and communities. This sensibility is a 'modern' one in the sense that it is embedded in the processes of transformation of the Ladakh region in the post-1947 period; in particular, the effects of state formation. Most studies about Ladakh, rooted in geo-political and Orientalist concerns, have chosen to ignore the structural cleavages that run through the community as a result of new forces and the release of emotional and physical energies. What directions these take, what concerns they express, what anxiety, pain, and creativity ensues, cannot be captured by looking merely at traditional ritual forms. I have deliberately chosen such cases which encapsulate the displacement of persons, things, and feelings as a result of new processes in the community. Not only is there a refashioning of the world of the villagers – through dress, new foods, the shrinking of distances, Hindi films, or occupational opportunities – but also a remaking of the sense of the sacred.

This sacred sphere no longer inheres merely in the locations of a traditional culture – *lhatos*, monasteries, or mosques – or through certain prescribed modes of ritual action – *skangsol* ceremonies, *lapsangs*, and so on. The alteration in the territory of the sacred and the need for fresh limits to be drawn for ritual action is captured in the belief expressed by the Khardung *lhaba* who explained: 'With the Chinese occupation of Tibet, *lhatos* were destroyed along with the homes of villagers. Not only did people become refugees, but so did the gods. These exiled gods are now seeking habitation in people's bodies'. Along with the 'inner refugees' of cultural change and nation-state formation in the Ladakh region, Chamshing sought a home in Gelong's body. This home-coming and visitation were accompanied by signs and events which were designed towards the creation of a new home and world for the community as well. It came as the culmination of a series of cases which signalled the lines of fracture of the old world. A recasting of the bodies of persons and the social body, the struggle with the demons of change and social decay, was experienced in the four long months of the winter of 1990-1.

Notes

1. There are no recent census figures available for linguistic practices in the region. Zutshi 1994 states that out of a total of 105291 persons in the Ladakh division in 1971, 53.90 percent are Ladakhi speakers, 37.07 percent, Balti speakers, and the rest are speakers of Dogri, Hindi or Gojri, Kashmiri, Punjabi and Shina. In 1981, out of a total of 134372 persons, 52.12 percent were Ladakhi speakers, 34.89 percent, Balti speakers and, the rest, speakers of the other languages.
2. See Koshal 1979:1-4 et passim.
3. For example, Pandit (1988:3-7), who classifies the various types of language contact situations in India.
4. c.f. Koshal 1979.

5. Other authors have drawn attention to this factor as well. See for example, Gal 1987; Irvine 1989; and Woolard 1985. Ripley 1996 also points to the centrality of food in Ladakh, its ability to bear different levels of linguistic and social meaning, and its implication in different processes of exchange.

6. See Turner 1968:26.

7. See ibid.,:152.

8. See Volosinov 1987 [1927]:85.

9. See ibid., : 79.

10. Linguistics has been aware of the phenomena of code-switching since Ferguson 1959 and Weinreich 1963 whose studies showed that speakers could switch from one language to another according to appropriate changes in the speech situation (and interlocutors or topics) and that society could contain various varieties of a language according to different domains. Others since then have added an ethnographic dimension to code-switching practices and a socio-cultural context to language contact situations (see for instance, Fishman 1972; Gumperz 1982; Hymes 1971; Saville-Troike 1982)

11. See Gluckman 1954 and Turner 1969.

12. See Aggarwal's powerful analysis of the *skyinjug* in her thesis (1994, chapter six, pp. 198-236). I owe many of the observations in this paragraph to her.

13. My ideas about the carnival are derived chiefly from Bakhtin's classic work on the elements of the carnival (Bakhtin 1968 [1965]).

14. See Aris 1988:1-45 et passim.

15. See Nebesky-Wojkowitz 1993 [1956]: 88-93.

16. This is an important thesis in Day 1990 and Samuel 1993. Samuel cites two interesting stories similar to the one told about Chamshing in Nubra, i.e. the intervention of a fierce *yul-lha* against enemy forces, in this case against the Chinese in the Tibetan-Chinese wars in this century (ibid.p.103-4).

17. See Tucci 1980 [1970]:200.

18. Mills 1995 recognizes this significant feature; this is also acknowledged by Tucci (1980 [1970]:163-212) in his chapter on folk religion in Tibet.

19. I follow Tucci in the interpretation of many of the festivities of the religious calendar of Tibetan Buddhism. (See Stein 1972 [1962]:211-8 et passim; Tucci 1960 [1970]:147-52 et passim).

20. For example, in the first period of Christianity, docetism was the corollary of some Gnostic systems. These took from the Gospel, the name of Jesus as the leading champion of the world of the spirit, if not the final emanation from God, and because the world of matter was made by the powers of darkness and evil, it was believed that the Saviour could have no body. All references to his flesh were in the domain of mere appearance. Some schools solved the problem in another way: by denying any essential union between Christ, the spiritual saviour and Jesus, the man, foreshadowing Nestorianism that sees the Incarnation as uniting within himself two persons, the Logos and the man. This makes the life which is an example to men, an apparent one. There were also sects that believed that at birth, Christ received another body, a spiritual one and when his material body

was crucified, his soul put on this other body (Hastings 1927 [1912]:832-5 et passim).

21. See ibid., : 835-6.
22. See Filliozat 1991:128-129.
23. See Samuel 1994.
24. Tucci 1980[1970]:195.
25. See, for instance, Cutten 1927; Goodman 1971; 74; 76; Malony and Lovekin 1985.
26. Mumford 1990 looks at the interaction between Tibetan monks and Gurung shamans within the frame of Bakhtin's work. For other areas, Boddy 1994 reviews some of the main studies on spirit possession using concepts drawn from the Bakhtinian repertoire.
27. My analysis builds on such earlier studies, though not for Ladakh, such as by Comaroff 1985; Desjarlais 1992; and Taussig 1987.

Epilogue

'Separated all the skin and meat, but left the tail.'

– A Nubra proverb

In the summer of 1993, I returned to Ladakh for a month, a period of two years after I left the valley of my fieldwork. I was in the process of writing my Ph.D. dissertation and felt the need to again walk down the roads and by lanes of Leh bazaar, and the paths through the fields and by the houses of the villages I had resided in. I also came to Leh to present a paper at the Sixth Colloquium of the International Association of Ladakh Studies held in Leh that year.

While I listened to papers being presented by participants there, a good number of whom were Ladakhis, and exchanged notes with my age-set of fellow researchers, I mused over my new role. It was not till I reached Tegar village some days later, crossing once again the Khardung pass by bus as I had done numerous times in the year 1990–1, that I understood in what ways relationships had changed. As usual, a crowd of villagers had gathered on the highway which passes through the village to greet the bus. There were some men from the Ladakh Scouts returning to the village and their homes for a few days; a few monks from the Samstanling *gompa*; villagers who had gone to Leh for their shopping or to visit relatives or the office of the District Commissioner; bags of flour, biscuits, a few chickens; and me. I asked myself wistfully would anyone remember me?

A couple of children shouted – "*Ani* is here!' I was, it seemed, no longer *pomo* (girl child), but *ani*, aunt. I was taken to the house of a *phaspun* member of my family, because members of my family were away from the village that day. I spent time talking to the *abbe* there, a ninety-two year old woman, who had been my main informant for the genealogies of village families, *Abbe*, after she had shed a few tears upon my arrival, wanted to fill in details of new marriages, births and deaths in my charts. Was I still not married and when was I going to bring my family to see her? After a while, Tsewang Lullu, another companion, arrived and we caught up on the news of the past few years. The highway was being tarred, he told me, though the dam at Sumur village had still not been completed, and the wind-mill put up by the army had fallen down. My school-teacher friend, Tsering Yangchen, and the nurse, Lhamo, had been transferred to other villages. 'And what of Gelong?'I asked.

Gelong arrived a day later, quieter and more withdrawn than I remembered him. He was no longer the *manekhang* priest, but was now a monk at the monastery. It appeared that a month or so after I left Nubra valley, Chamshing had stopped visiting him. He was now an ordinary monk in the *gompa*, no longer *luyar*, the vessel of god. He looked curiously at the photographs I had brought with me taken at the time of his possession. All through the possession of Gelong by Chamshing, the latter allowed the *Luyar's girgan* (the teacher of the vessel of god, i.e. me) to take photographs of different periods of the embodiment; indeed, masterfully demanded it. But he examined with greater interest the ones of my home and my family. He said he was planning to ask for a position at Bylekuppe, a Tibetan refugee settlement in Karnataka which has a large number of monks from Ladakh. He would come and visit me in Bangalore, he said. I can never walk down the area of the main bus stand in Bangalore and see a couple of Buddhist monks in their yellow and red clothes without wondering whether Gelong will make a reciprocal visit. What kind of role reversal would that involve?

In the house that I had lived in for one long year very little had changed. The boys were bigger, the mustard grinding mill had more business, and it was suggested that on my next visit I study the solar electrification that had been done of many of the villages in the Nubra valley.

News had filtered through the village that the *Dikanbo* (writer) was back and I was hosted at various houses for dinner and lunch. I rather sadly reflected that indeed the intense period of my fieldwork was really over – I was now a writer of books, not a pupil in a culture which had been generous and kind to me as I ineptly struggled with their language and their tools (the sight of me carrying a basket with vegetables never failed to make them smile). They never once let it be known that I may have been interfering in private matters, and at all times were tolerant of my numerous questions. Some things had changed in the village too, at first not apparent to the eye. I saw Fatima, the daughter of the Sunni Muslim family in Tegar walking down the road past the *manekhang* with her closest friend, a Buddhist girl. The boycott against Muslims had long since been called off and exchanges of all kinds – of farm tools, social visits, and so on – had begun again. Now all the talk in the village was about whether the Indian government would hold true to its promise of Hill Council status for Ladakh and what that would mean in terms of elections from various areas. I was also questioned if news about the opening of trade links between Ladakh and Tibet could be corroborated. If commercial intercourse began again, it might mean that local products – barley, apricots, and wool – would have a market once again as it had done earlier. I was told that this year there would be no play from the monastery, but some village youth were planning to stage a 'modern' drama about Ladakhi life.

Work in the fields continued as usual. The trees were full of apricots, the barley and mustard stalks stood at half-height, and the *dzos* were up in the mountain pastures with some of the village men. As I made my way by the postal truck to Hundar village a few days later, I found that changes had occurred there as well. The *abba* of the family had retired from his position at the school though he continued to be the priest at the *masjid*. There was news that the Sunni *Arghuns* were also to be given Scheduled Tribe status along with others in Ladakh, something which would go a long way in establishing good faith between the two religious communities.

When I left Nubra after some days, I reflected on the various routes that I had taken in the culture of the villages of this valley. A researcher can only take those paths which the society that she is studying allows her to. A shaman, like my friend, Gelong, is in part a sociologist who divines the mysterious workings of his society and the travails of persons in it. I could only allow a certain loss of my soul and let myself be inhabited by the voices of others. I will never know how thorough that soul-loss was: did I manage to understand what were the causes for change, grief, or humour? Was I able to uncover the hidden rationale for villagers doing what they did in their culture? I can only hope that beyond the linguistic, discursive, economical enterprise that writing about cultures has become, I have shown that culture is an experiencing, soulful being which once in a while becomes the privilege of the sociologist to witness.

The day I left Leh for Delhi, *Abba* Kalon, in whose house I had spent many days, had left for a meeting with the LBA. Halfway down the incline from the house, he turned the jeep back to wish me goodbye. Gruffly he hugged me, while I tearfully said I would come back and visit. 'There have been many travellers here, *pomo*, most forget us and few come back' he said. I hope this book has been a return that you understand, *Abba*.

Glossary of Local Terms

Aakhri Jumma – the last Friday prayer during Ramzan
Abad-i-de – land under settlement
abba (and appa) – father, mother's elder sister's husband, father's elder
     brother
abbe – mother's mother or father's mother
ache – elder sister
acho – elder brother
agu – father's younger brother, mother's younger sister's husband
ajang – mother's elder and younger brother
Akhikat – occasion of naming child among Muslims
akhun – Muslim priest
amma – mother, mother's elder sister, father's elder brother's wife
ani – father's younger and elder sister, mother's brother's wife
Arghun – generally those of mixed descent, but here in the book offspring
    of Ladakhi Buddhist women and Kashmiri Muslim men
azan – Muslim prayer call

Babas – costumed figures who appear at New Year at Khalaste village
Bag-pa – masked persons who appear at New Year at Tegar
Balti – people from Baltistan
Bandobast – land settlement
Bardo – intermediate realm between this world and the other world
beda – minstrel
begar – labour for carriage requirements
bo – a wooden mug used as a measure
Bodhi (Bhoti) – Tibetan, literary Ladakhi
Botos – a term sometimes used for Ladakhi Buddhists

bukhari – room heater using wood
bum – kernel
Bumskor – a ritual where scriptures are taken around the settlement by
        monks and laymen, usually in the sixth Buddhist month

chams – monastic drama or mime
chang – barley beer
Changpas – pastoralists, especially of Changthang
cholok – joke; literally, the Dharma reversed
chomo – nun
chorten – place for sacred relics
chos – scripture, Dharma, the holy word
choskhang – altar
choskyong – protectors of religious law
chospun – ritual siblings
chotpa – dough offering of good (spiritual) forces
chonga – fifteenth
chuknispa – twelfth
chukshikpa – eleventh
chulda – orchard
chupji – fourteenth
chupa – tenth
churspon – officer in charge of the irrigation system
churuk – sixteenth
chutayi – boiled dumplings

da – arrow
dawa – moon, also used to refer to lunar month
Dharmakaya – universal Buddha
dharmapala – protector of the faith
dikanbo – writer
dogpa – nomad, shepherd
Dolma Yudos storma – effigies to strengthen life-force of a person
dorje – metal thunder bolt
dre – demon/malevolent spirit
dua – prayer
duba – hermit/mad saint

dud – malevolent spirits who feed on flesh
dug – sorrow
dukhang – altar room of temple or monastery
duniya – this world
dunpa – seventh
dzo – male cross between yak and cow

fagir namaaz – dawn prayers
fitr – a tithe given to the poor during Id

Galdan Namchot – Tsong Khapa's birthday
gara – blacksmith
Gay – a kind of Buddhist Lent in fifth and sixth Buddhist months
gelong – initiated full monk
girgan – teacher
goba – village headman
gompa – monastery
goncha – everyday wear of Ladakhis
gowe-lha – personal protective deities
gupa – ninth
gustor – calendrical festival at a monastery
Gyagar – a term commonly meaning area south of Kashmir, i.e. India
gyatpa – eighth
gyatuk – Ladakhi noodles
gyelpo – spirits of failed/evil kings and monks
gyut – group of people with common ancestor, family/parentage

Id-ul-fitr – celebration of the end of the Muslim fasting period of Ramzan
idak – tortured spirit with a voracious appetite
idi – gifts given to children during Id in Hundar
Id mubarak – greetings exchanged during Id
iftar – the daily evening meal that breaks the Ramzan fast
iftarspun – local-level ritual group among Muslims
imam – priest of a mosque
Isahi – Christian

Jamabandi – periodical additions to the land settlement
jipa – fourth
jipa chukshik – eleventh day of fourth Buddhist month
jipe chonga – fifteenth day of fourth Buddhist month
jumma – Friday congregation at mosque

Kaaba – holy building in Mecca
Kache-pa – Muslims
Kache-yul – Kashmir
kalchor or karchor – sign of good omen generally held by women such as
    curds and milk
Kalon – chief minister
Kalon-pa – people of the Kalon family
kertse – a local pulse
Khalsa Sircar – government land
khambir – local bread
khampa – homestead
khangchen – main house of an extended group of families
khangchun – term for minor house in the Leh area
Kharpon – master of the castle
khataks – ceremonial scarf
kholak – local barley porridge
khunak – salty tea decoction
khutu – minor house of an extended group of families
khyim-lha – deity associated with women and family's welfare
Koran – Muslim scripture
kotwal – officer of the law
kura – fried crisps
kushok – a reincarnate monk

la – pass
la – life-force
lama – monk
lapsang – purification of the gods
larje – doctor
lashing – tree of the life-force of a person
lha – deity

lhaba – male oracle
lhamo – female oracle
lhapchok – initiation
lhashun – dance of the lhas
lhato – place where a deity resides
linga – scapegoat, dough effigy
Lonpo – minister
lopchak – triennial trade and gift missions from Ladakh to Tibet
Losar – Ladakhi New Year
loze – blank verse recounting heroic/tragic narratives
lu – spirits of the underworld, aquatic deities
lung – instruction, spiritual exhortation
lus – body
luyar – vessel of the spirit/ god

machung – mother's younger sister, father's younger brother's wife
magpa – husband
magrib namaaz – prayer at dusk
malik – owner of land
mane – abbreviation of "Om Mane Padme Hum", Buddhist prayer
mane – stone and mud structure on which are placed plaques with sacred
          formulae
manekhang – temple
markur – local biscuits
maryak – a yak figure made from butter
marzan – local porridge with butter.
masjid – mosque
mdo (and gto) – rituals of exorcism of and protection against evil forces
meme – father's father or mother's father
mikha – people's mouths, more literally, their speech
Mikha Dolzok storma – effigies made to get rid of ill effects of people's
                    talk
mimangs – middle-ranking strata
mok-mok – meat dumplings
mo-lha – god associated with women and family's well being
mon – musician

Mon Lam – vow or promise; a festival of solemn promise to affirm the
　　　　　Buddhist Law/Dharma
moulvi – Muslim scholar/theologian
mubarak – greetings/good wishes
mulazzim – official
Mussalman – Muslim

namaaz – five times daily prayers of Muslims
namgang – twenty-ninth day of the tenth Buddhist month
Namroz – festival of Shias, celebrated on third day of Ramzan
namshes – soul
nangmi – family
nangskor – meadow
neespa – second
ngamtuk – soup made from barley flour
ngyen – spirits who live on earth, trees, etc.
Nirmanakaya – fabricated body of the Buddha
nomo – younger/elder daughter, younger sister
nono – elder/younger son, younger brother
Nubra–pa – people of Nubra
nyen – kin

onpo – astrologer

pa – people
paktuk – local noodles
papolo – a local bread
pari – angel
pha-lha – the deity of the phaspun
phaspun – local level ritual group among Buddhists
phetik – a white design made from flour
Pichokchok – a festival of children at Losar
po-lha – god of household defense associated with men
pomo – girl child
poori – a fried food item
pumpa – sacred pots containing seeds inside a shrine

qayamat – day of judgement
quom – race, community

Ramzan – Muslim month of fasting
rgyal-rig – royalty
ri – mountain
rig – strata, rank
rigsnan – outcastes
rinpoche – reincarnated monk
ru – bone
ruh – spirit
ruspa – those with whom common 'bone'/descent is shared

sa – malevolent planetary deities
sadag – lords of the soil
Sakha – day ritually marking the beginning of the agricultural season
sangrak – horse race during Losar in Tegar
sangs – cleansing
sar – the daily pre-dawn meal during the Ramzan fast
sems – heartmind
sepahi – soldier
Shab – night long vigil and prayer of Muslims
shakspa – forgiveness
Shamskat – dialect of western Ladakh
Shimi – a ritual event for feeding ancestors during Losar
shinkan – carpenter
shrungma – monastic protector
shrupla – first (harvest) cutting of grass/barley
shukpa – juniper
skangsol – a ritual of offering, usually after harvest
skew – dumplings
skora – circle
skutag – nobility
skyinjug – songs of farewell sung by a bride at weddings
sngapa – fifth
Sonam Losar – Farmer's or People's New Year
soni-yam – annual donation of household to monasteries

spang – pasture
sparka – life-force or strength
spun – siblings
srunga – a magical charm used to ward off evil
storma – a dough representation of evil and good forces
storme-par – a wooden board used to make dough representations
Stotskat – dialect of eastern Ladakh
sumpa – third
sunpa – weariness of soul, pain of loss, isolation
sunnat – circumcision
sur – powdered mixture of barley flour, sugar and mustard oil

tag – blood
tagi – bread
tamzey – mendicant
tangpo – first
temo – a evil female spirit or witch
thanka – a cloth painting usually representing religious iconography among
          Himalayan Buddhists.
thangskam – desert
thap – stove
thelba – shame
tib – pollution
ti-mok-mok – steamed cake
Trikaya – three bodies scheme of Vajrayana Buddhism
trongpa – land-owning peasant households
tsangpo – river
tsao – daughter's son, sister's son, brother's son, son's son
tsomo – daughter's daughter, sister's daughter, son's daughter, brother's
          daughter
tsen – spirits of the earth
tsespachik – first day of the eleventh month
tsherka – heartache, pain of loss
tsogs – a barley offering of butter, chang and butter milk
Tsokspa – a term used for LBA branch in Nubra, but generally any association
tuk – six
tukpa – sixth

tukpe chonga – fifteenth day of sixth Buddhist month
tutbing – 'smoke', household, a separate hearth
tzangs – simulated modesty

yaksa – celestial being
yidam – patron deities
yul – region, place or village
yul-lha – god of village or settlement
yultak – threshing ground

Yultsa lhato – name of the dwelling of a god associated with Tegar village
zamindar – land owner
zan – a type of porridge
zat – patrilineal group
Zatpa – acts of the Buddha
Zimskang – distinguished family in the village conferred that title usually
           by the king
zingbatpa – farmers or peasants

References

AGGARWAL, PARTAP C. 1971. *Caste, Religion and Power: An Indian Case Study* New Delhi: Shri Ram Centre for Industrial Relations and Human Resources.

AGGARWAL, RAVINA. 1994. From Mixed Strains of Barley Grain: Person and Place in a Ladakhi Village. Ph.D thesis, Indiana University.

AHMAD, IMTIAZ. ED. 1976. *Family, Kinship and Marriage among Muslims in India* New Delhi: Manohar.

ANDERSON, BENEDICT. 1983. *Imagined Communities. Reflections on the Origin and Spread of Nationalism* London: Verso.

ARIS, MICHAEL. 1988. ''The boneless tongue': alternative voices from Bhutan in the context of lamaist societies'. In P.BANERJEE and S.K. GUPTA EDS. *Man, Society and Nature* Shimla: Indian Institute of Advanced Study: 1-45.

ATKINSON, PAUL. 1990. *The Ethnographic Imagination. Textual Constructions of Reality* London/New York: Routledge.

AZIZ, BARBARA, N. 1978. *Tibetan Frontier Families* New Delhi: Vikas.

BAKHTIN, M.M. 1968 [1965]. *Rabelais and His World* Cambridge, Massachusetts: MIT Press.

BAKHTIN, M.M. 1981. *The Dialogic Imagination. Four Essays* London/Austin: University of Texas Press.

BARTH, FREDERIK ED. 1969. *Ethnic Groups and Boundaries: The Social Organisation of Cultural Difference* Boston: Little, Brown and Co.

BERTELSEN, KRISTOFFER BRIX. 1995. 'Early modern Buddhism in Ladakh. Proceedings of the Seventh Colloquium of the International Association for Ladakh Studies, Bonn.

BODDY, JANICE. 1994. 'Spirit possession revisited: beyond instrumentality.' *Annual Review of Anthropology* Vol. 23:407–34.

BRANT, CHARLES, S. and MIMI KHAING. 1951. 'Burmese kinship and the life cycle: an outline'. *Southwestern Journal of Anthropology* Vol. 7:437-454.

BRAUEN, MARTIN. 1980. *Feste in Ladakh* Graz: Akademische druck und Verlagsanstalt.

BRAY, JOHN with NAWANG TSERING SHAKSPO. 1989. *A Bibliography of Ladakh* Warminister: Aris and Phillips.

BRAY, JOHN. 1990. 'A history of the Moravian Church's Tibetan Bible translations.' In L. ICKE-SCHWALBE and G. MEIER EDS.:66-79.

BRAY, JOHN. 1990a. 'The lapchak mission from Ladakh to Lhasa in British Indian foriegn policy.' *The Tibet Journal* XV, No.4:75-96.

BRAY, JOHN. 1991. 'Ladakhi history and Indian nationhood.' *South Asia Research* Vol. 11, No.2:115–33.

BRAY, JOHN. (forthcoming). 'The Roman Catholic mission in Ladakh, 1888-98.' In HENRY OSMASTON and NAWANG TSERING EDS. *Recent Research on Ladakh 6.* University of Bristol, Bristol.

CENSUS OF INDIA 1961. Jammu and Kashmir Distict Census Handbook 4. Ladakh District, Jammu and Kashmir: Director of Census Operations.

CENSUS OF INDIA 1971a. Series 8. Jammu and Kashmir. Part 1-B. General Report. Jammu and Kashmir: Director of Census Operations.

CENSUS OF INDIA 1971c. Series 8. Jammu and Kashmir. Parts X-A & B. Town and Village Directory, Village and Townwise Primary Census Abstract. Ladakh District. Jammu and Kashmir: Director of Census Operations.

CENSUS OF INDIA 1981. Series 8. Jammu and Kashmir. Part IVA. Social and Cultural Tables. Jammu and Kashmir: Director of Census Operations.

COHEN, ABNER. 1965. *Arab Border-Villages in Israel. A Study of Continuity and Change in Social Organisation* Manchester: Manchester University Press.

COMAROFF, JEAN. 1985. *Body of Power. Spirit of Resistance: The Culture and History of a South African People* Chicago: University of Chicago Press.

CROOK, J.H. and H. OSMASTON EDS. 1994 *Himalayan Buddhist Villages* Delhi: Motilal Banarsidass.

CROOK, J.H. 1994. 'Social Organisation and Personal Identity in Zangskar'. In J.H. CROOK and H. OSMASTON EDS.:475-518.

CUNNINGHAM, ALEXANDER. 1970 [1854]. *Ladak: Physical, Statistical and Historical with Notices of the Surrounding Countries* New Delhi: Sagar Publications.

CURZON, G.N. (LORD). 1907. 'Frontiers'. Romanes Lecture, Oxford.

CUTTEN, GEORGE B. 1927. *Speaking with Tongues* New Haven: Yale University Press.

DAVID-NEEL, A. 1931. *With Mystics and Magicians in Tibet* London: John Lane The Bodley Head.

DAY, SOPHIE. 1989. Embodying Spirits: Village Oracles and Possession Ritual in Ladakh, North India. Ph.D. thesis, London School of Economics and Political Science.

DAY, SOPHIE. 1990. 'Ordering spirits: The initiation of village oracles in Ladakh'. In L. ICKE-SCHWALBE and G. MEIER EDS.:206-22.

DENDALECHTE, CLAUDE and PATRICK KAPLANIAN EDS. 1985. *Ladakh, Himalaya Occidental: Ethnologie, Ecologie. Recent research No.2* Pau: Acta Biologica Montana 5.

DESJARLAIS, ROBERT R. 1992. *Body and Emotion. The Aesthetics of Illness and Healing in the Nepal Himalayas* Delhi: Motilal Banarsidass.

DOLLFUS, PASCALE. 1989. *Lieu de neige et de genevriers: Organisation sociale et religieuse des communities bouddhistes du Ladakh* Paris: Editions du CNRS.

DOLLFUS, PASCALE. 1995. 'The history of Muslims in central Ladakh'. *The Tibet Journal* Vol. XX, no. 3:35-58.

DREW, FREDERICK. 1976 [1875]. *Jummo and Kashmir Territories. A Geographical Account* New Delhi: Cosmo Publications.

ECONOMIC REVIEW. 1991. For the year 1990-1, Leh district, District Statistical and Evaluation Agency, Leh.

ELIADE, MIRCEA. 1964 [1951]. *Shamanism: Archaic Techniques of Ecstasy* New York: Pantheon.

EVANS-PRITCHARD, E. E. 1940. *The Nuer* Oxford: Clarendon Press.

FERGUSON, C.A. 1959. 'Diglossia.' *Word* Vol.15:325-40.

FILLIOZAT, JEAN. 1991. 'Docetism in Christianity and in India.' *Religion, Philosophy, Yoga* Delhi: Motilal Banarasidass: 127–34.

FISHER, MARGARET W. ET.AL. 1963. *Himalayan Battleground. Sino-Indian Rivalry in Ladakh* New York/London: Frederick A. Praeger.

FISHMAN, JOSHUA. A. 1972. *Language in Socio-cultural change. Essays* Stanford: Stanford University Press.

FORTES, MEYER. 1940. 'The political system of the Tallensi of the northern territories of the Gold Coast'. In MEYER FORTES and E.E. EVANS-PRITCHARD EDS. *African Political Systems* London:Oxford University Press:238-271.

FRANCKE, A.H. 1977 [1907]. *A History of Ladakh* New Delhi: Sterling Publishers Pvt. Ltd.

FRANKENBERG, RONALD. 1957. *Village on the Border. A Social Study of Religion, Politics and Football in a North Wales Community* London: Cohen and West.

FRASER, DAVID. 1986 [1910]. *Trans-Himalaya Unveiled* 2 vols. New Delhi: Cosmo Publications.

FRASER, S. 1977. Ladakh Expedition 1976. Report. University of Southhampton.

FREEMAN, J.D. 1961. 'On the concept of kindred'. *Journal of the Royal Anthropological Institute of Great Britain and Ireland* Vol. 91, Part 2: 192-220.

FURER-HAIMENDORF, C. VON ED. 1964. *The Sherpas of Nepal: Buddhist Highlanders* London: John Murray.

GAL, SUSAN, 1987. 'Codeswitching and consciousness in the European periphery.' *American Ethnologist* Vol. 14: 637-53.

GAZETTEER OF KASHMIR AND LADAK. 1974 [1890]. Delhi: Vikas Publishing House.

GERGAN, JOSEB. 1976. *La dwags rgyal rabs 'chi med gter.* New Delhi: Sterling Publications.

GILLARD, DAVID. 1977. *The Struggle for Asia 1828-1914. A Study in British and Russian Imperialism* London: Metheun and Co. Ltd.

GLUCKMAN, MAX. 1954. *Rituals of Rebellion in South-east Africa* Frazer Lecture (1952). Manchester: Manchester University Press.

GLUCKMAN, MAX. 1965. *Politics, Law and Ritual in Tribal Society* Oxford: Basil Blackwell.

GOKHALE-CHATTERJEE, SANDHYA. 1987. 'Stratification and change in contemporary Ladakhi society.' In M.K. RAHA ED. *The Himalayan Heritage* Delhi: Gian Publishing House: 456–68.

GOLDBERG, HARVEY E. 1977. 'Rites and riots: the Tripolitianian pogrom of 1945.' *Plural Societies* 8(1): 35-56.

GOLDSTEIN MELVYN C. and P. TSARONG. 1987. 'De-encapsulation and change in Ladakh'. In M.K. RAHA ED. *The Himalayan Heritage* Delhi: Gian Publishing House: 443–55.

GOODMAN, FELICITAS. 1971. 'The acquisition of glossolalia behaviour.' *Semiotica* 3:77-82

GOODMAN, FELICITAS. ET.AL. 1974. *Trance, Healing and Hallucination. Three Field Studies in Religious Experience* New York: John Wiley and Sons.

GOODMAN, FELICITAS. 1976. 'Shaman and priest in Yucatan Pentecostalism'. In AGEHANANDA BHARATHI ED. *The Realm of the Extra Human, Agents and Audiences* The Hague/Paris: Mouton: 159–65.

GRIST, NICOLA. 1990. 'Muslim kinship and marriage in Ladakh'. Proceedings of a conference on the Anthropology of Tibet and the Himalaya, Zurich.

GRIST, NICOLA. 1990a. 'Land tax, labour and household organization in Ladakh'. In L. ICKE-SCHWALBE and G.MEIER EDS.: 129–40.

GRIST, NICOLA. 1995. 'Muslims in western Ladakh'. *The Tibet Journal* Vol. XX, no. 3:59-70.

GUMPERZ, JOHN J. 1982. *Discourse Strategies* New York: Cambridge University Press.

GUTSCHOW, KIM. 1993. 'The politics of irrigation in three Tibetan societies: `Lords of the fort', `lords of the water' and no lords at all'. Proceedings of the Sixth Colloquium of the International Association for Ladakh Studies, Leh.

GUTSCHOW, KIM. 1996. 'Kinship in Zangskar: idiom and practice.' In HENRY OSMASTON and PHILIP DENWOOD EDS.:337–47

GYALSTSAN, JAMYANG. 1993. 'Introduction of Buddhism in Ladakh.' Proceedings of the Sixth Colloquium of the International Association for Ladakh Studies, Leh.

HASTINGS, JAMES. 1927 [1912]. *Encyclopaedia of Religion and Ethics* Vol. 4 . Edinburgh: T. and T. Clark/New York: Charles Scribner's Sons.

HEBER, A. REEVE and KATHLEEN M. HEBER. 1976 [1923]. *Himalayan Tibet and Ladakh* New Delhi: Ess Ess Publications.

HITCHCOCK, JOHN T. and REX L. JONES EDS. 1976. *Spirit Possession in the Nepal Himalayas* Warminister: Aris and Phillips.

HOLMBERG, DAVID. 1989. *Order in Paradox. Myth, Ritual and Exchange among Nepal's Tamang* Ithaca/London: Cornell University Press.

HYMES, DELL. ED. 1971. *Pidinization and Creolization* London: Cambridge University Press.

ICKE-SCHWALBE, LYDIA and GUNDRUN MEIER EDS. 1990. *Wissenchaftsgeschichte und gegenwartige Forscungen in Nordwest-Indien* Dresden Museum of Ethnology.

IMPERIAL GAZETTEER OF INDIA, THE. 1908. *The Indian Empire* Vol. 1. New edition. Oxford at the Clarendon Press.

IRVINE, JUDITH T. 1989. 'When talk is'nt cheap : language and political economy'. *American Ethnologist* Vol.16: 248–67.

JAESCHKE, H. 1975 [1881]. *A Tibetan-English Dictionary* Delhi: Motilal Banarsidass.

KANTOWSKI, D. and R. SANDER EDS. 1983. *Recent Research on Ladakh: History, Culture, Sociology, Ecology* Munich: Weltforum Verlag.

KAPLANIAN, PATRICK. 1981. *Les Ladakhi du Cachemire* Paris: CNRS

KAUL, H.C. and SRIDHAR KAUL. 1992. *Ladakh through the Ages. Towards a New Identity* New Delhi: Indus Publishing House.

KHAN, HASHMUTALLAH. 1939. *Tarikh Jammun, Kashmir, Laddakh aur Baltistan.* Lucknow.

KIPLING, RUDYARD, 1987 [1901]. *Kim* Harmondsworth, England: Puffin Books.

KOSHAL, SAMYUKTA. 1979. *Ladakhi Grammar* Delhi: Motilal Banarsidass.

LAMB, ALASTAIR. 1968. *Asian Frontiers. Studies in a Continuing Problem* London: Pall Mall Press.

LATTIMORE, OWEN D. 1968 [1956]. 'The frontier in history'. In ROBERT A. MANNERS and DAVID KAPLAN ED. *Theory in Anthropology, A Source Book* London: Routledge and Kegan Paul: 374–86.

LEVINE, NANCY. 1981. 'The theory of ru. Kinship, descent and status in a Tibetan society'. In CHRISTOPHER VON FURER-HAIMENDORF ED. *Asian Highland Societies in Anthropological Perspective* New Delhi: Sterling Publishers Pvt. Ltd: 52-78.

MALONY, H. NEWTON and LOVEKIN, A. ADAMS. 1985. *Glossolalia: Behavioural Science Perspectives on Speaking in Tongues* New York: Oxford University Press.

MANN, R.S. 1986. *The Ladakhi: A Study in Ethnography and Change* Calcutta: Anthropological Survey of India.

MEHRA, PARSHOTAM. 1992. *An 'Agreed' Frontier. Ladakh and India's Northermost Borders, 1846-1947* Delhi: Oxford University Press.

MILLER BEATRICE D. 1956. 'Ganye and Kidu: two formalized systems of mutual aid among the Tibetans.' *Southwestern Journal of Anthropology* Vol.12: 157–70.

MILLER, BEATRICE. D. 1961. 'The web of Tibetan monasticism'. *Journal of Asian Studies* Vol XX, No.2: 197-203.

MILLS, MARTIN A. 1995. 'The religion of locality: local area gods and the characterization of Tibetan Buddhism'. Proceedings of the Seventh Colloquium of the International Association for Ladakh Studies, Bonn.

MUMFORD, STAN ROYAL. 1990. *Himalayan Dialogue. Tibetan Lamas and Gurung Shamans in Nepal* Kathmandu: Tiwari's Pilgrims Book House.

MURDOCK G.P. 1968. 'Cognatic forms of social organisation'. In PAUL BOHANNAN and JOHN MIDDLETON ED. *Kinship and Social Organisation* New York: The Natural History Press: 235–53.

NASH, DENNISON. 1963. 'The ethnologist as stranger: an essay in the sociology of knowledge'. *Southwestern Journal of Anthropology* 19:149–67.

NEBESKY-WOJKOWITZ, RENE DE. 1993 [1956]. *Oracles and Demons of Tibet: The Cult and Iconography of the Tibetan Protective Deities* Kathmandu: Book Faith India.

OKADA, FERDINAND E. 1957. 'Ritual brotherhood: a cohesive factor in Nepalese society'. *Southwestern Journal of Anthropology* Vol.13: 212–22.

OKELY, JUDITH and HELEN CALLAWAY EDS. 1992. *Anthropology and Autobiography* London/New York: Routledge.

ORTNER, SHERRY B. 1979 [1978]. *Sherpas through their Rituals* New Delhi: Vikas Publishing House.

OSMASTON, HENRY and PHILIP DENWOOD EDS. 1996. *Recent Research on Ladakh 4 & 5* Delhi: Motilal Banarasidass.

OSMASTON, HENRY and NAWANG TSERING EDS. (forthcoming). *Recent Research on Ladakh 6* The University of Bristol, Bristol.

PALLIS, MARCO. 1974 [1939]. *Peaks and Lamas* London: Woburn Press.

PANDIT, P.B. 1988. 'Prospects in sociolinguistics.' In LACHMAN KHUBCHANDANI ED. *Language in a Plural Society* Delhi: Motilal Banarasidass/Shimla: Indian Institute of Advanced Studies: 3-7.

PETER, PRINCE OF GREECE AND DENMARK. 1963. *A Study of Polyandry* Mouton: The Hague.

PETER, PRINCE OF GREECE AND DENMARK. 1979. 'Tibetan oracles.' *Tibetan Journal* 4(2): 51–6.

PHYLACTOU, MARIA. 1989. Household Organisation and Marriage in Ladakh, Indian Himalaya. Ph.D. Thesis, London School of Economics.

RABGYAS, TASHI. 1984. *Mar yul la dwags kyi sngon rabs kun gsal me long* Leh, Ladakh.

RABGYAS, TASHI and HENRY OSMASTON. 1994. 'The Tibetan calendar and astrology in the regulation of Zangskari agriculture.' In J.H.CROOK and H.OSMASTON EDS.:111–19.

RIBBACH, S.H. 1986 [1940]. *Culture and Society in Ladakh* New Delhi: Ess Ess Publications.

RIPLEY, ABBY. 1996. 'Food as Ritual.' In HENRY OSMASTON and PHILIP DENWOOD EDS.:165–75.

RIZVI, B.R. 1987. 'Muslims of the Kashmir valley and Kargil'. In M.K. RAHA ED. *The Himalayan Heritage* Delhi: Gian Publishing House: 427-441.

RIZVI, JANET. 1995. 'Leh to Yarkand: travelling the trans-Karakoram trade route.' Proceedings of the Seventh Colloquium of the International Association for Ladakh Studies, Bonn.

SAHLINS, MARSHALL. 1972. *Stone Age Economics* New York: Aldine Publishing Co.

SAMUEL, GEOFFEREY. 1982. 'Tibet as a stateless society and some Islamic parallels'. *Journal of Asian Studies* Vol. XLI: 215–29.

SAMUEL, GEOFFEREY. 1993. *Civilized Shamans: Buddhism in Tibetan Societies* Washington D.C.: Smithsonian Institution Press.

SAMUEL, GEOFFEREY, HAMISH GREGOR and ELISABETH STUTCHBURY EDS. 1994. *Tantra and Popular Religion in Tibet* New Delhi: International Academy of Indian Culture and Aditya Prakashan (Sata-Pitaka Series 376).

SAVILLE-TROIKE, MURIEL. 1982. *The Ethnography of Communication* Oxford: Basil Blackwell.

SHAKSPO, NAWANG TSERING. 1990. 'Historical perspectives of Nubra in Ladakh'. In L. ICKE-SCHALBE and G.MEIER EDS.: 100–6.

SHAKSPO, NAWANG TSERING. 1996. 'The significance of Khuksho in the cultural history of Ladakh.' In HENRY OSMASTON and PHILIP DENWOOD EDS.:181–87.

SHAW, ROBERT. 1984 [1871]. *Visits to High Tartary, Yarkand and Kashagar* Oxford: Oxford University Press.

SHEIKH ABDUL GHANI. 1996. 'A brief history of Muslims in Ladakh.' In HENRY OSMASTON and PHILIP DENWOOD EDS.:189–92.

SINGH, HARJIT. 1977. 'Territorial organisation of gompas in Ladakh.' In 'Ecologie et Geologie de l'Himalaya. Colloques Internationaux CNRS', Paris.

SINGH, HARJIT. 1978. *Ladakh - Problems of Regional Development in the Context of Growth Point strategy*. Ph.D. thesis, Jawaharlal Nehru University, Delhi.

SRINIVAS, SMRITI. 1991. 'The lost horizon? Problems in a strategic spot.' *Frontline* October 26-November 8: 81-87.

SRINIVAS, SMRITI. 1993. 'Hope on the horizon. A rapprochement'. *Frontline* November 19: 52-55.

SRINIVAS, SMRITI. 1994. 'The kindred and political patriliny: two styles in extra-local integration in Nubra valley, Ladakh'. *Sociological Bulletin* 43(2): 193–213.

SRINIVAS, SMRITI. 1995. 'The dialogic mode, role reversal and fieldwork'. In CLIVE THOMSON and HANS RAJ DUA EDS. *Dialogism and Cultural Criticism* London, Canada: Mestengo Press: 111–49.

SRINIVAS, SMRITI. 1995a. 'Conjunction, parallelism and cross-cutting ties between Muslims and Buddhists in Nubra valley, Ladakh'. *Tibet Journal* Vol. XX, no.3: 71-95.

STATE BANK OF INDIA. 1991. Annual Credit Plan for Leh (1990–1). Lead Bank of State Bank of India, Leh. Manuscript.

STEIN, ROLF. A. 1972 [1962]. *Tibetan Civilization* London: Faber and Faber Ltd.

STEWARD, JULIAN H. 1955. *Theory of Culture Change* Urbana: University of Illinois Press.

TAUSSIG, MICHAEL. 1987. *Shamanism, Colonialism and the Wild Man: A Study in Terror and Healing* Chicago: University of Chicago Press.

TERRAY, EMMANUEL. 1972 [1969]. *Marxism and 'Primitive' Societies* New York/London: Monthly Review Press.

THOMSON, THOMAS. 1978 [1852]. *Western Himalayas and Tibet. A Narrative on Ladakh and Mountains of Northern India* New Delhi: Cosmo Publications.

TSERING, NAWANG. 1979. *Buddhism in Ladakh* New Delhi: Sterling.

TUCCI, GUISEPPE. 1980 [1970]. *The Religions of Tibet* London/Henley: Routledge and Kegan Paul.

TURNER, V.W. 1957. *Schism and Continuity in an African Society. A Study of Ndembu Village Life* Manchester: Manchester University Press.

TURNER, V.W. 1968. *The Drums of Affliction. A Study of Religious Processes among the Ndembu of Zambia* Oxford: Clarendon Press.

TURNER, V.W. 1969. *The Ritual Process: Structure and Anti-Structure* London: Routledge and Kegan Paul.

UBEROI, J.P.S. 1962. *Politics of the Kula Ring. An Analysis of the Findings of Bronislaw Malinowski* Manchester: Manchester University Press.

UBEROI, J.P.S. 1964. Social Organisation of the Tajiks of Andarab Valley, Afghanistan. Partly published Ph.D. thesis, Australian National University.

VAN BEEK, MARTIJN and KRISTOFFER BRIX BERTELSEN. 1995. 'No present without past. The 1989 agitation in Ladakh.' Proceedings of the Seventh Colloquium of the International Association for Ladakh Studies, Bonn.

VAN BEEK, MARTIJN. 1996. Identity Fetishism and the Art of Representation: The Long Struggle for Regional Autonomy in Ladakh. Ph.D thesis, Cornell University.

VOHRA, ROHIT. 1996. 'Early history of Ladakh: mythic lore and fabulation.' In HENRY OSMASTON and PHILIP DENWOOD EDS.:215–33.

VOLOSINOV, V.N. 1973 [1930]. *Marsixm and the Philosophy of Language* New York/London: The Seminar Press.

VOLOSINOV, V.N. 1987 [1927]. *Freudianism. A Critical Sketch* Bloomington: Indiana University Press.

WARIKOO, K. 1995. 'Hemp drug (*charas*) trade between Ladakh and Xinjiang, 1846-1947.' Proceedings of the Seventh Colloquium of the International Association for Ladakh Studies, Bonn.

WEINRICH, URIEL. 1963. *Languages in Contact* The Hague: Mouton and Co.

WOODMAN, DOROTHY. 1969. *Himalayan Frontiers: A Political Review of British, Chinese, Indian and Russian Rivalries* London: Barrie and Rockliff, The Cresset Press.

WOOLARD, K. 1985. 'Language variation and cultural hegemony: towards an integration of sociolinguistic and social theory.' *American Ethnologist* 12 (4): 738-48.

ZUTSHI, BUPINDER. 1994. 'Changing spatio-cultural profile of Jammu and Kashmir.' Proceedings of a conference on 'Cultural Heritage of the Western Himalaya and its Future', New Delhi.

Index

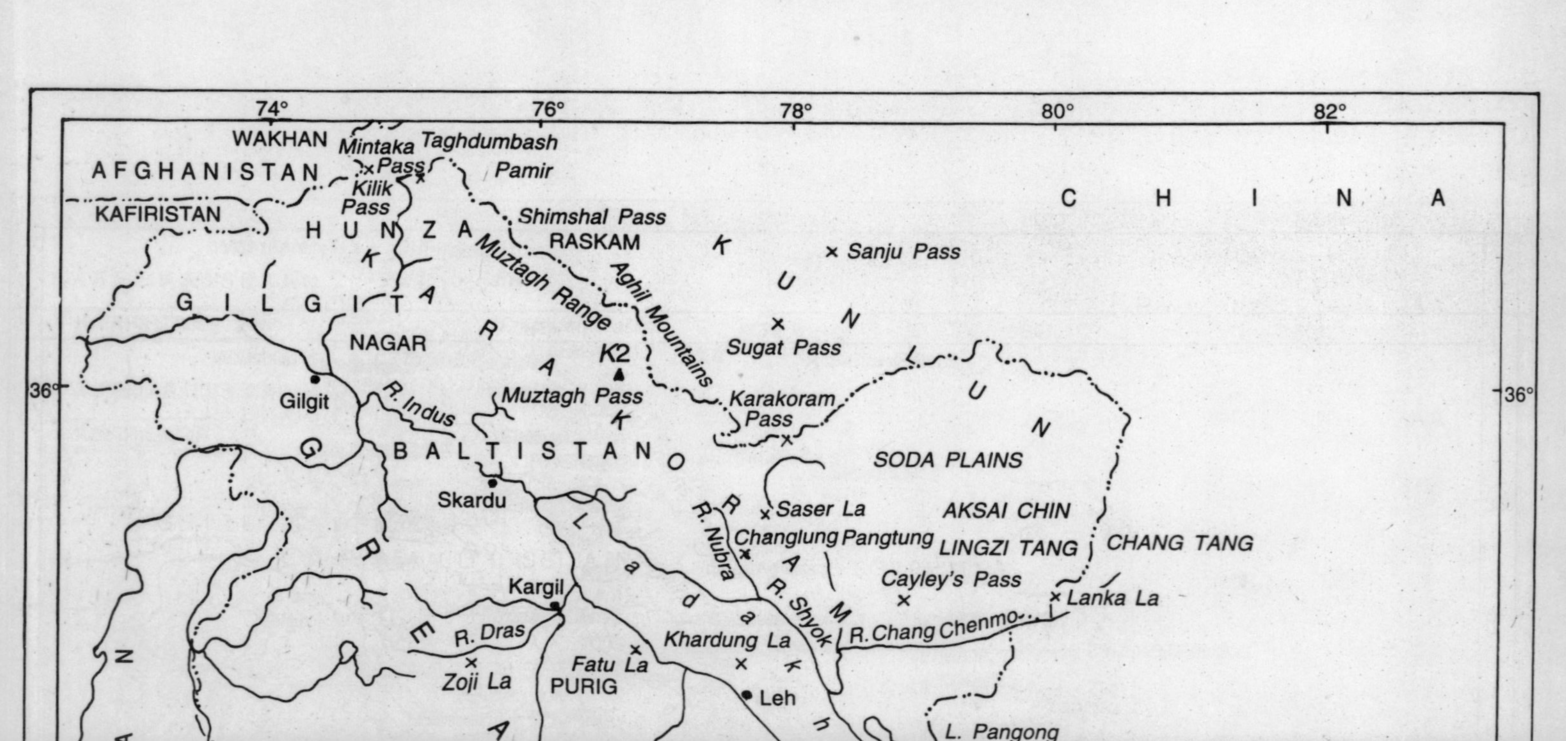

74°
76°
78°
80°
82°
36°
36°
WAKHAN
Mintaka
Pass
Taghdumbash
Pamir
AFGHANISTAN
KAFIRISTAN
Kilik
Pass
Shimshal Pass
RASKAM
CHINA
HUNZA
Muztagh Range
Aghil Mountains
KUN
× Sanju Pass
GILGIT
NAGAR
KARA
Sugat Pass
K2
Muztagh Pass
Karakoram
Pass
LUN
Gilgit
R. Indus
BALTISTANO
G
R
A
SODA PLAINS
Skardu
Ladakh
Saser La
AKSAI CHIN
R. Nubra
Changlung Pangtung
LINGZI TANG
CHANG TANG
R. Shyok
Cayley's Pass
×
× Lanka La
Kargil
R. Chang Chenmo
R. Dras
Khardung La
Fatu La
Zoji La
PURIG
Leh
L. Pangong